Many Faces at the Rec.

Mayar Akash

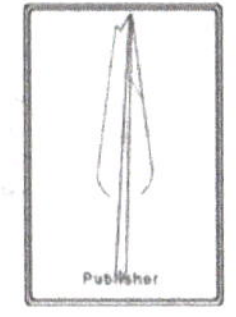

MA PUBLISHER

Published by MA Publishing (Penzance)
www.mapublisher.org.uk
Published in August, POD, UK
ISBN-13: 9781915958174

Cover designed, layout, pagination by Mayar Akash
Cover photos by Mayar Akash
Typeset and layout in Times New Roman by Mayar Akash
Title text: Time New Roman

Paper printed on is FSC Certified, lead free, acid free, buffered paper made from wood-based pulp. Our paper meets the ISO 9706 standard for permanent paper. As such, paper will last several hundred years when stored.

Dedication/Acknowledgement

My wife, Julie Ann Akash for her support in putting this together,

Jean Andrews my mother in law and Melvin John Durrant for their dedications and perseverance to uphold standards for the Princess May Recreation Gound.

Crammed!

Is what you have, photos and more photos, all sizes to fit in. In year order, but not months or days.
Something for everyone!

Aerial view of the ground

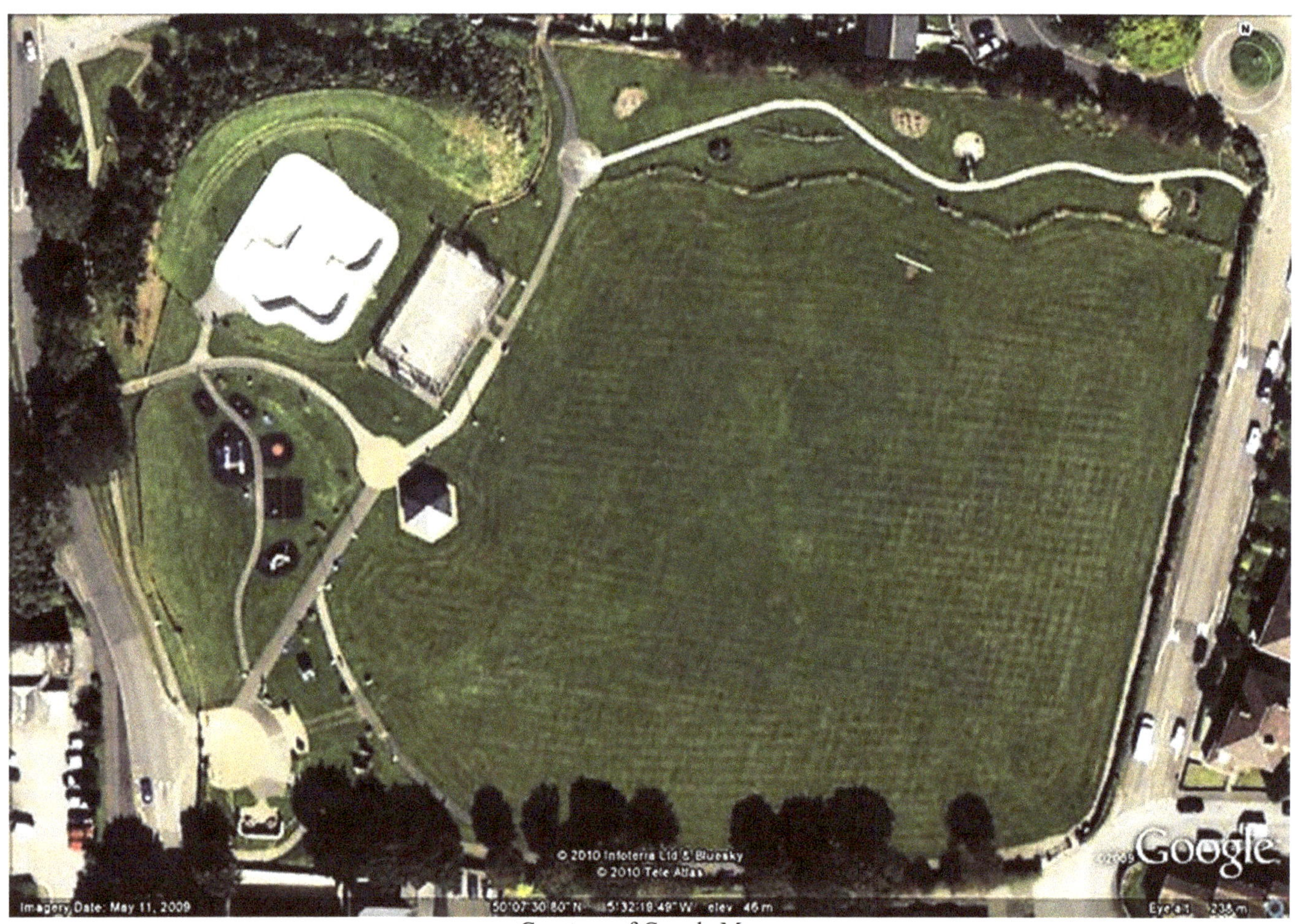

Courtesy of Google Maps.

Contents

1893

Background

The Princess May Recreation Ground in Penzance is named after Princess May of Teck, who later became Queen Mary, the wife of King George V. Queen Mary was born Victoria Mary Augusta Louise Olga Pauline Claudine Agnes on May 26, 1867, and was commonly known as Princess May before her marriage.

Princess May of Teck was engaged to Albert Victor, Duke of Clarence and Avondale, the eldest son of the Prince of Wales (later King Edward VII). However, after Albert Victor's untimely death, she became engaged to and married his younger brother, George, Duke of York, in 1893. George later became King George V, making Princess May Queen Mary, the queen consort of the United Kingdom from 1910 until 1936.

The Princess May Recreation Ground in Penzance was named in 1893. This naming coincided with the engagement and subsequent marriage of Princess May of Teck to Prince George, Duke of York, who later became King George V. The naming of the ground was a way to commemorate this significant royal event.

Princess May, who became Queen Mary, did not have a direct personal significance to Penzance or the immediate area. The naming of the Princess May Recreation Ground was more of a commemorative gesture rather than a reflection of a personal connection to the region. It was common practice during the Victorian and Edwardian eras to honour royal figures by naming public spaces, buildings, and institutions after them, especially around significant events such as engagements, marriages, and coronations.

In the case of the Princess May Recreation Ground, it was likely named to honour the marriage of Princess May to Prince George, Duke of York, in 1893, reflecting the local community's respect and admiration for the royal family. This kind of naming was a way to express loyalty to the crown and to celebrate national events on a local level.

2020

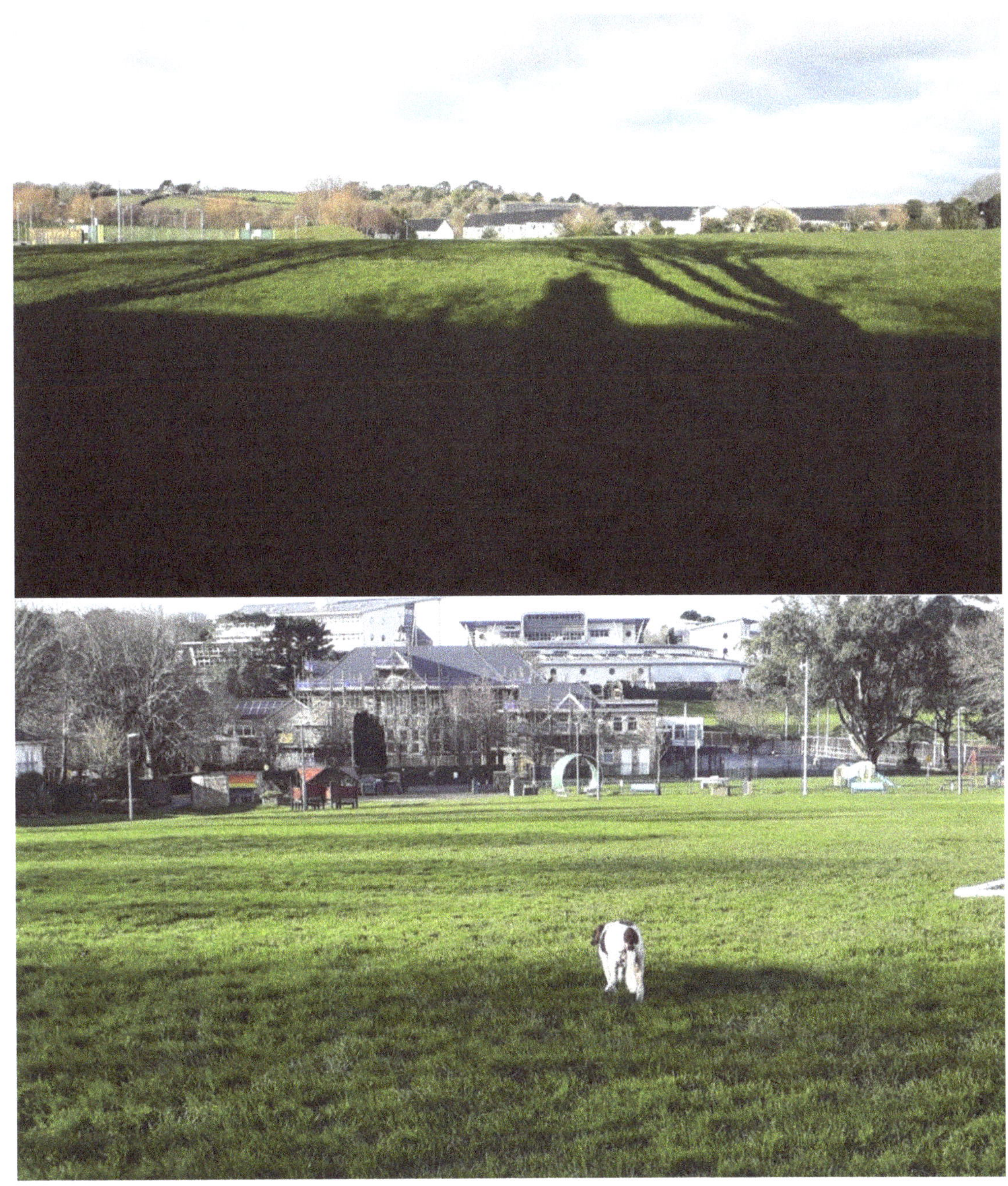

2021

Key aspects

The Princess May Recreation Ground in Penzance is known for being a well-used and cherished public space in the community. While it may not be "famous" in the sense of having wide international recognition, it has historically served as an important recreational area for the local population.

Key aspects of its significance include:

1. **Recreational Use**: The ground has provided a space for various sports and recreational activities, including football, cricket, and other outdoor games.
2. **Community Events**: It has been a venue for local events, fairs, and public gatherings, serving as a central spot for community engagement and social activities.
3. **Green Space**: As a green space, it has offered residents a place for leisure, relaxation, and enjoying nature, contributing to the overall well-being of the community.
4. **Historical Context**: Its naming after Princess May (Queen Mary) adds a historical and cultural dimension, linking it to a significant period in British royal history.

Overall, the Princess May Recreation Ground holds a place of local importance in Penzance as a communal and recreational hub.

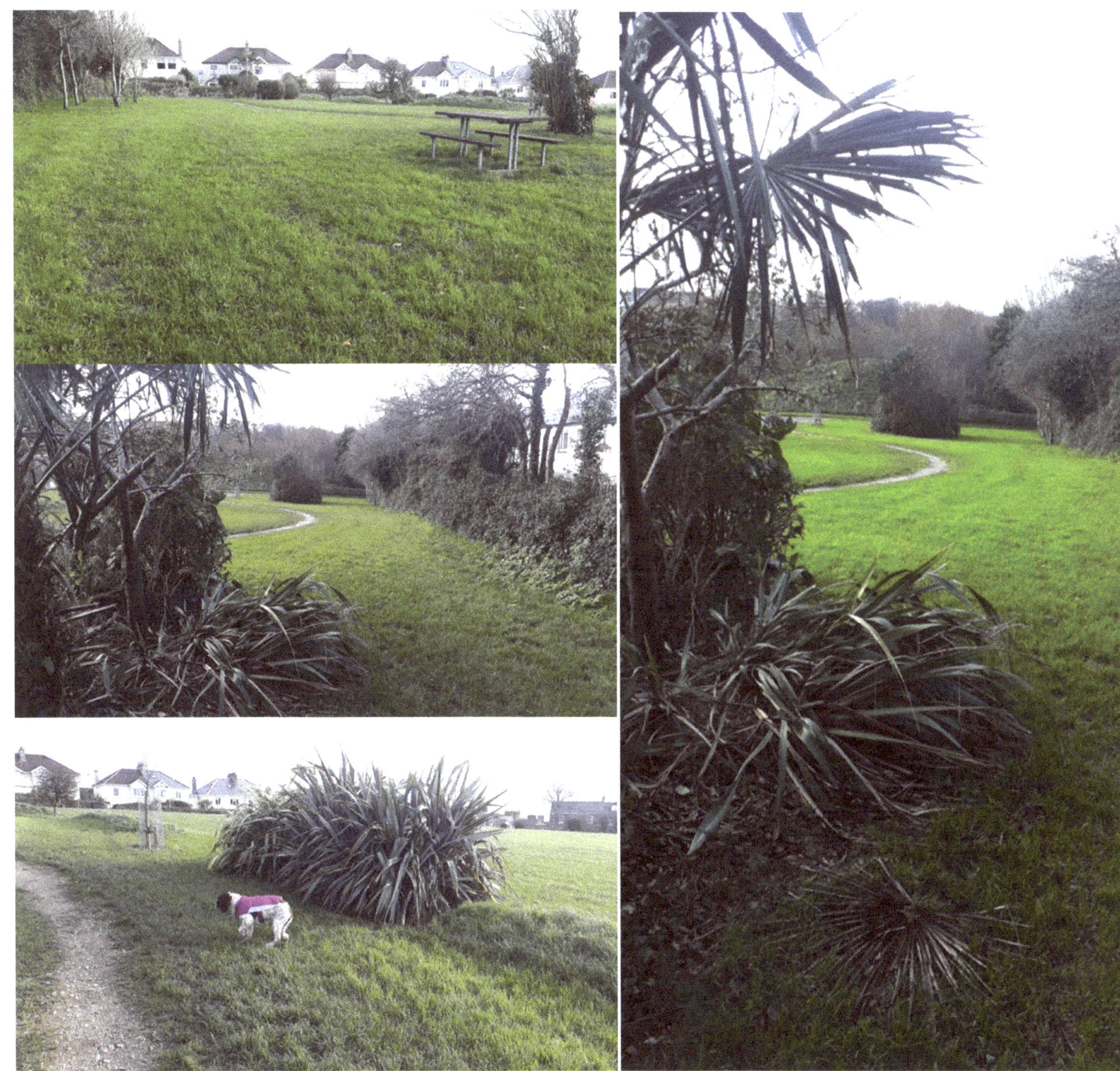

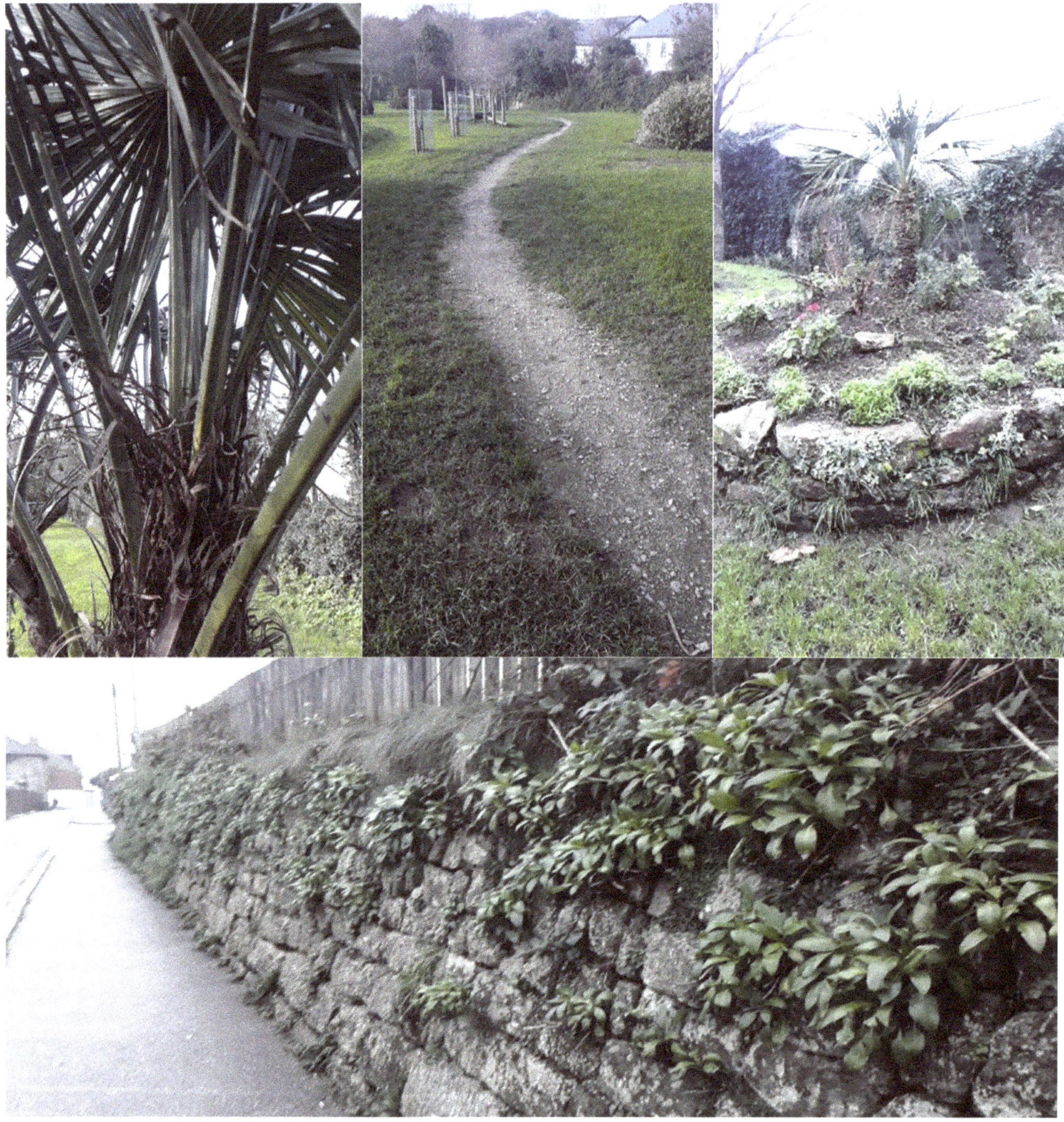

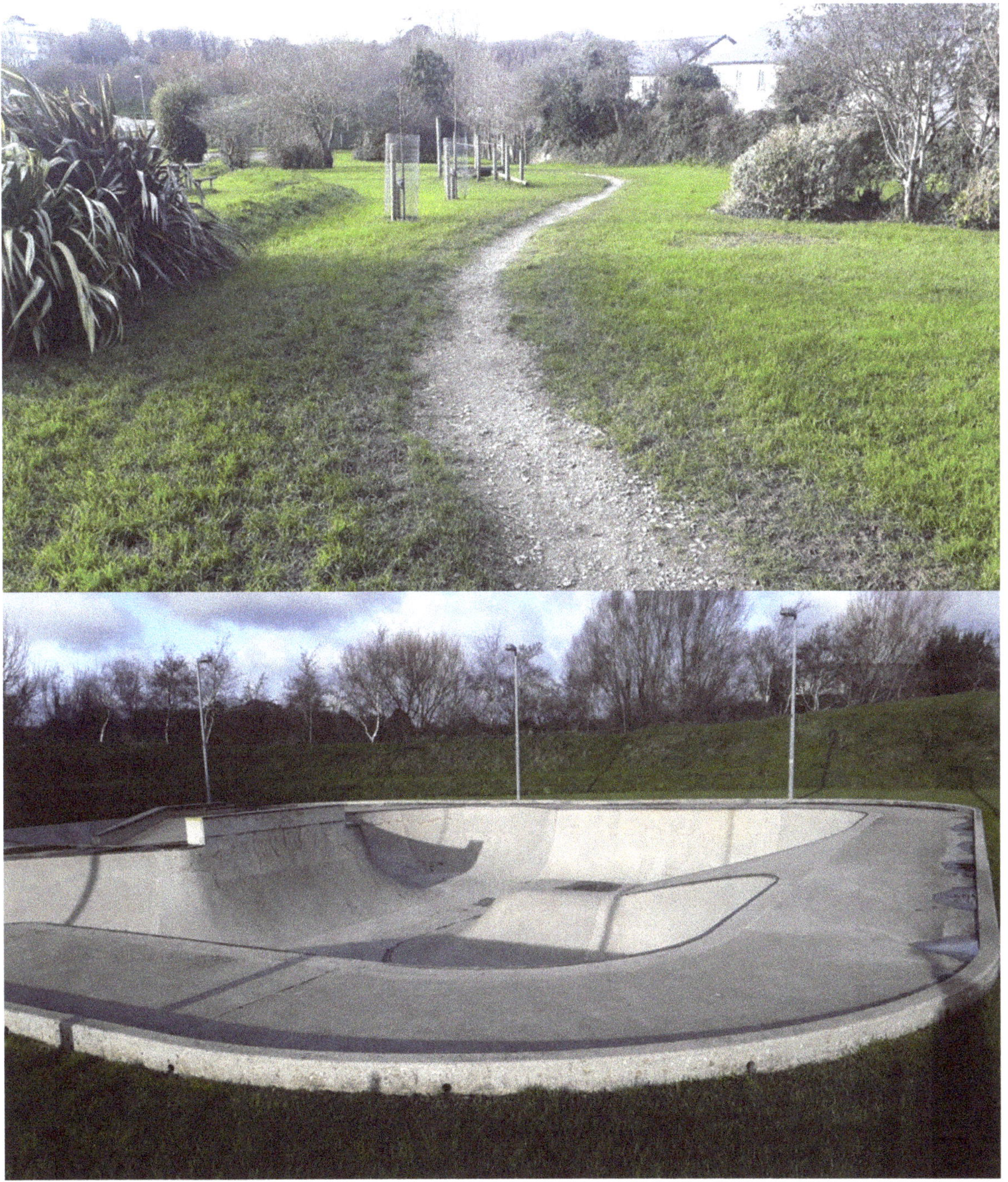

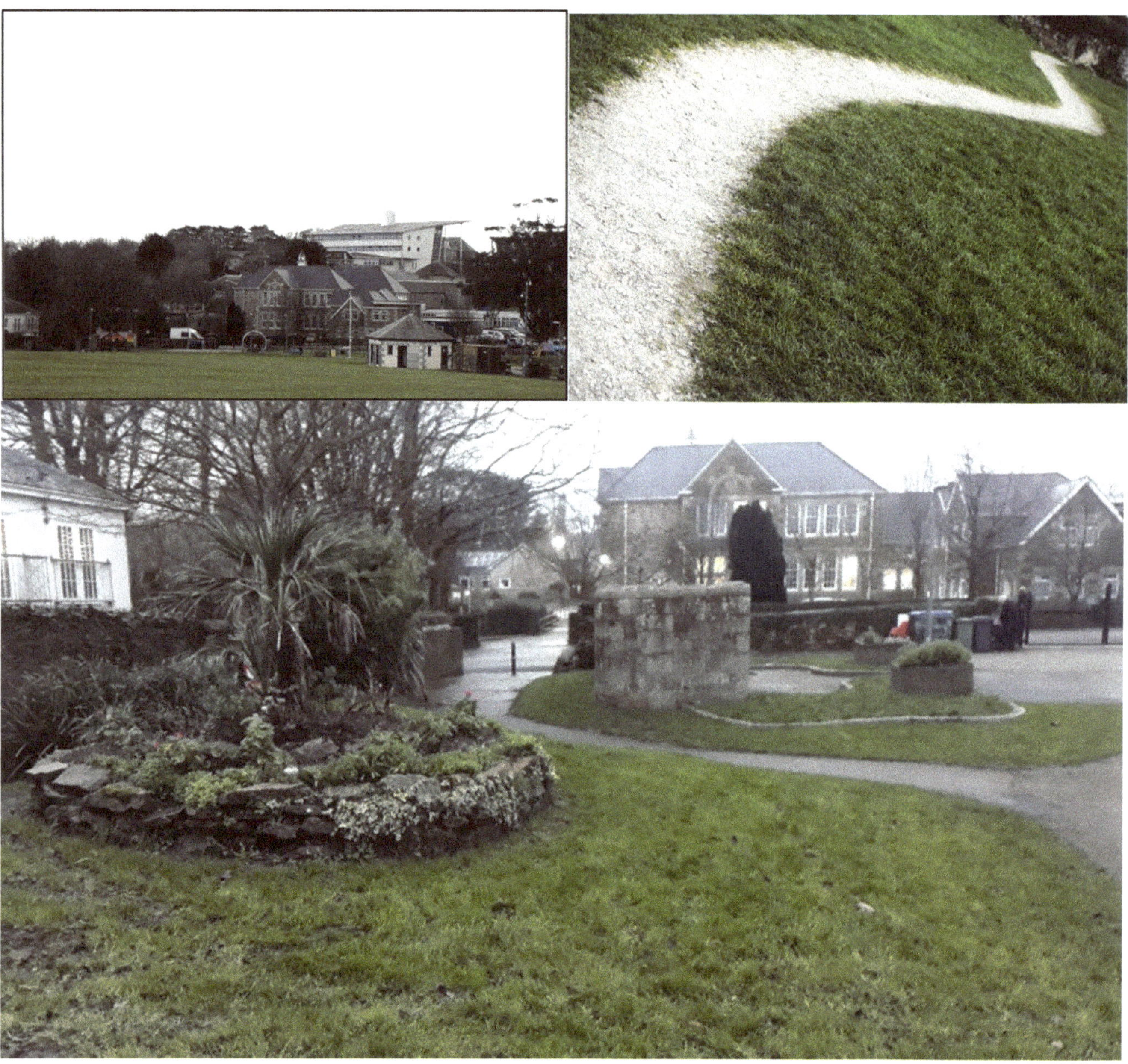

New gardening team, Jean Andrews & Melville Durrant

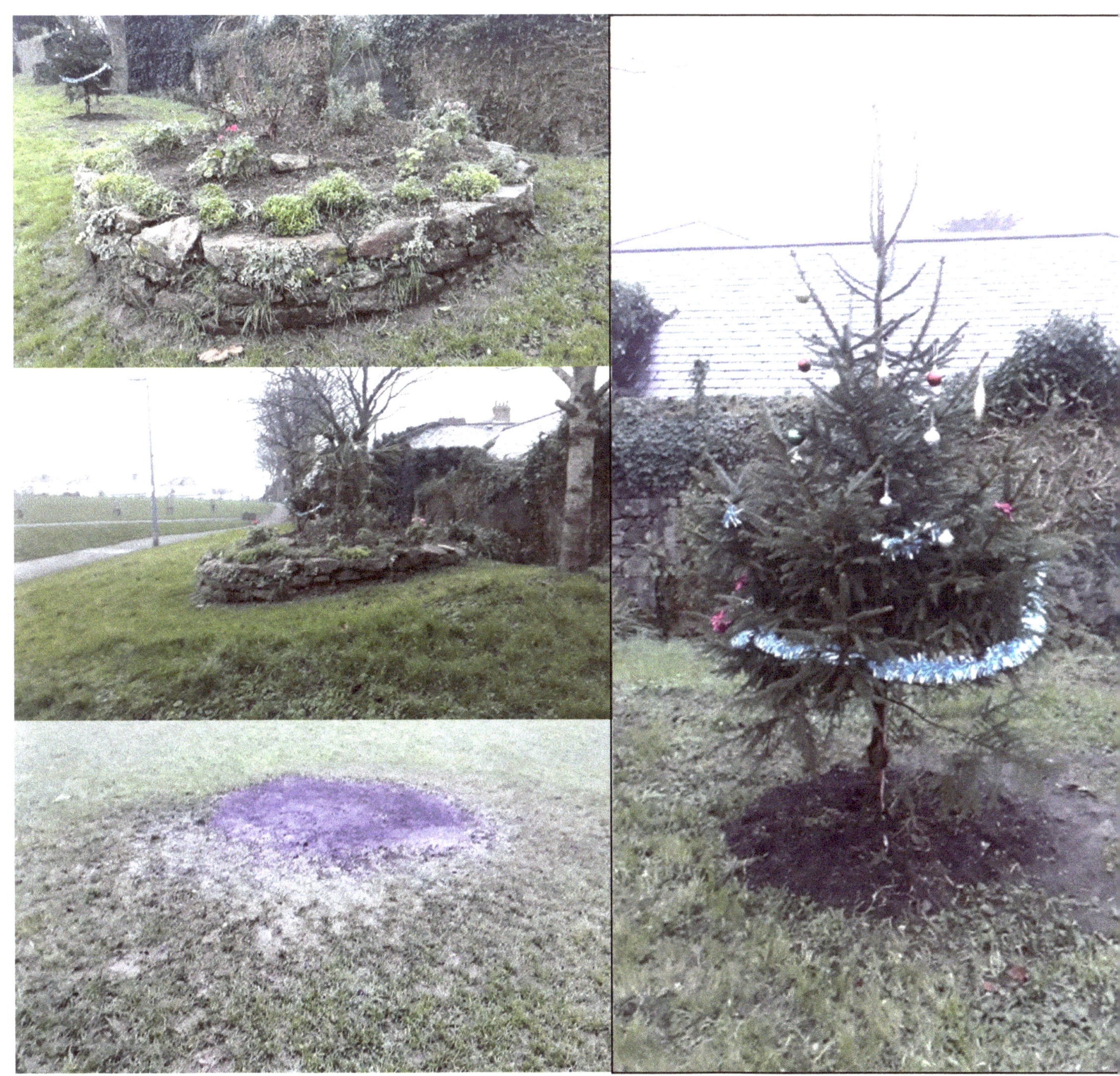

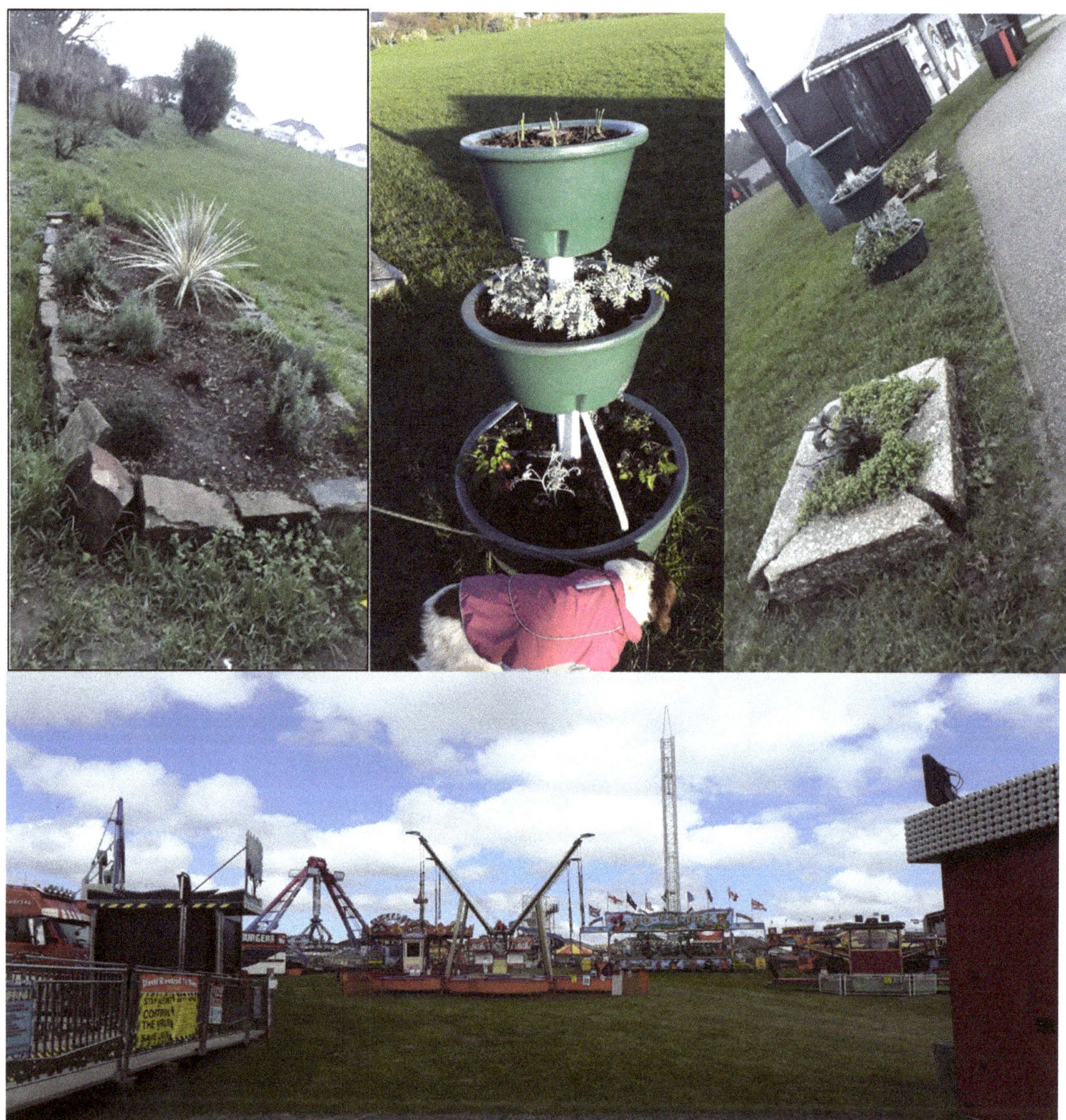

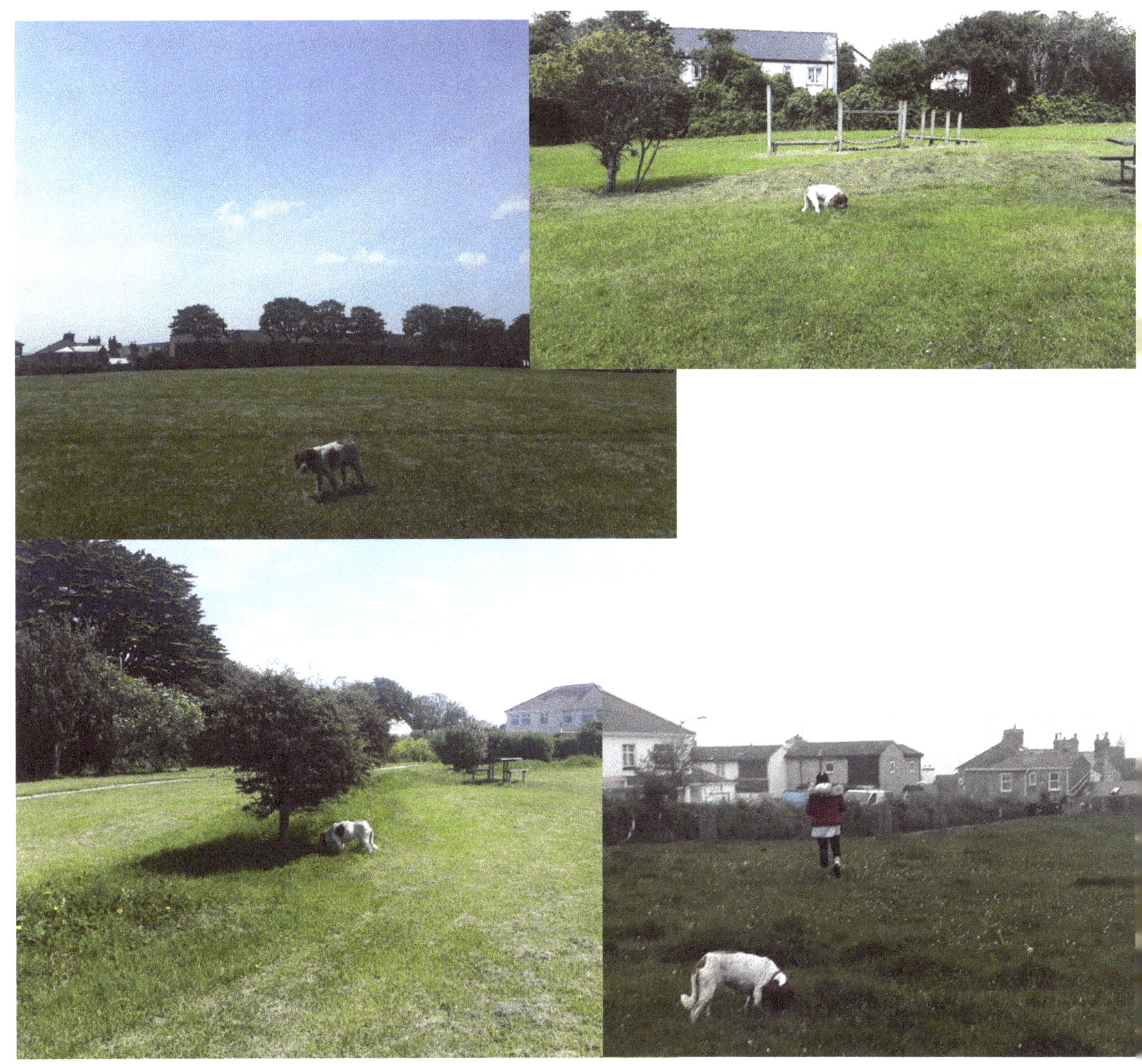

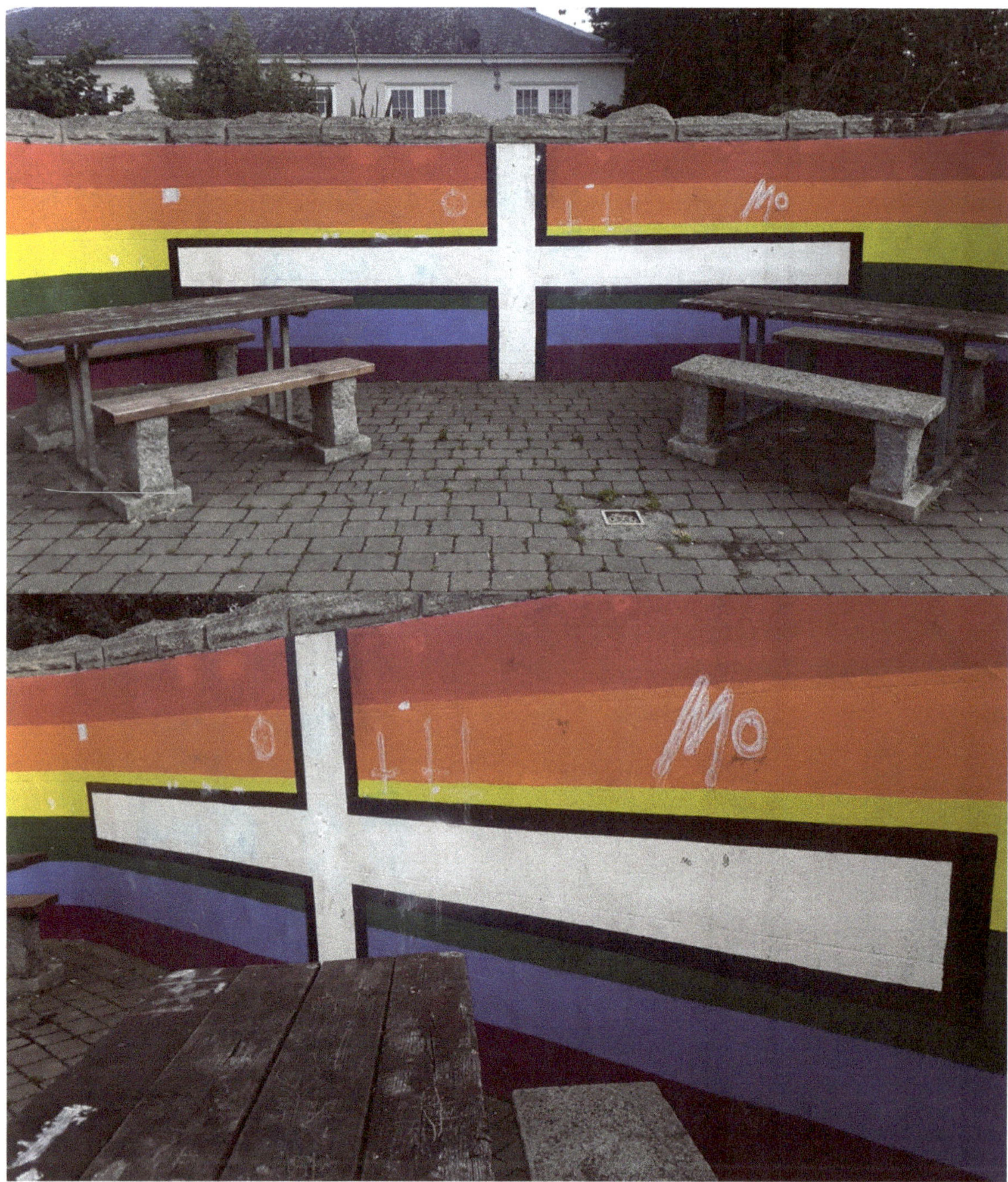
Mo
Mo

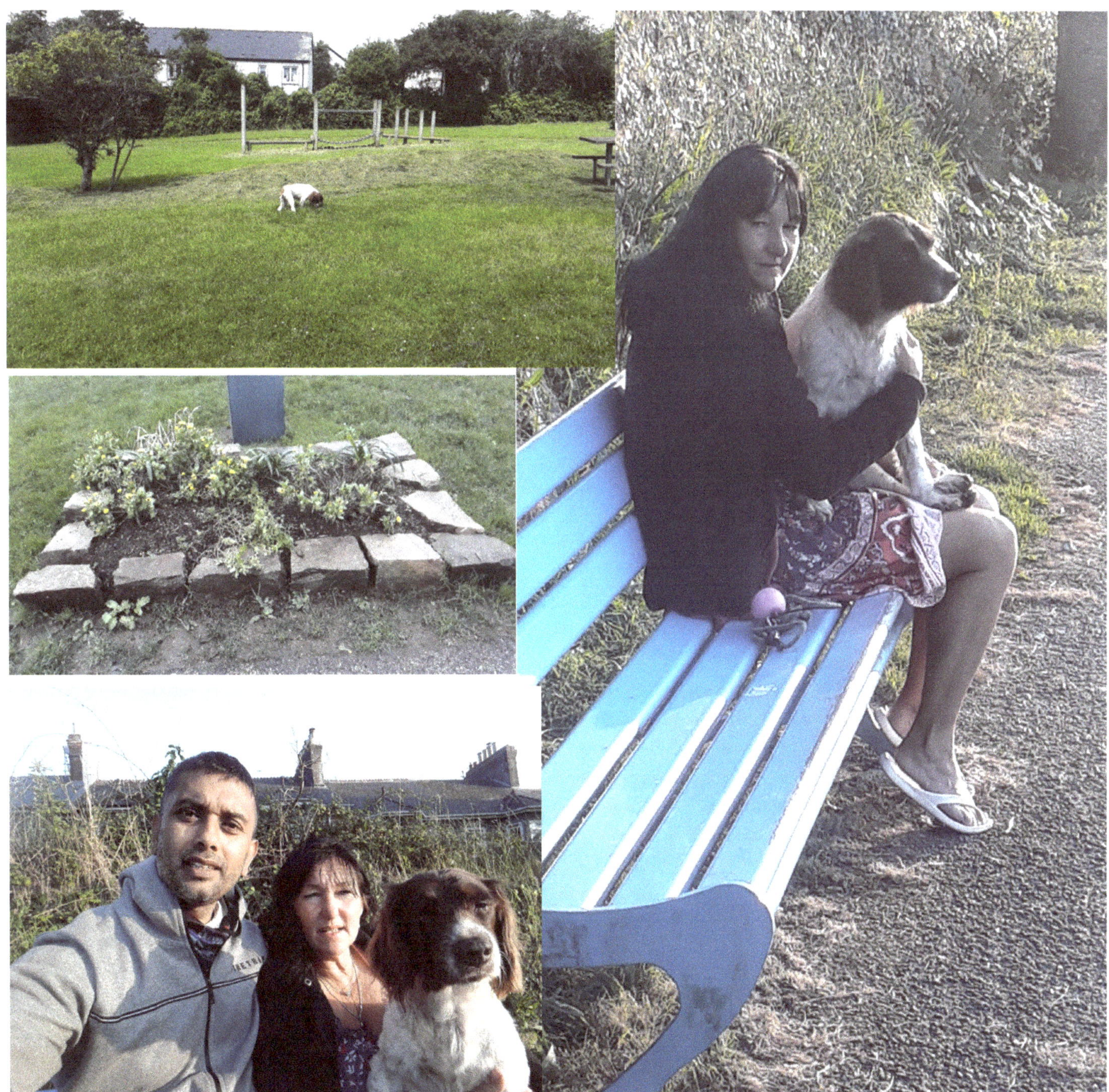

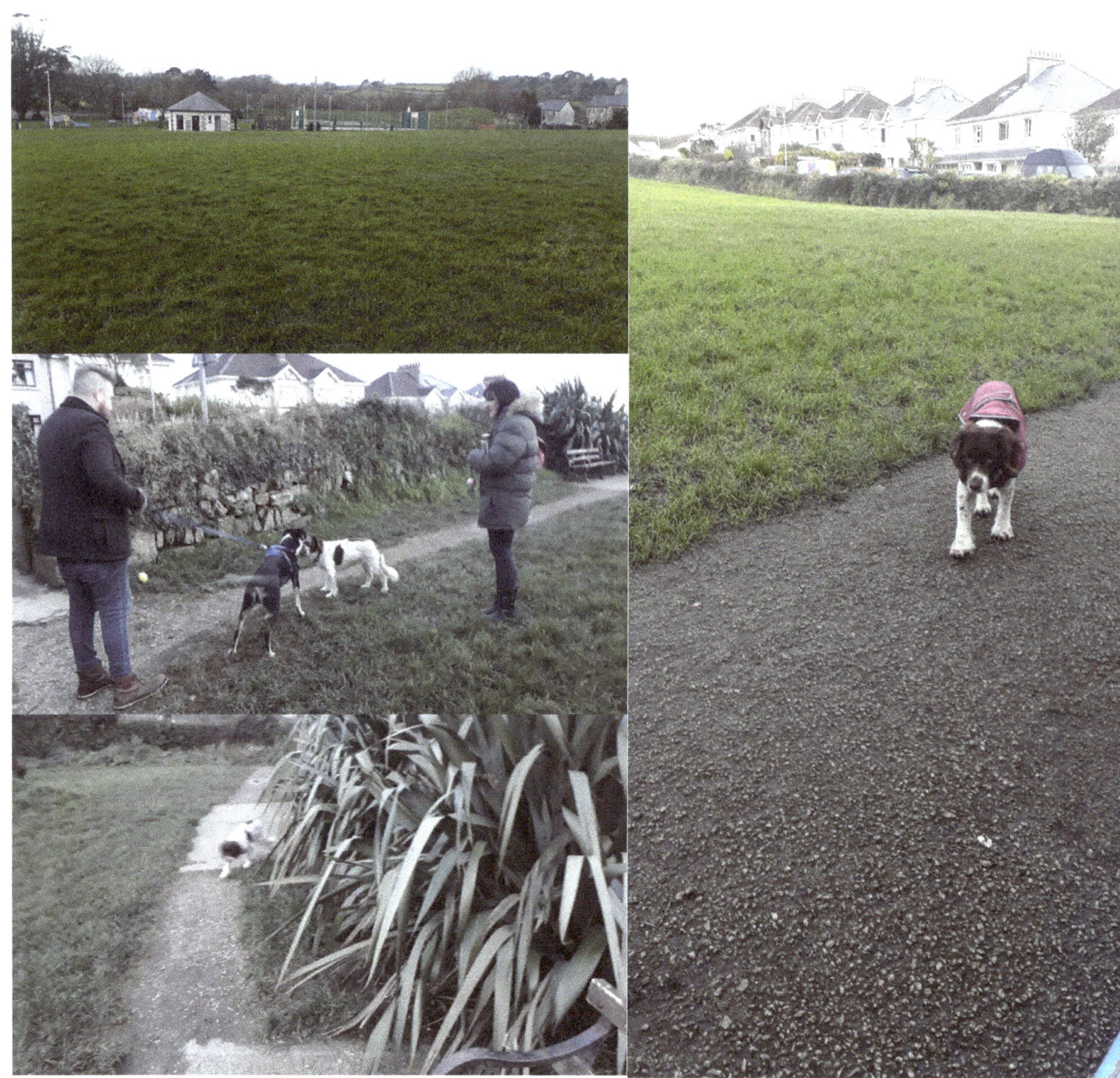

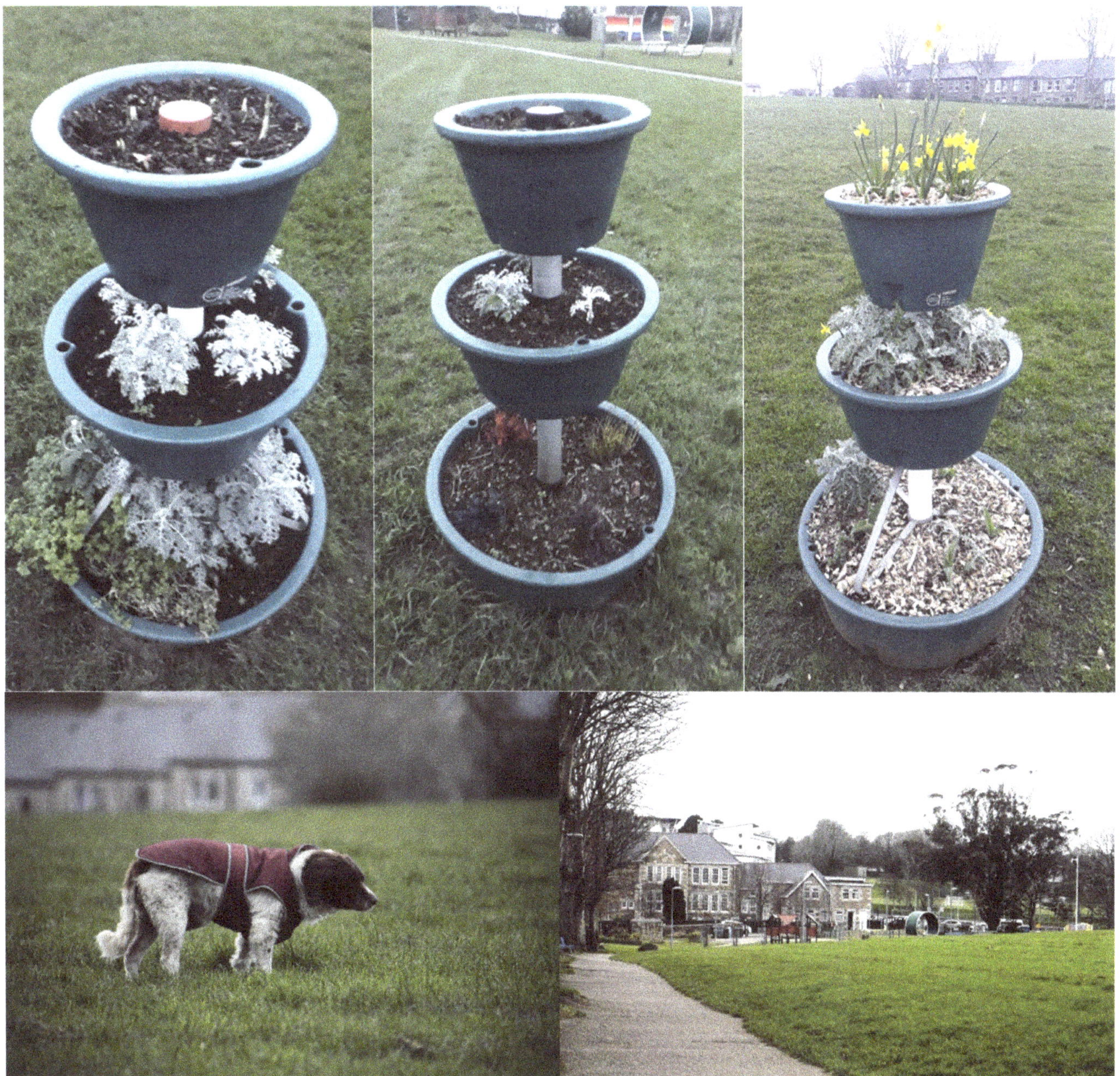

Many walks and friends made, come and gone, and now you're gone, rest in peace Kes Akash.

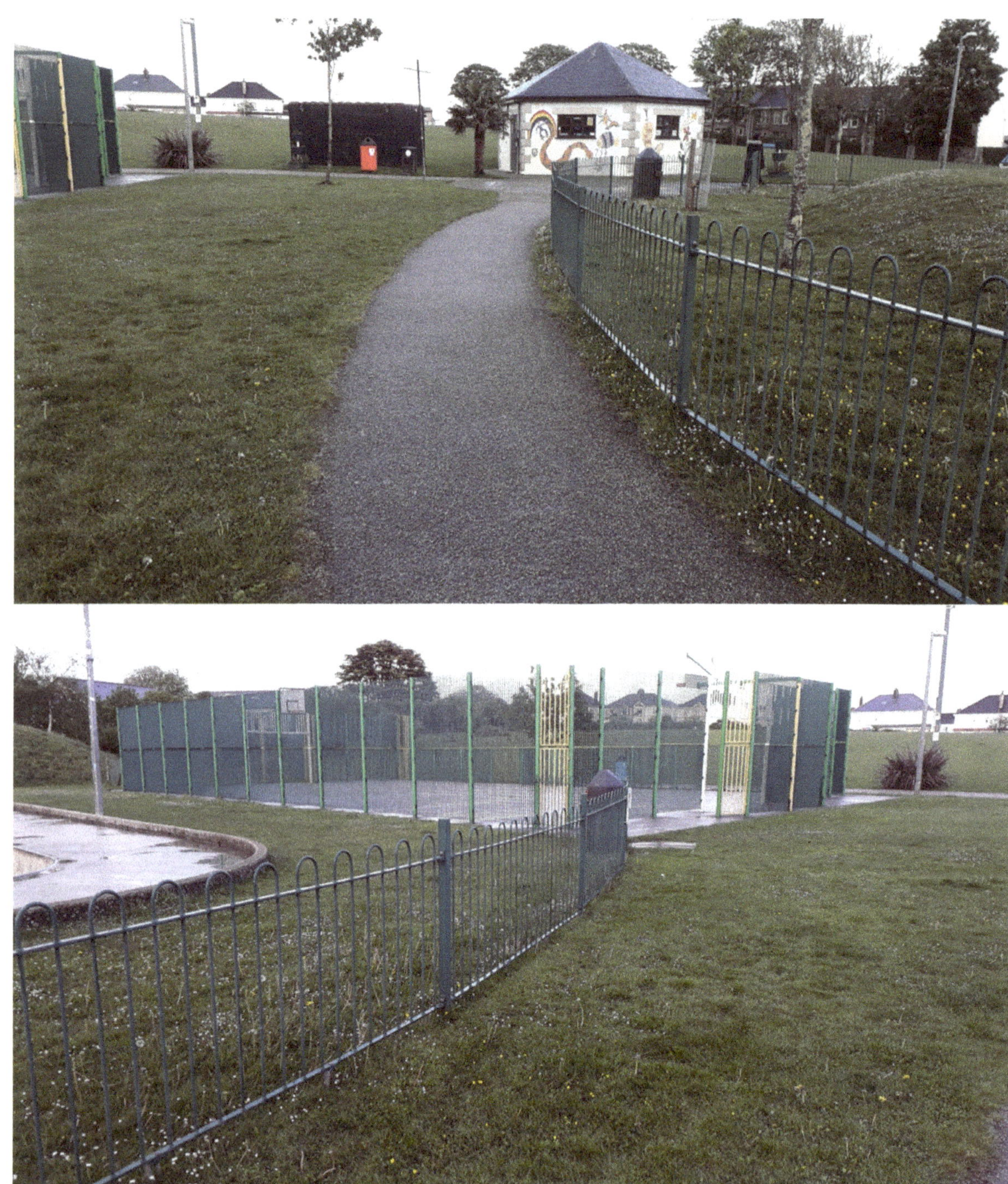

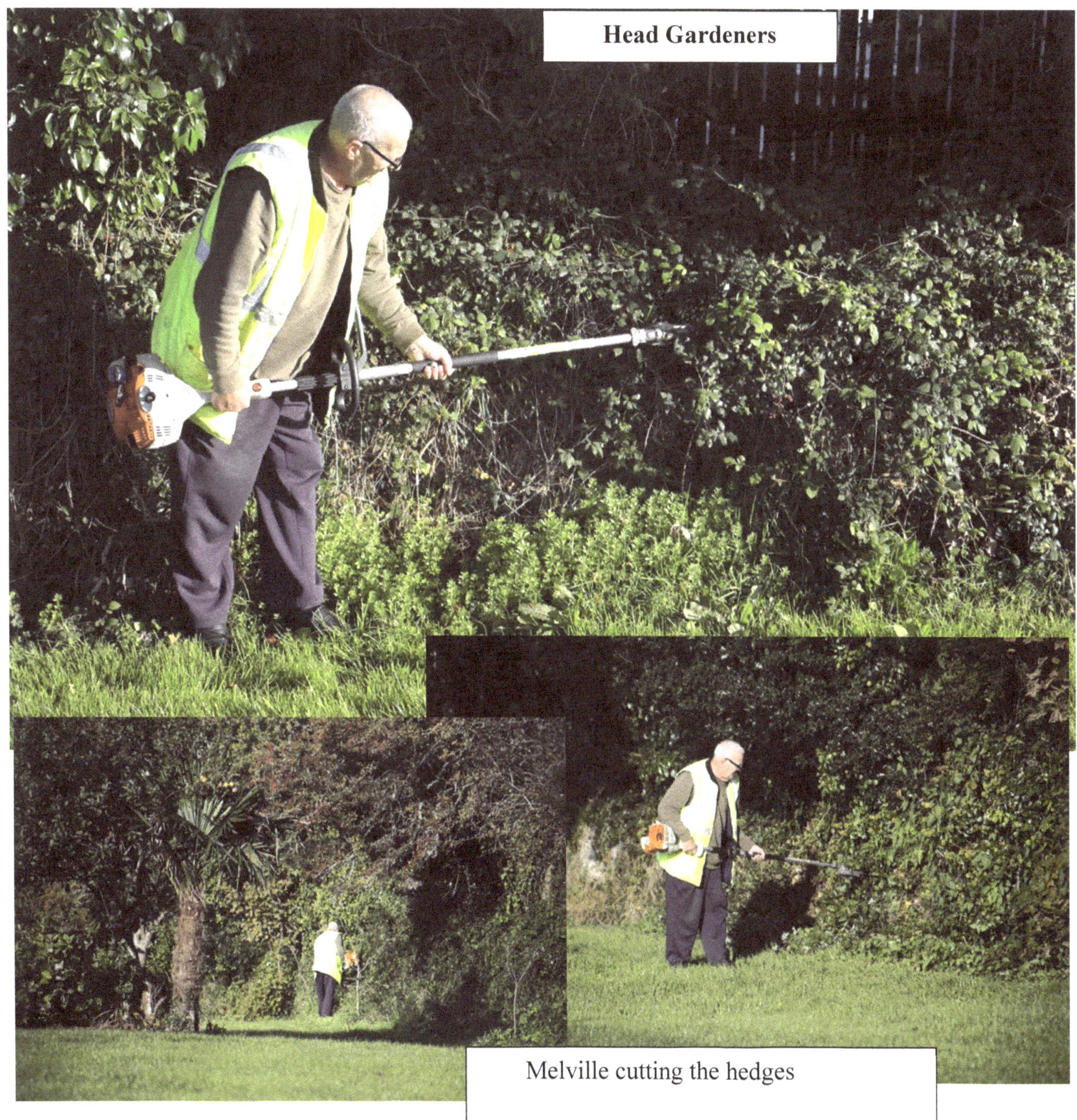

Head Gardeners

Melville cutting the hedges

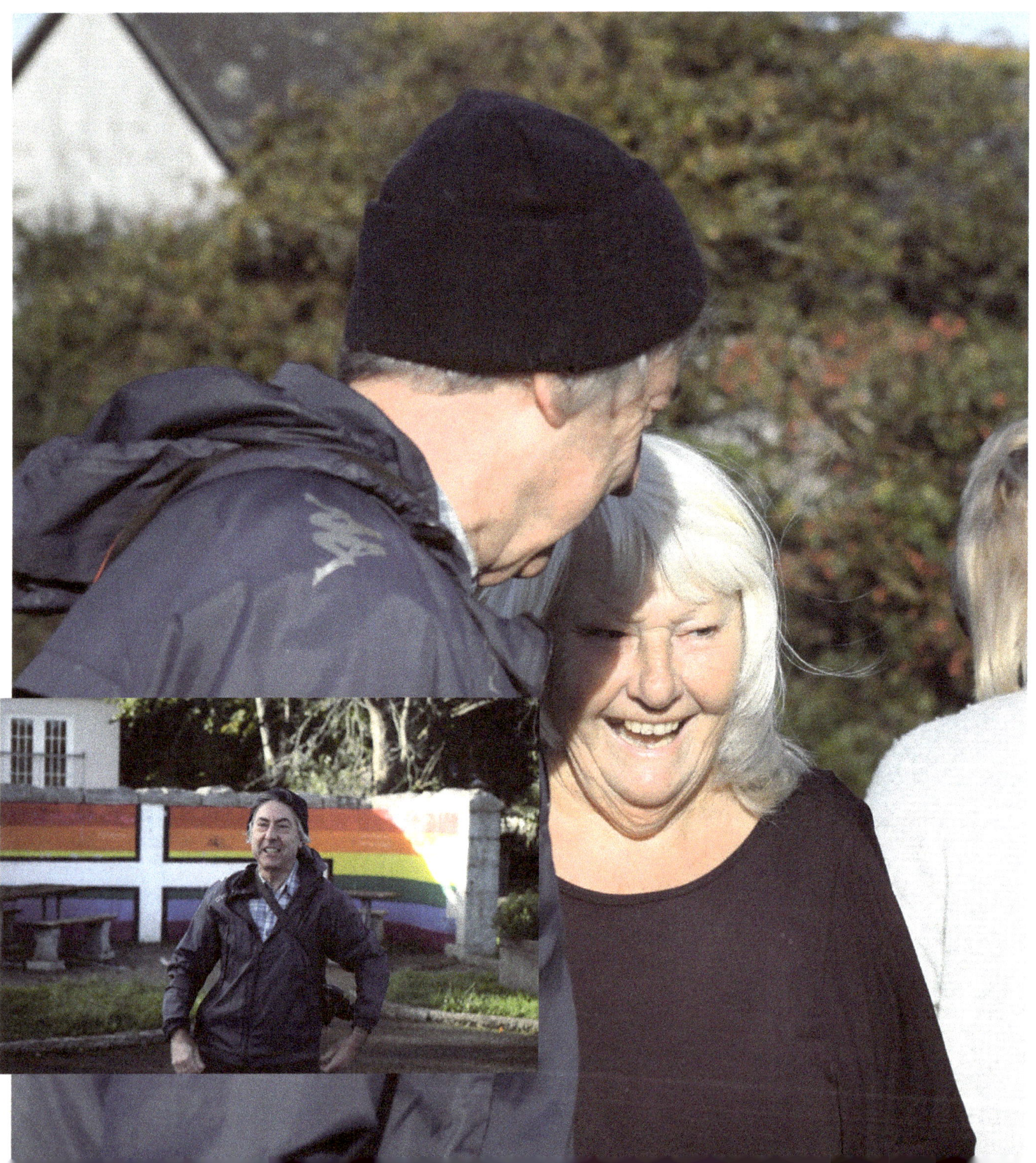

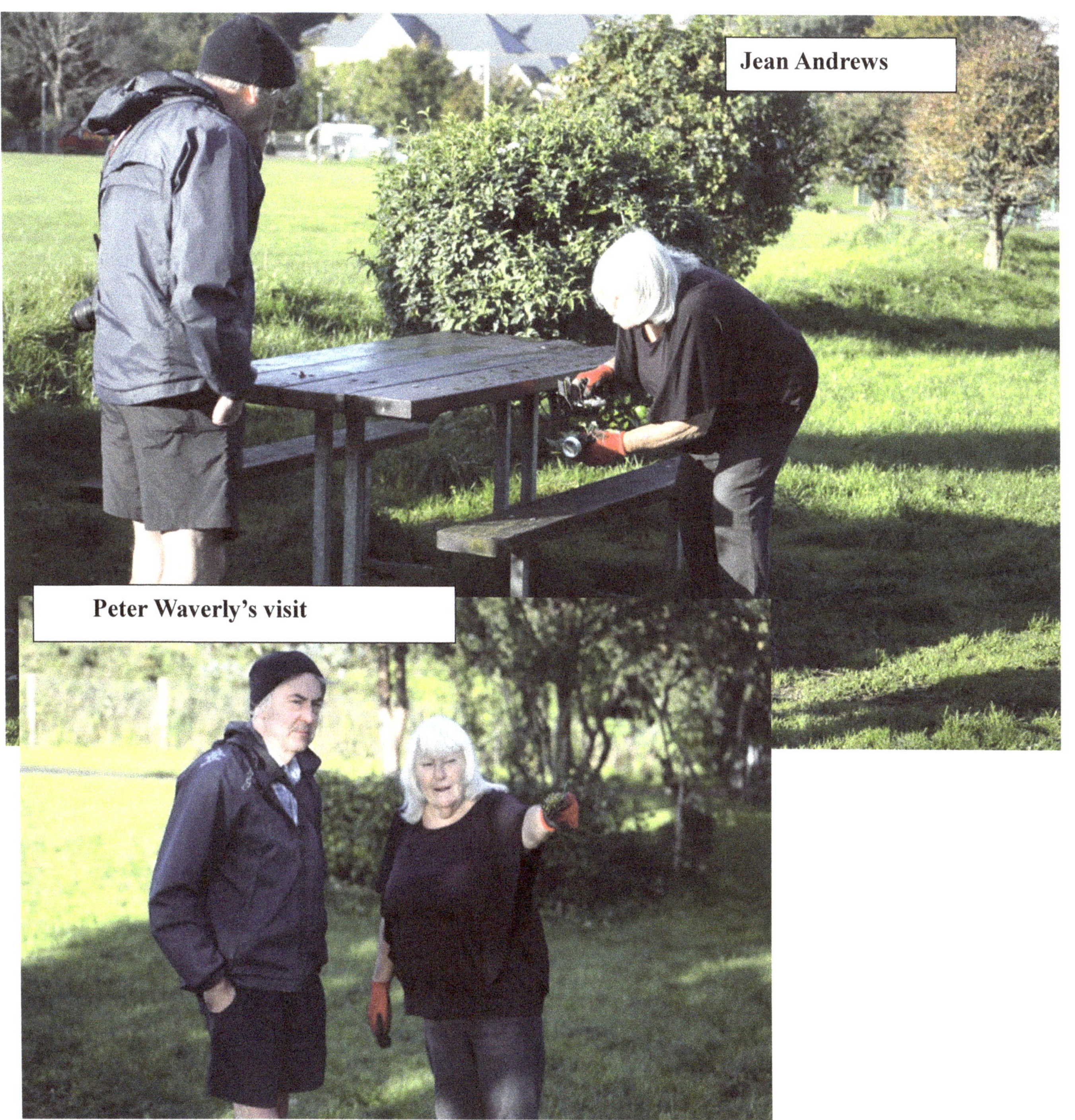
Jean Andrews
Peter Waverly's visit

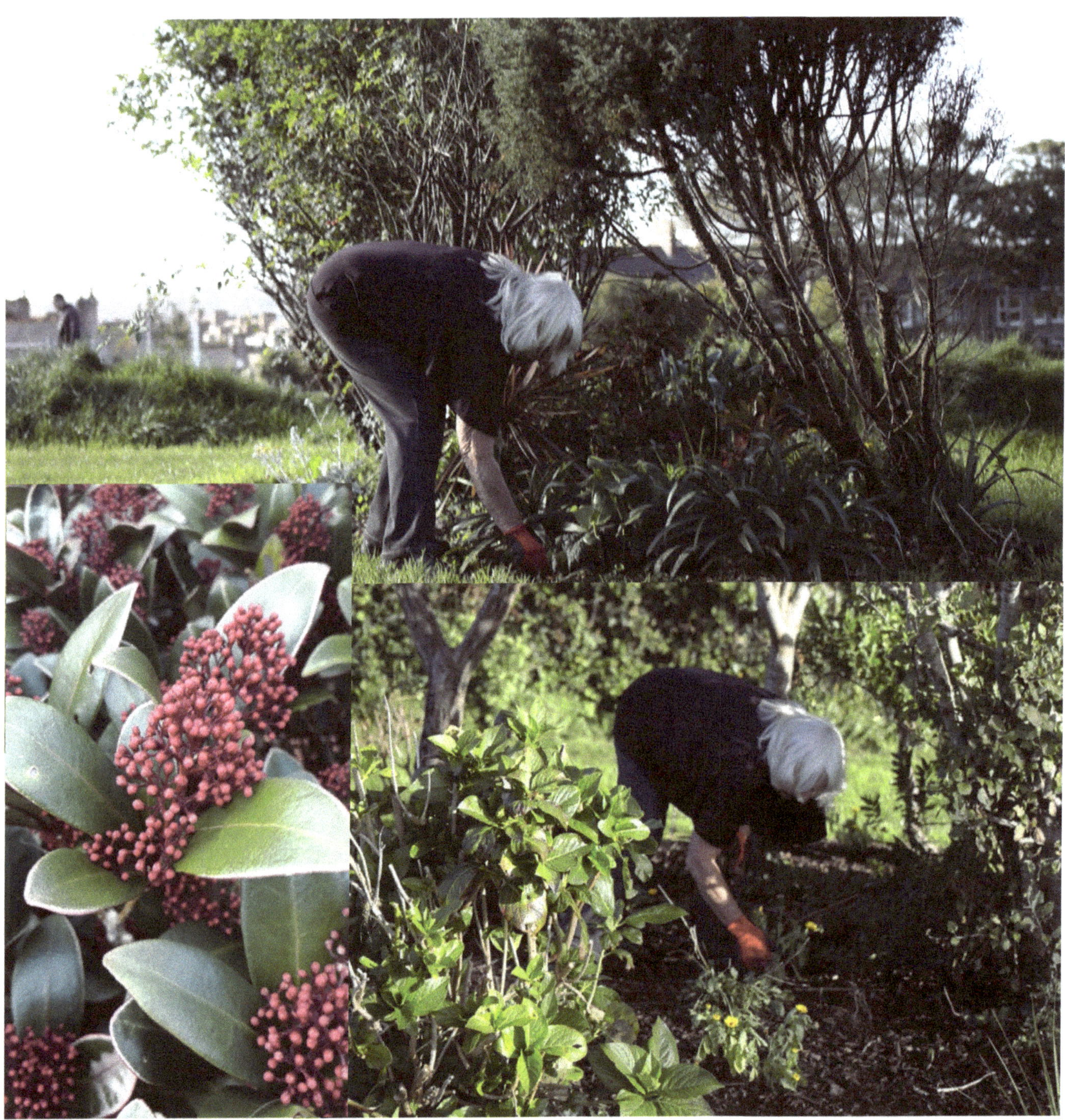

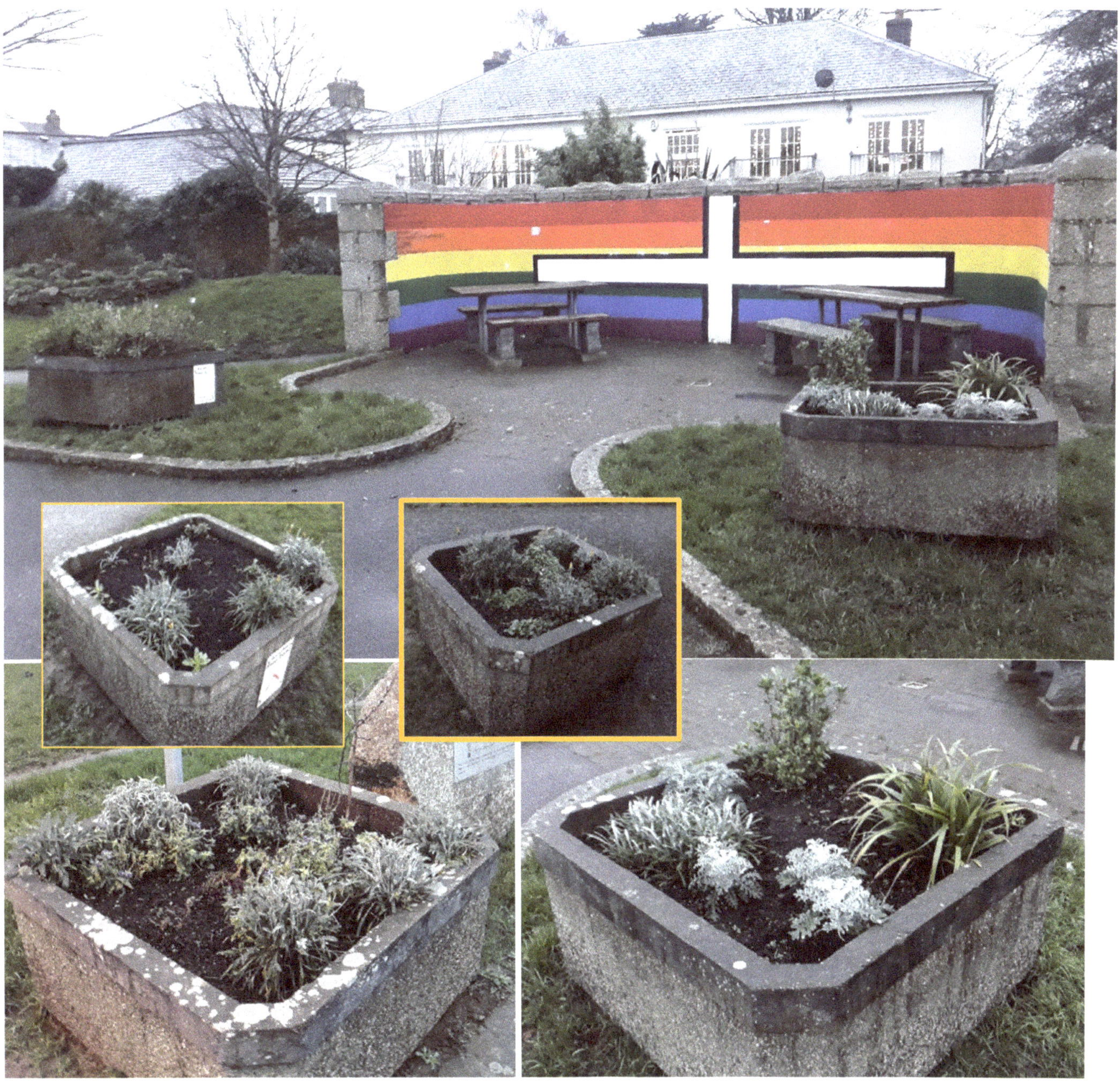

Planters

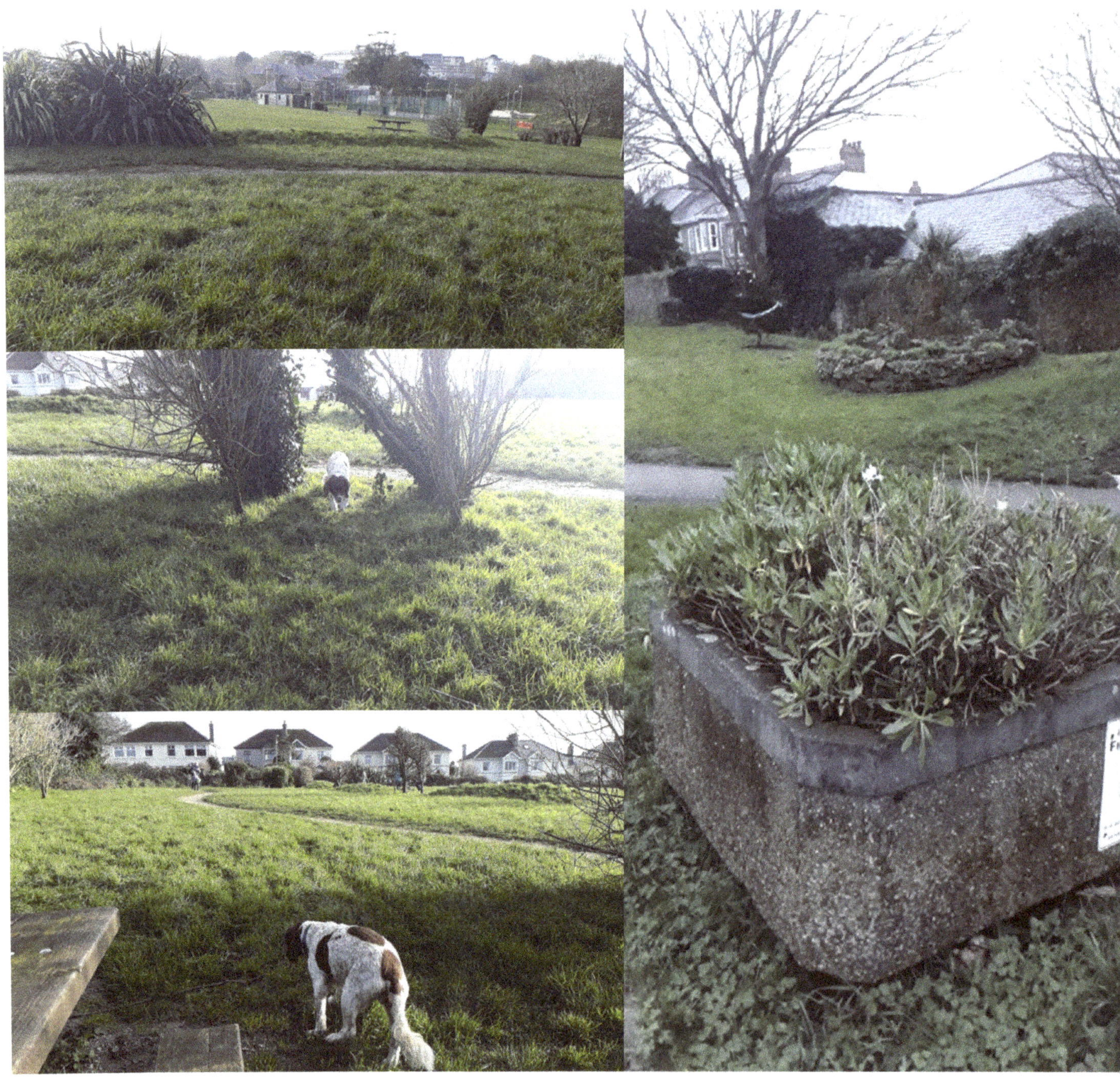

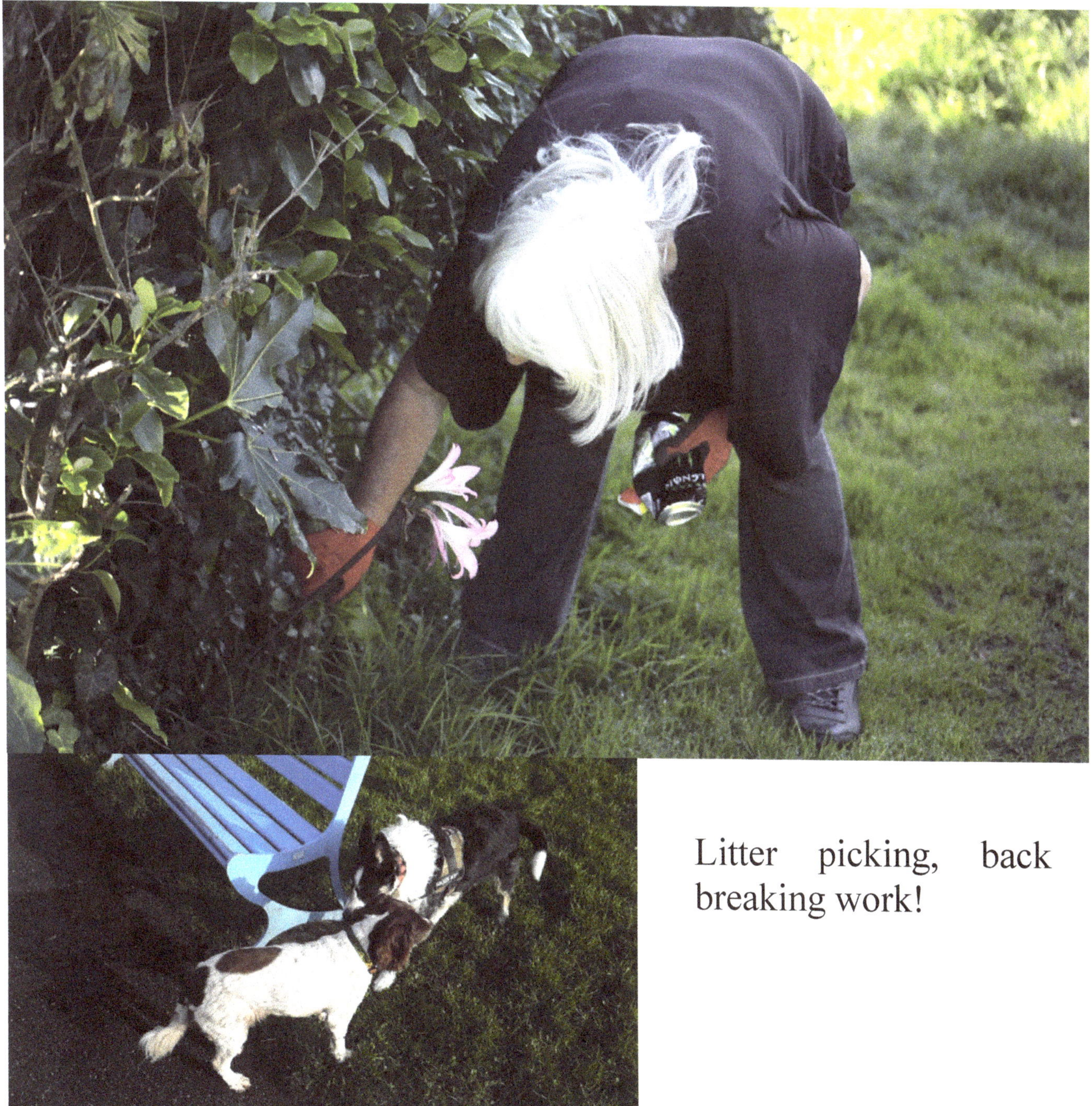

Litter picking, back breaking work!

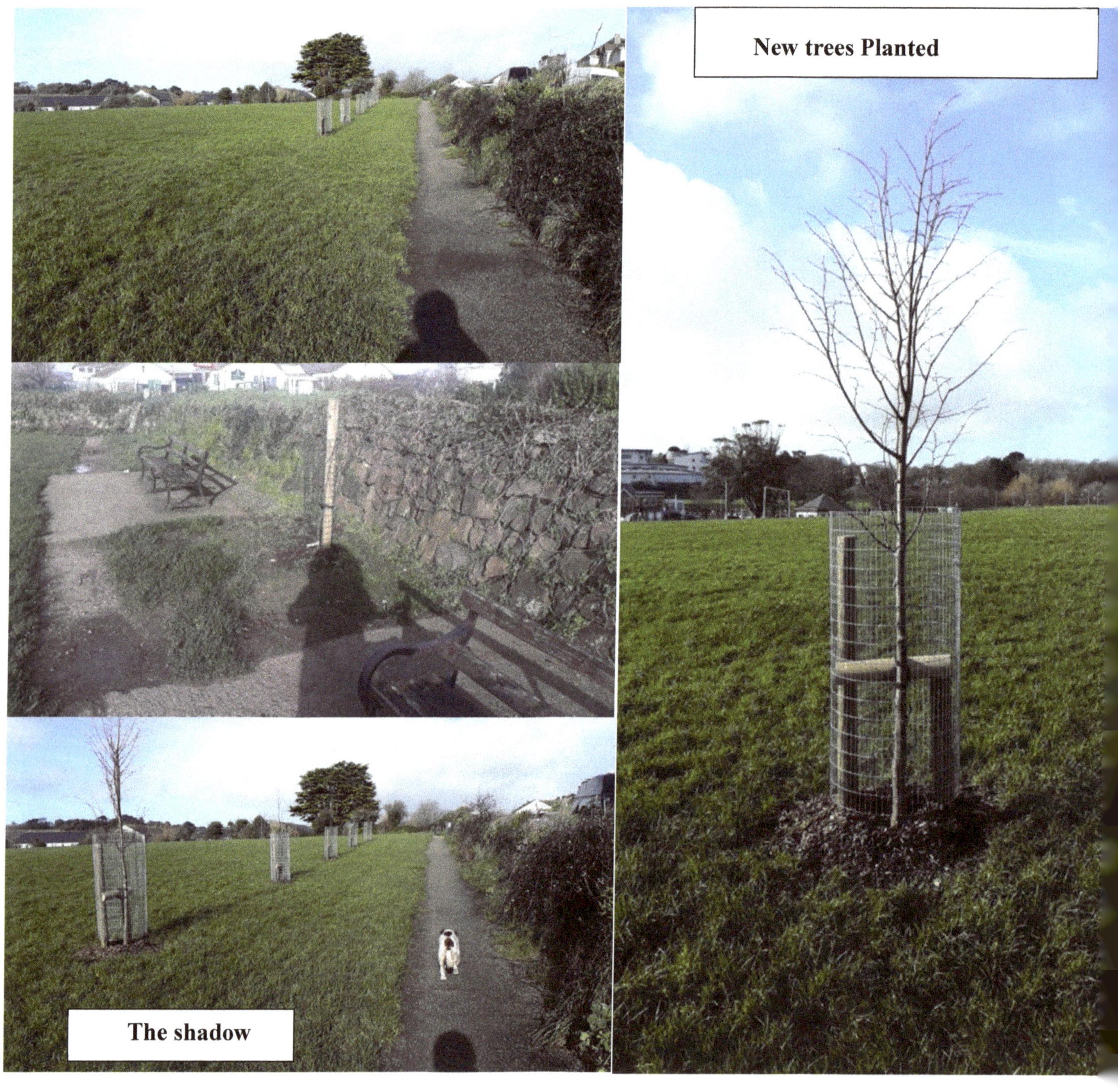
New trees Planted
The shadow

The Fair

THRILLER EXPRESS
Rowland's
FUN FAIR
Penzance Princess May
WEDS 19th APRIL
to SUN 23rd
6PM WEEKDAYS
2PM SAT & SUN
BIGGER AND BETTER THAN EVER

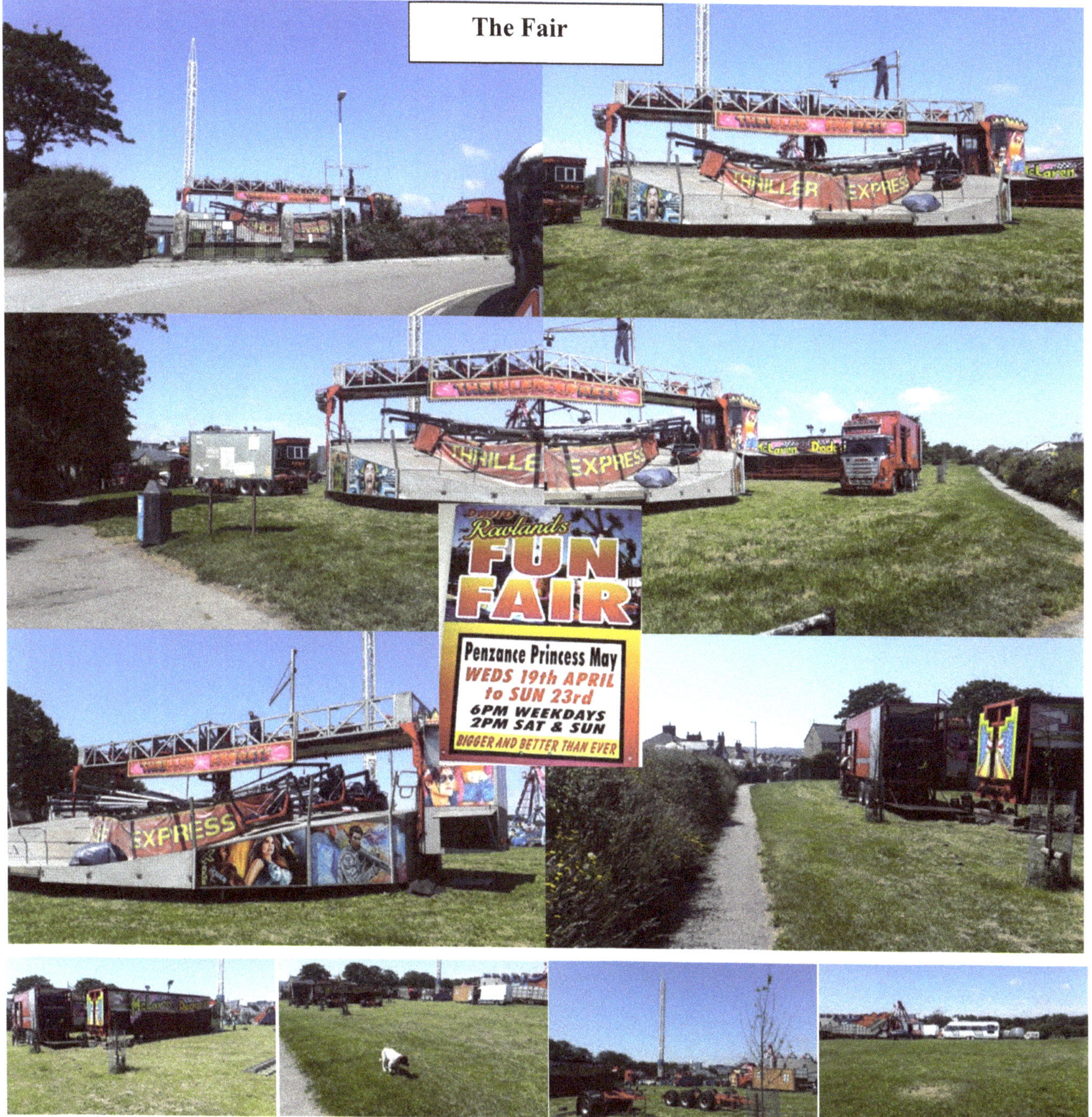

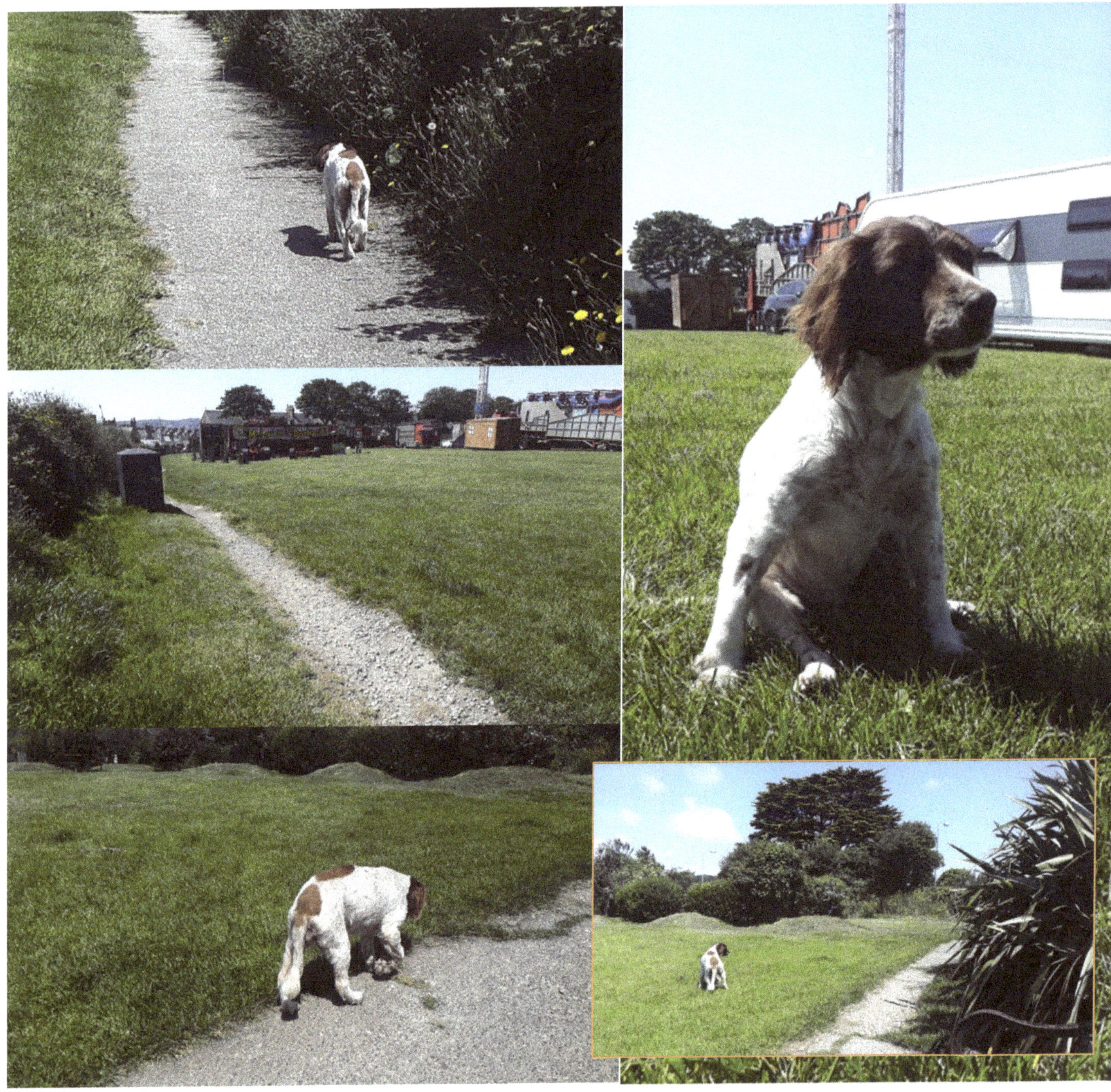

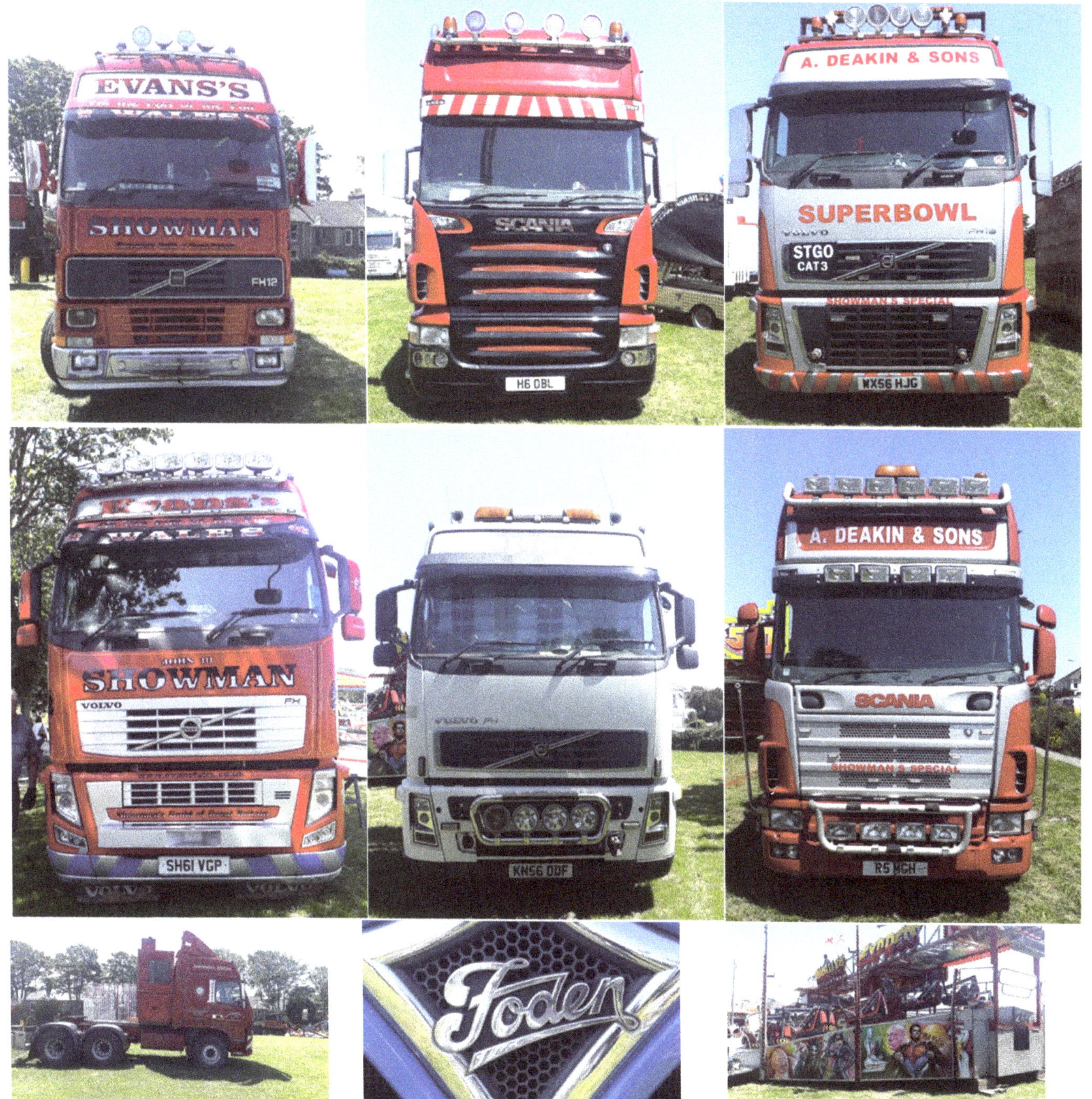
EVANS'S
SHOWMAN
FH12
SCANIA
H6 OBL
A. DEAKIN & SONS
SUPERBOWL
STGO
CAT 3
WX56 HJG
WALES
SHOWMAN
VOLVO
SH61 VGP
KN56 ODF
A. DEAKIN & SONS
SCANIA
SHOWMAN'S SPECIAL
R5 MGH
Foden

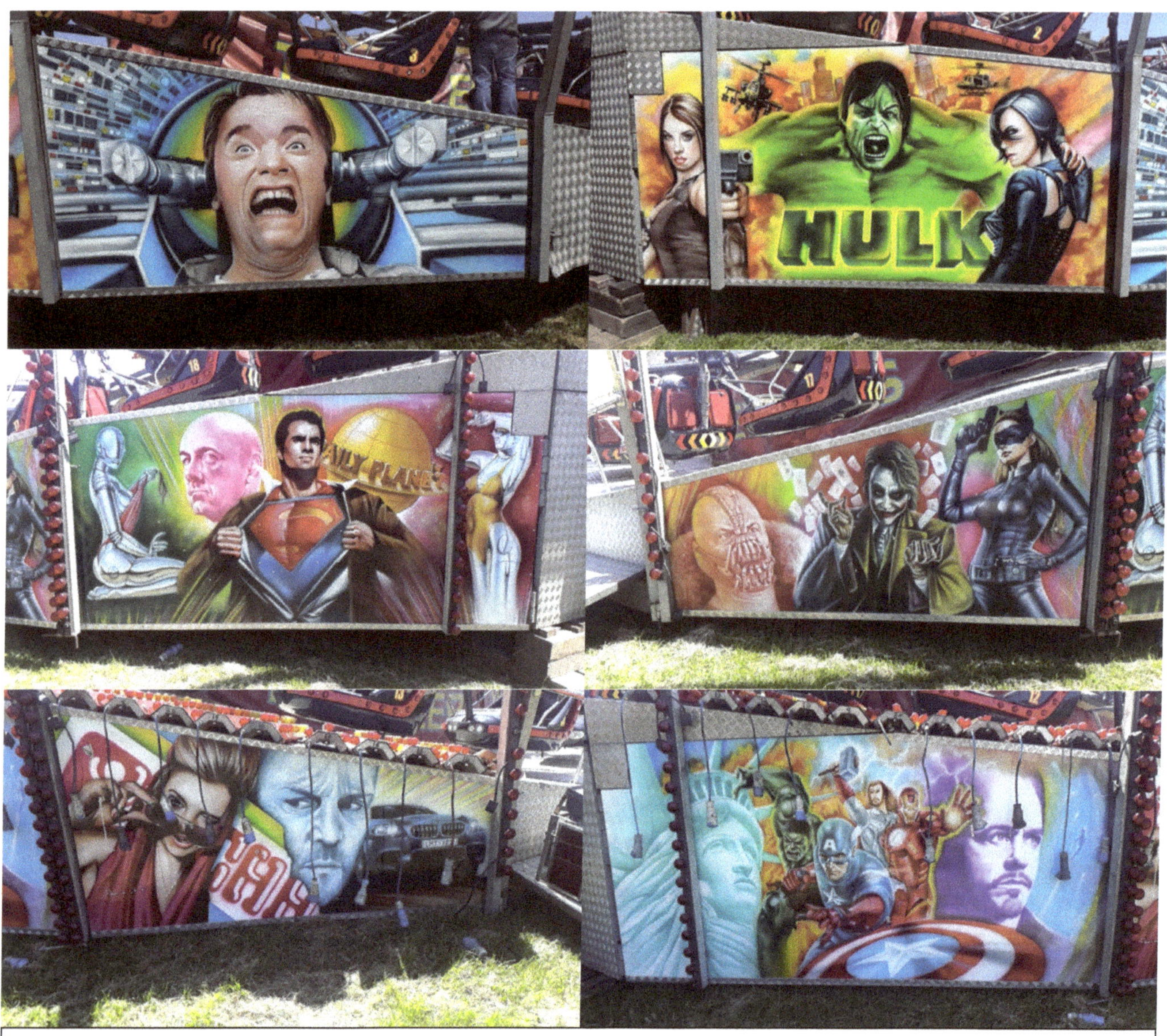

When the fair comes to town

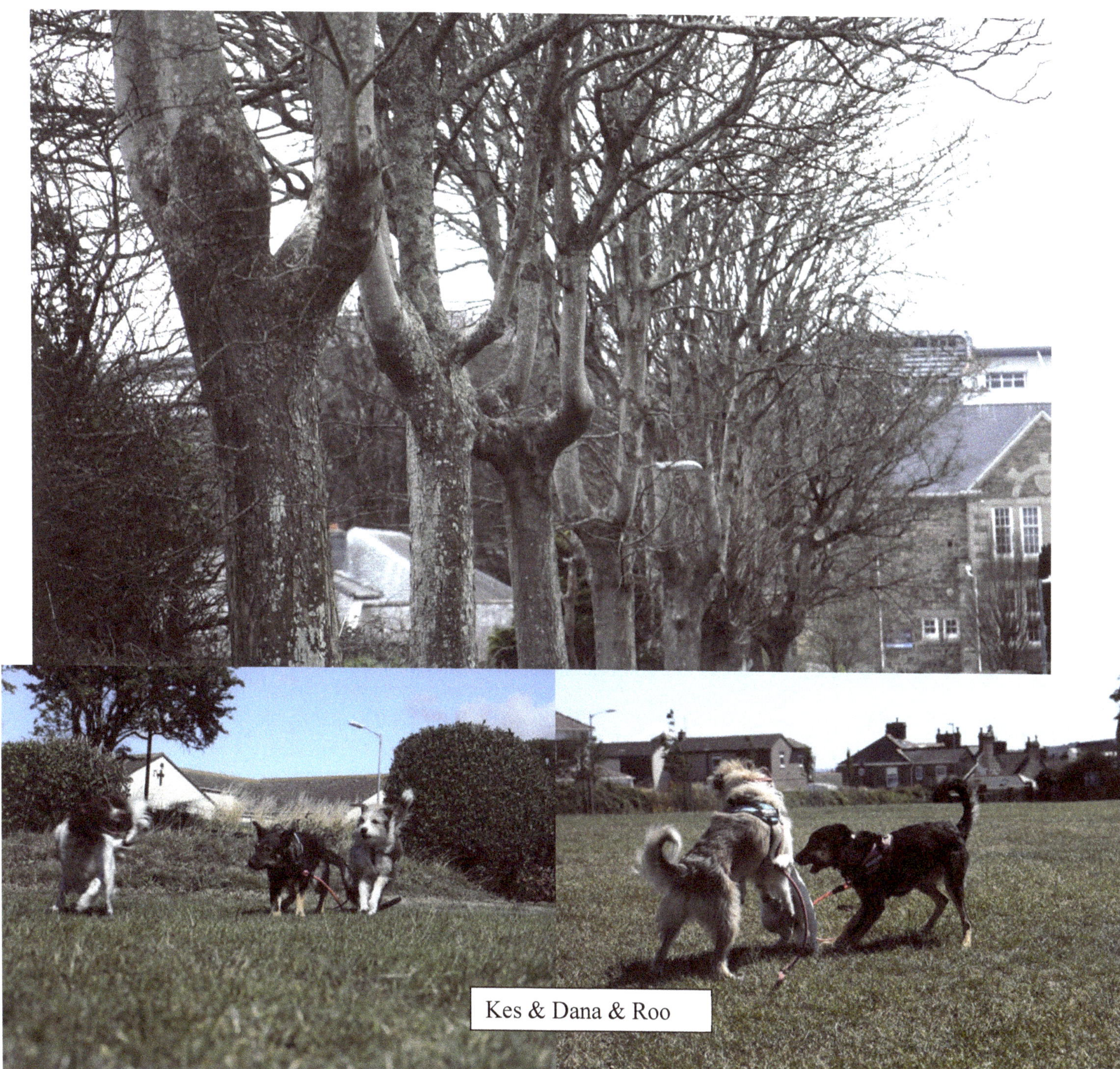

Kes & Dana & Roo

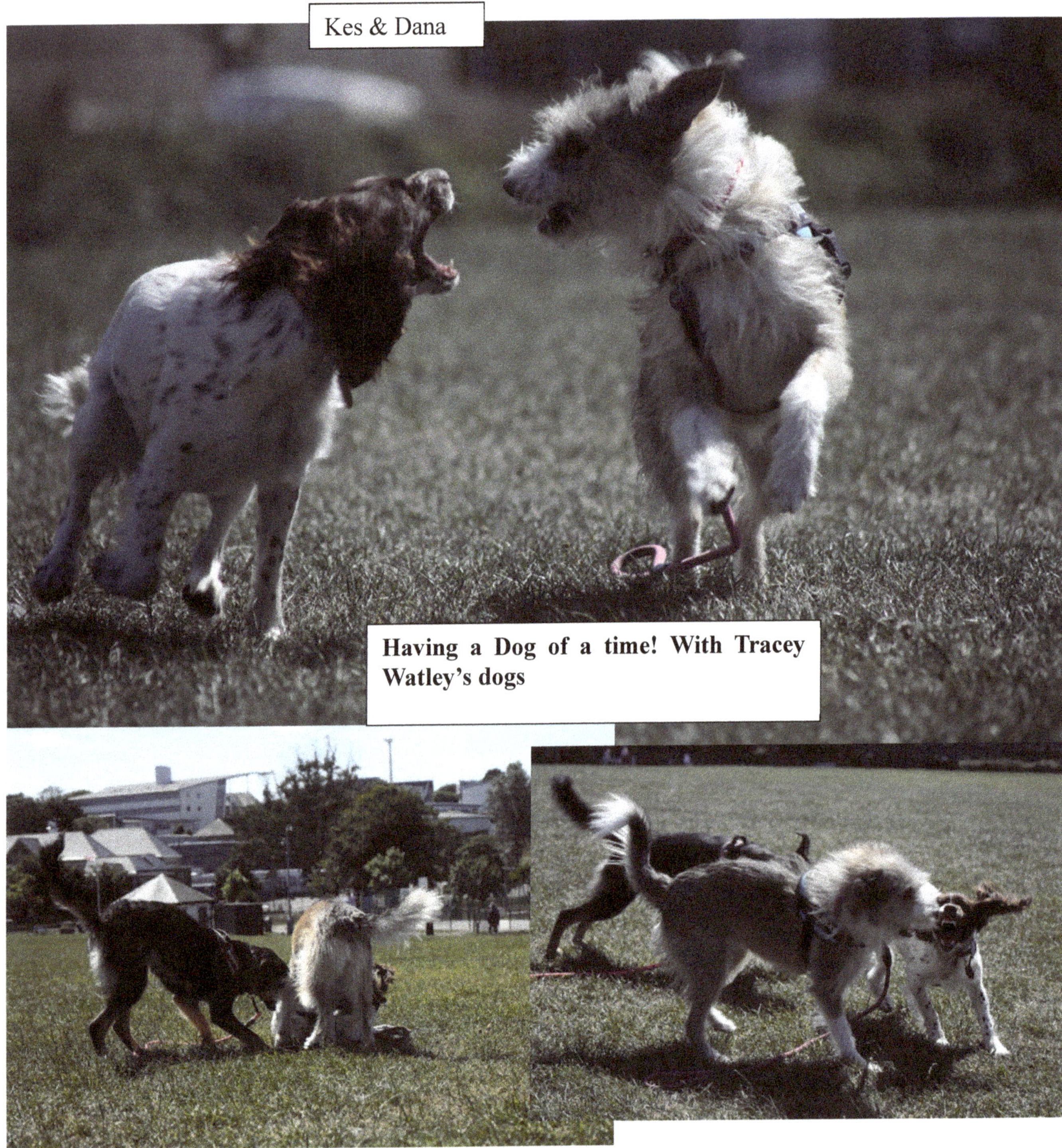
Kes & Dana
Having a Dog of a time! With Tracey Watley's dogs

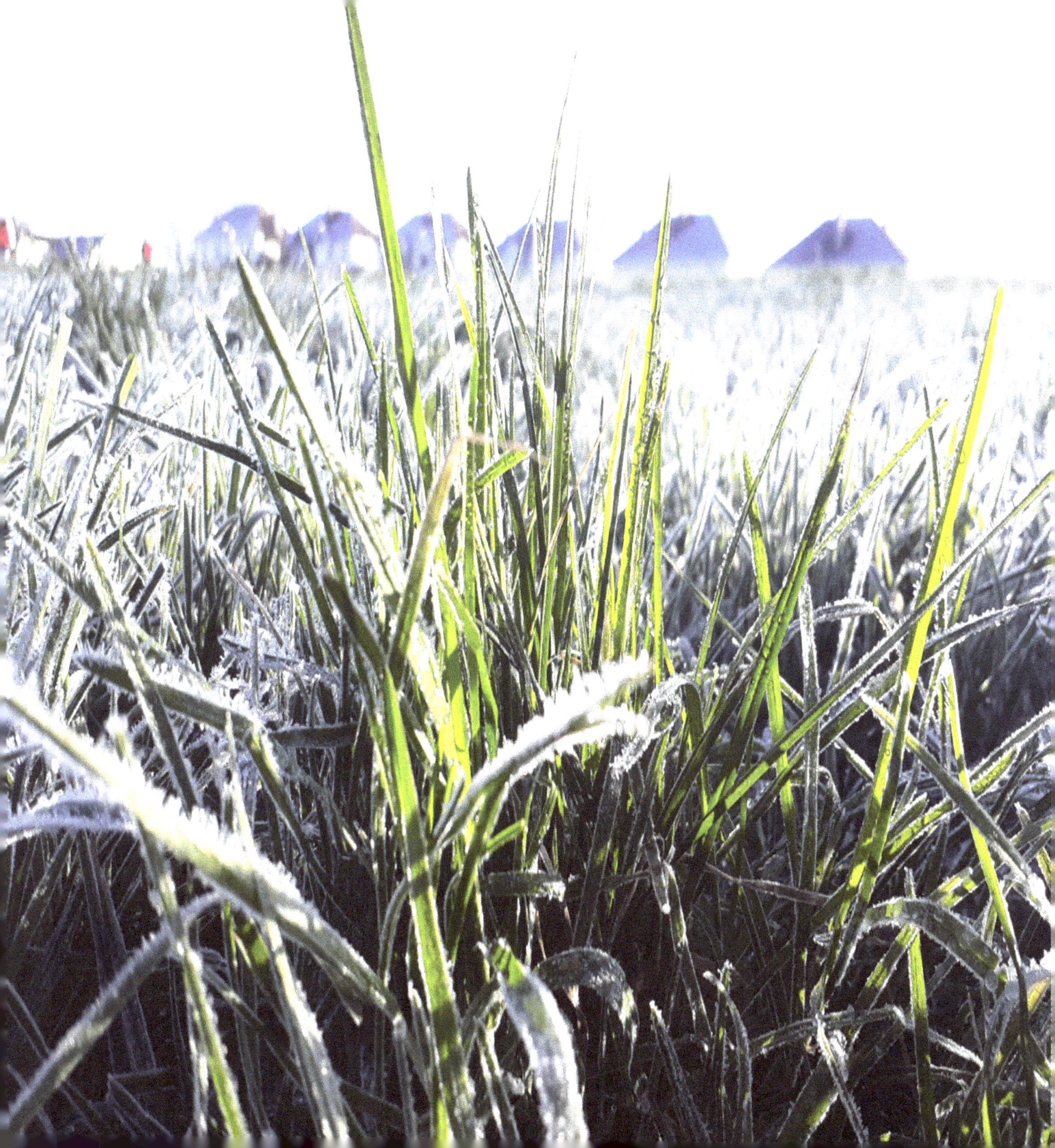

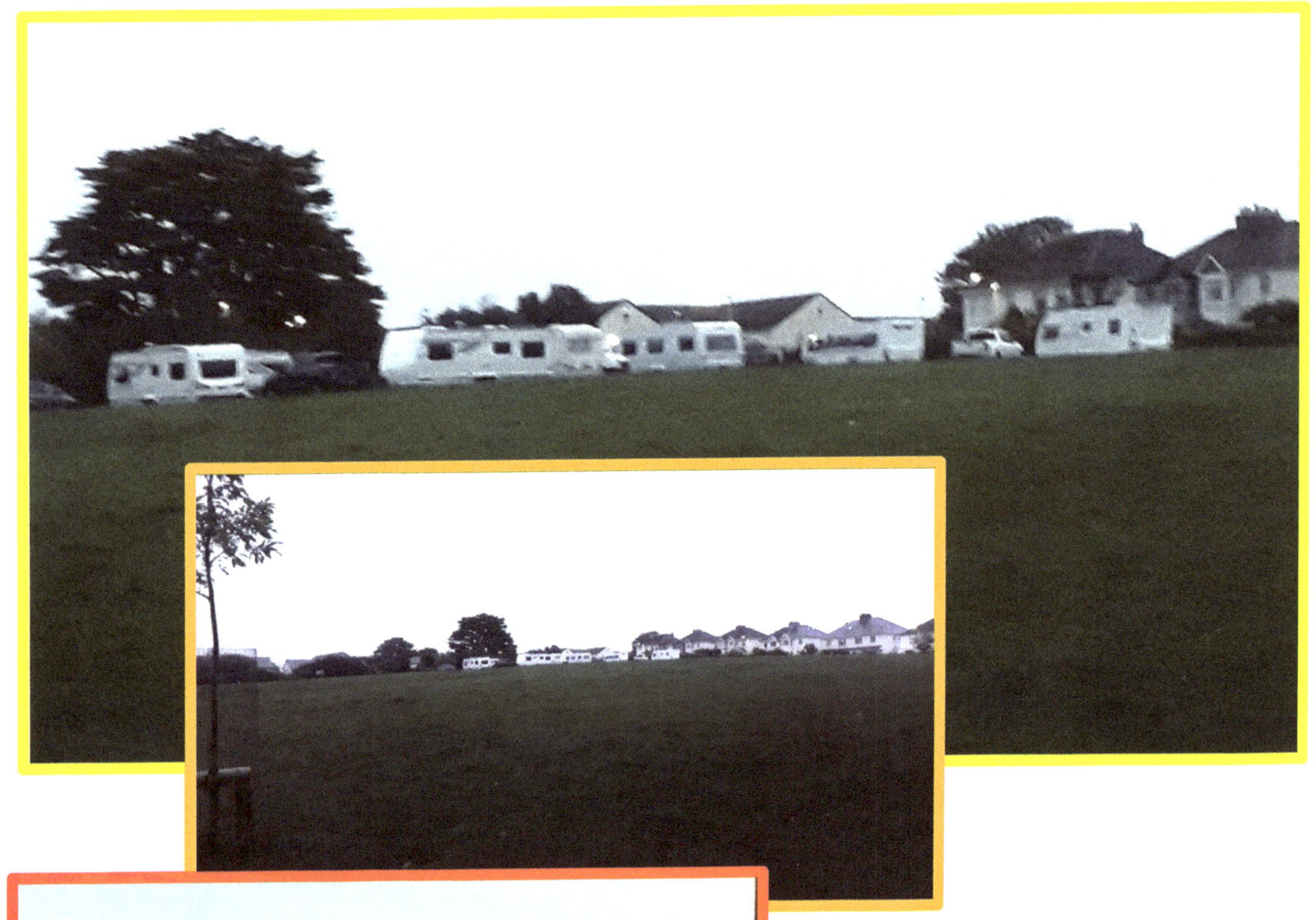

Travellers

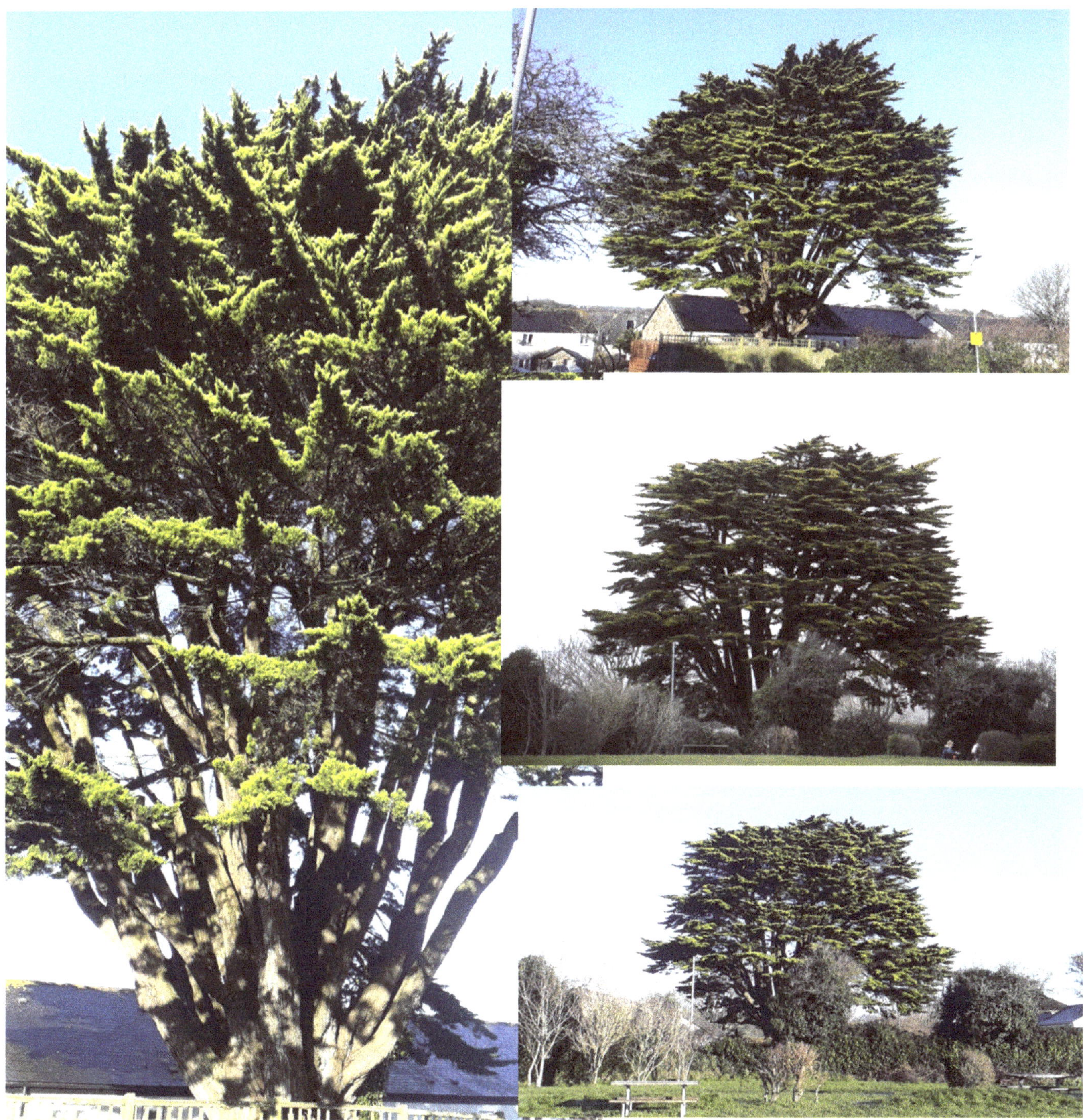

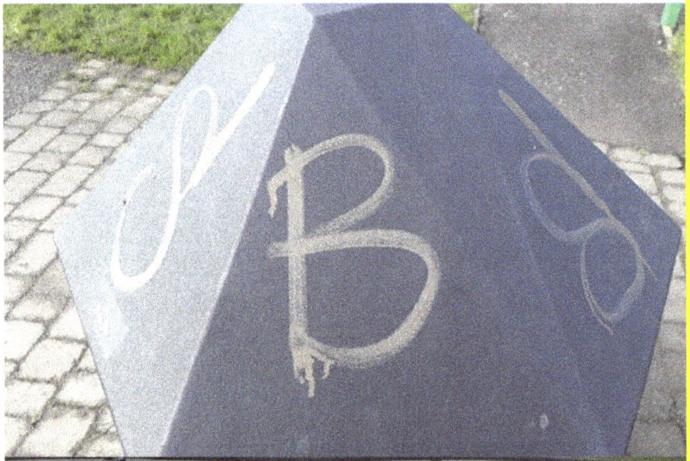

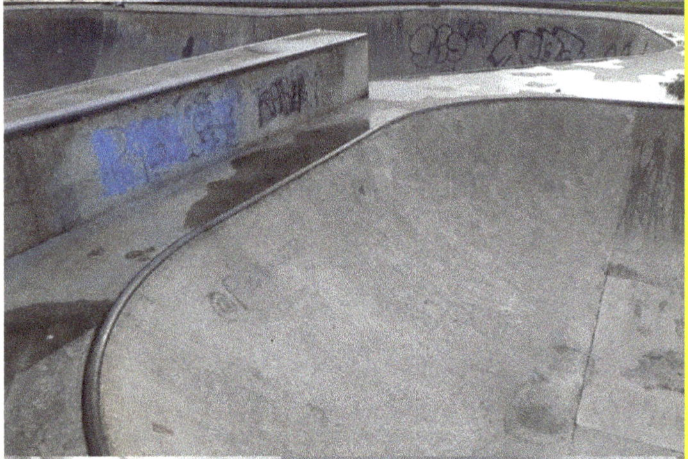

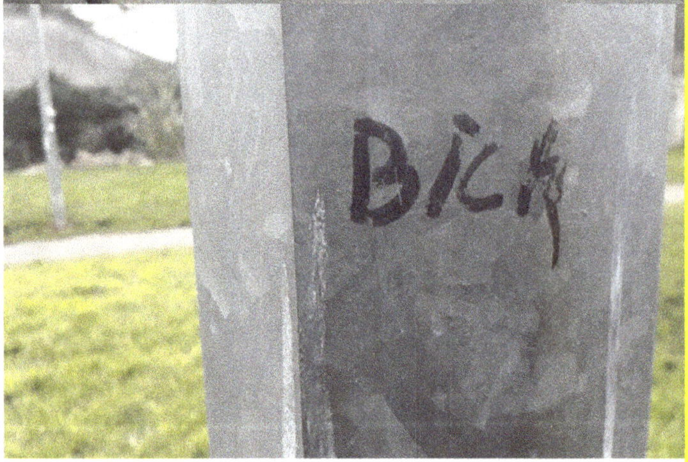

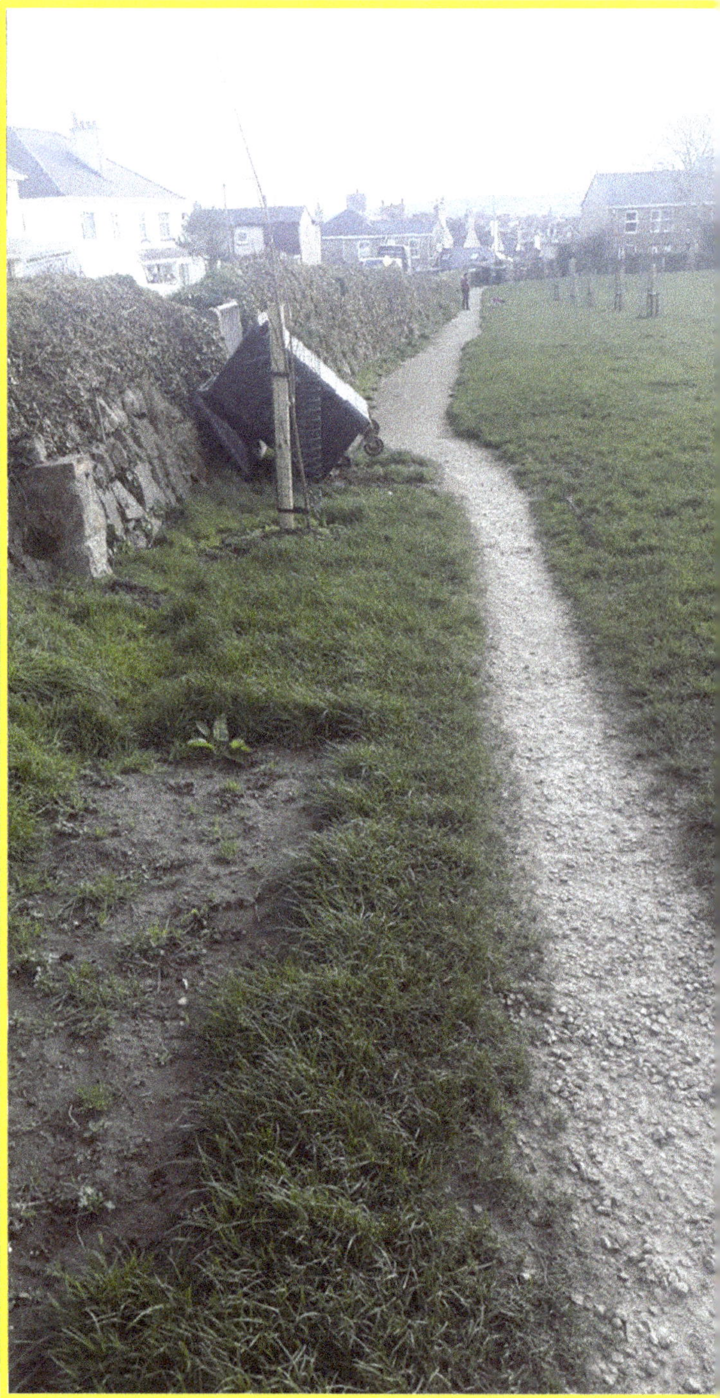

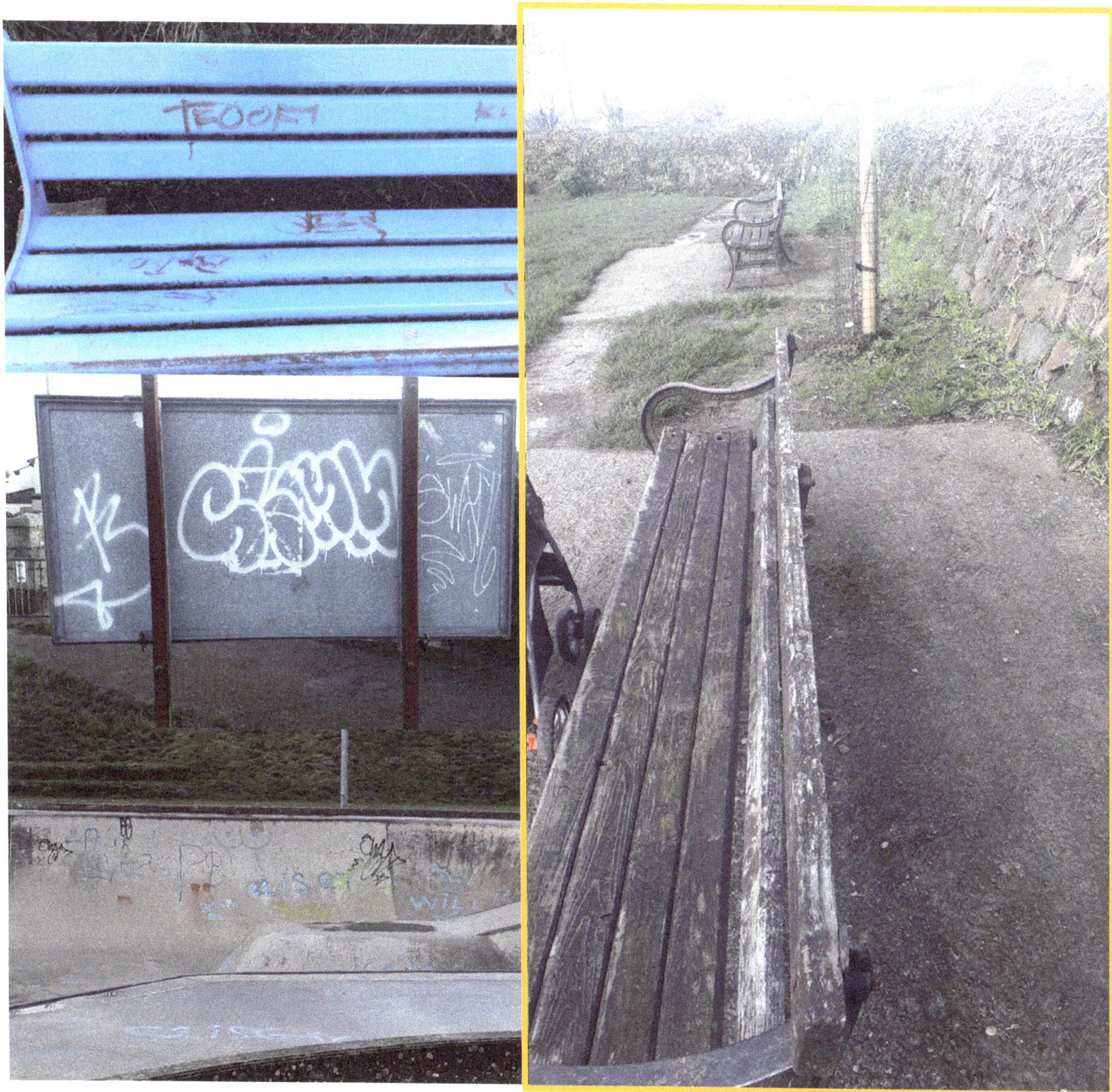

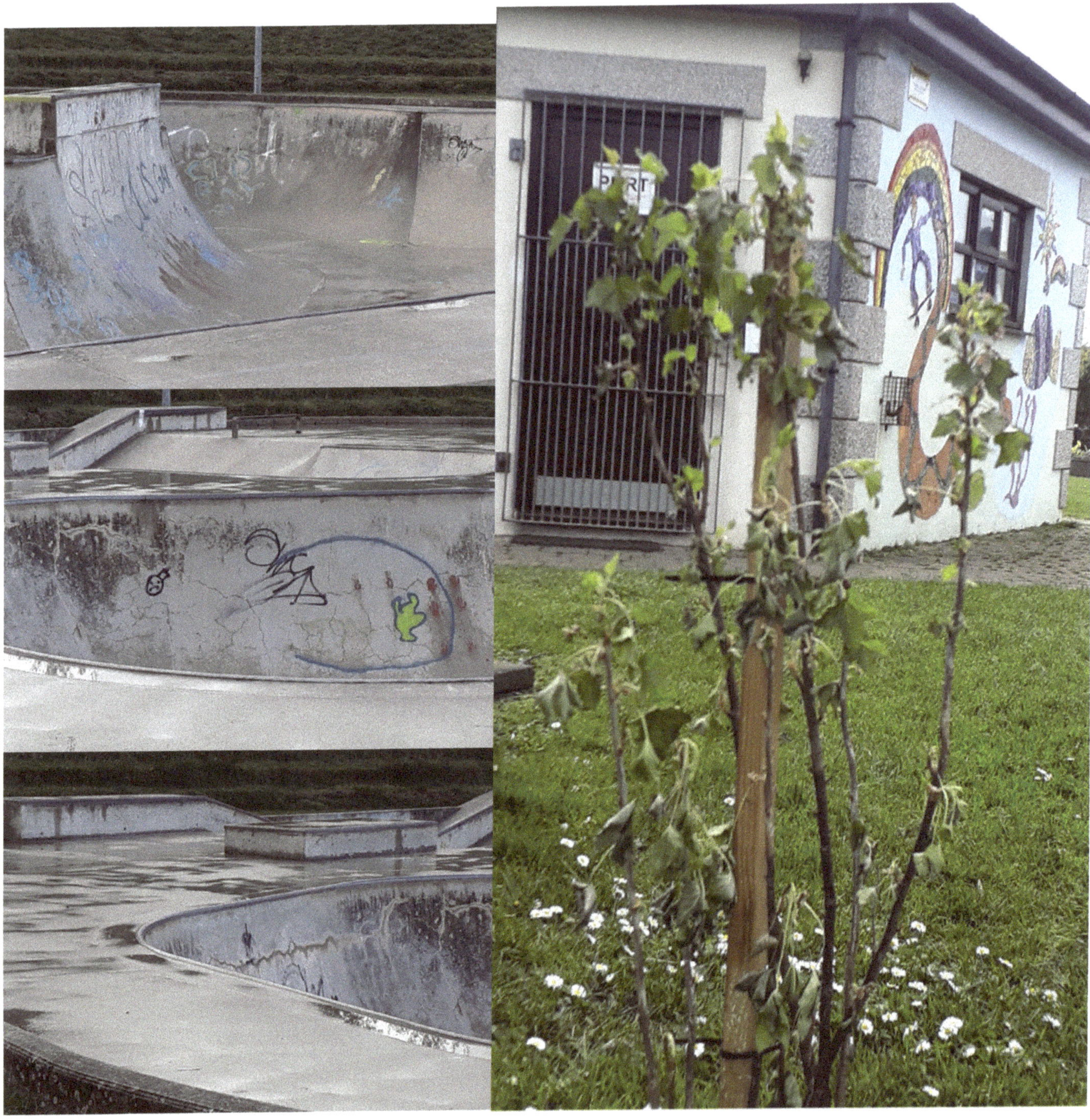

Queen's Last Jubilee

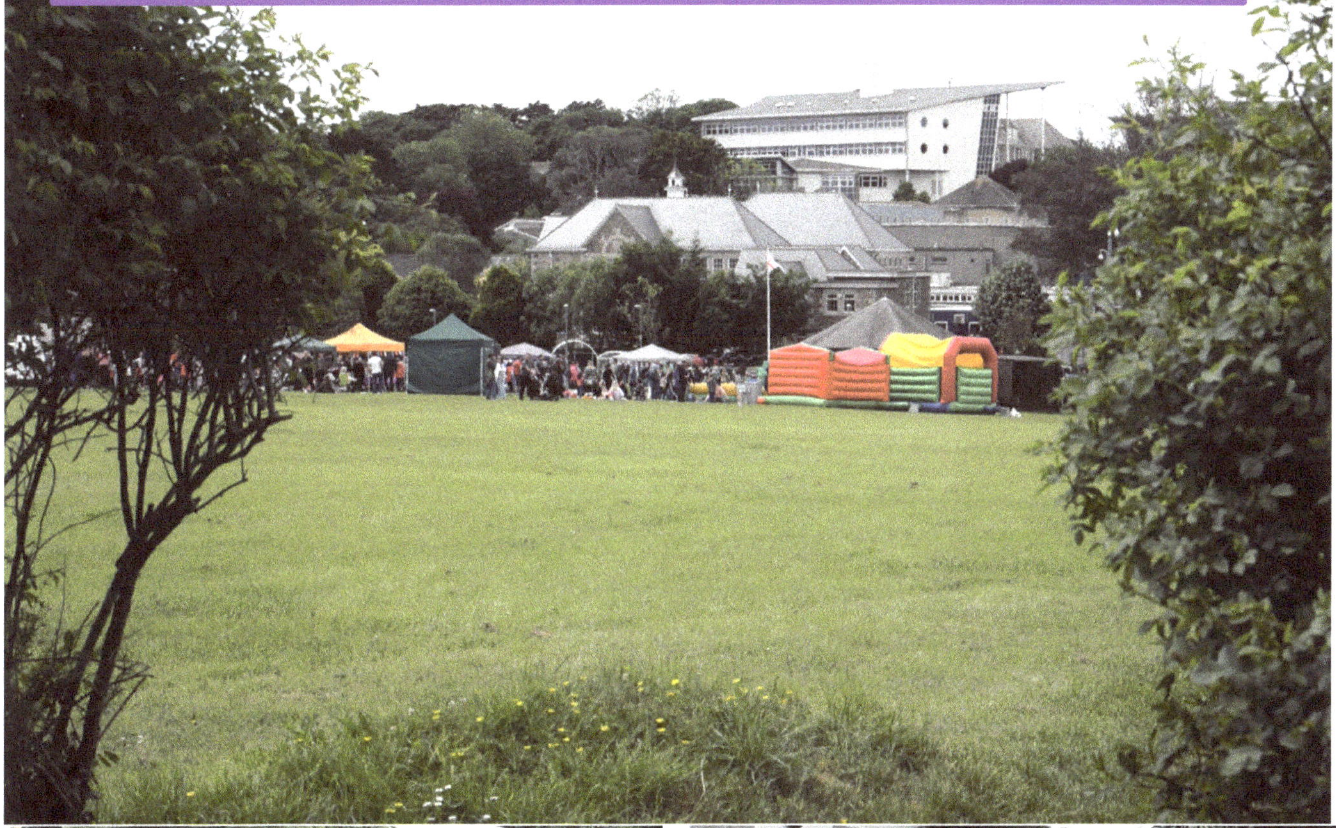

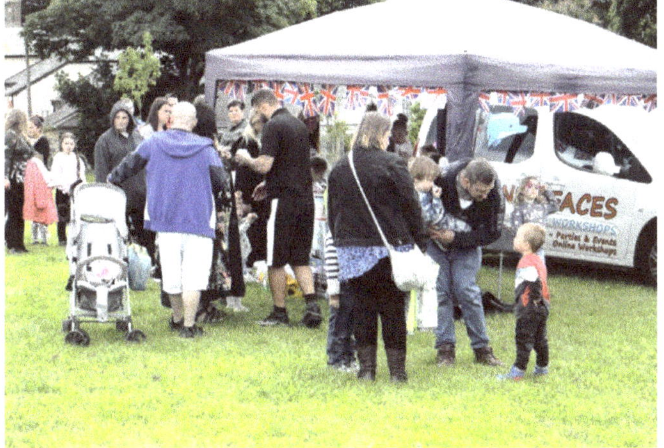

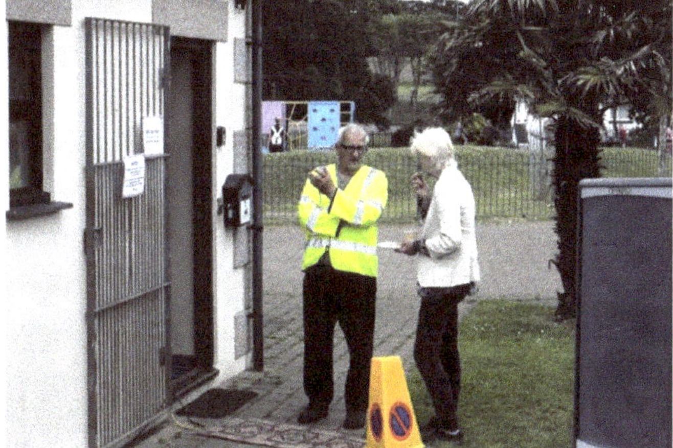

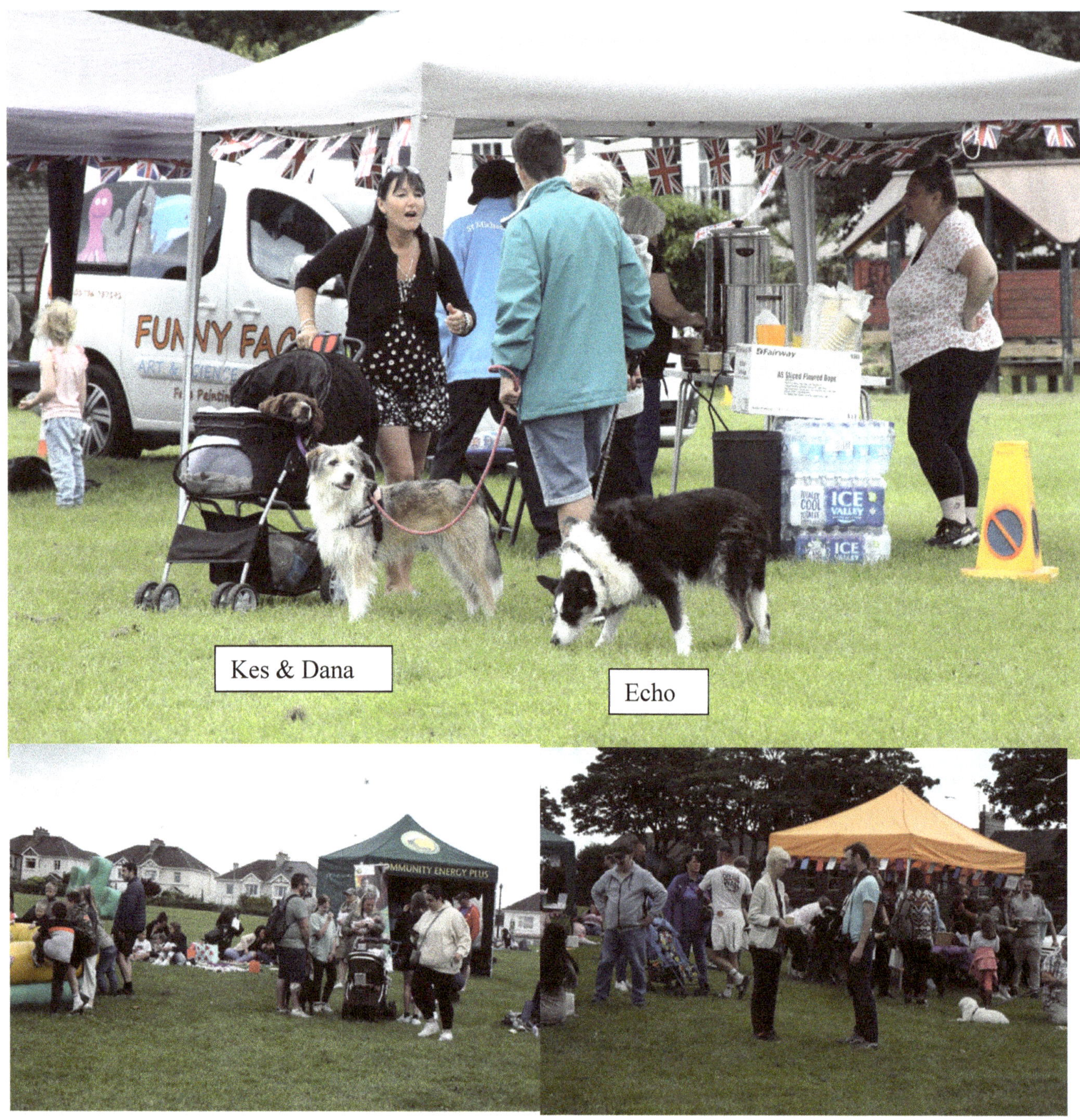

Kes & Dana

Echo

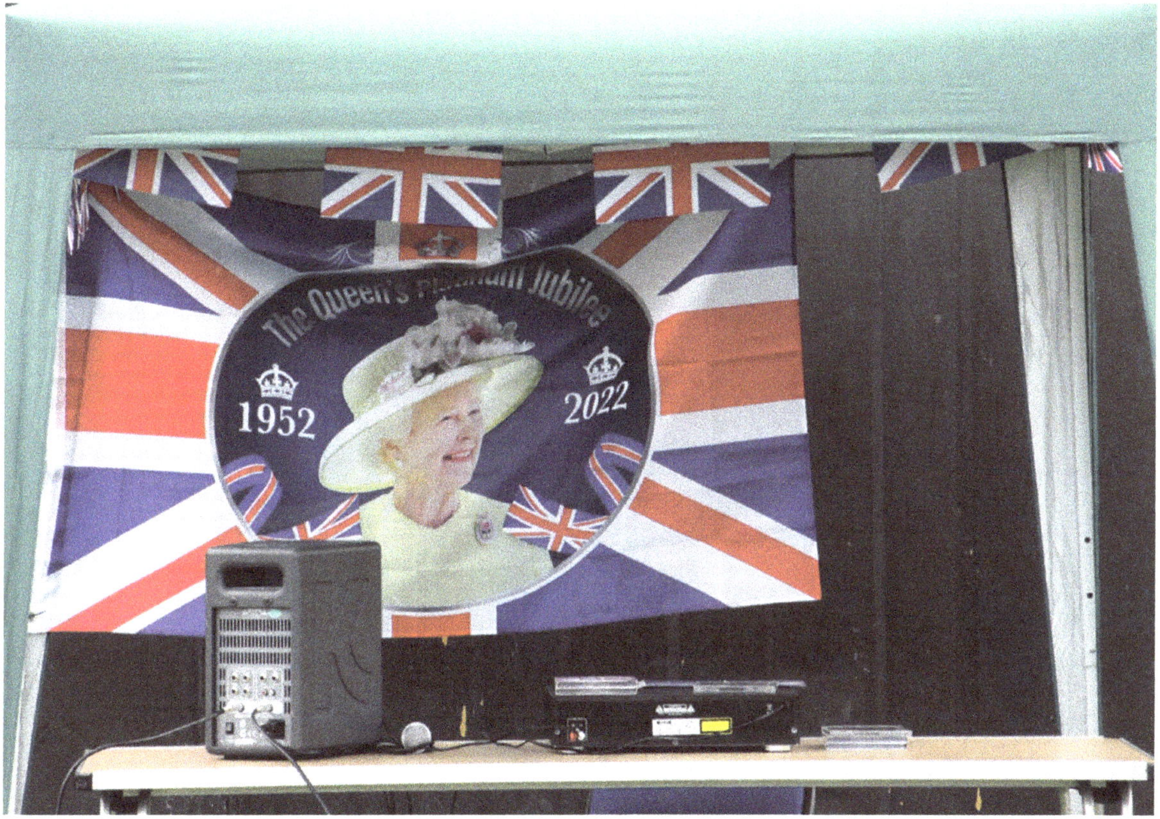

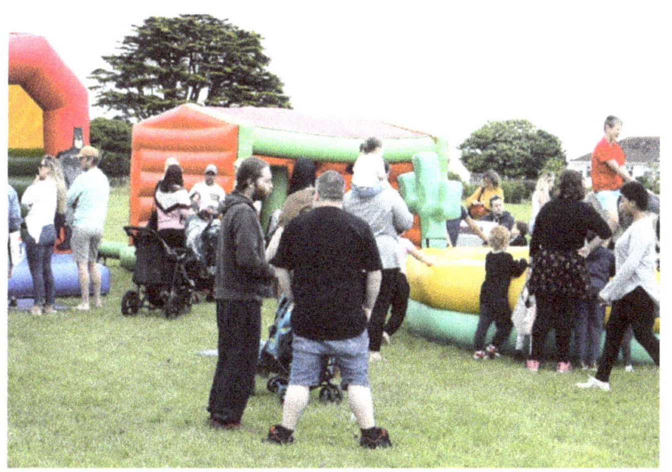

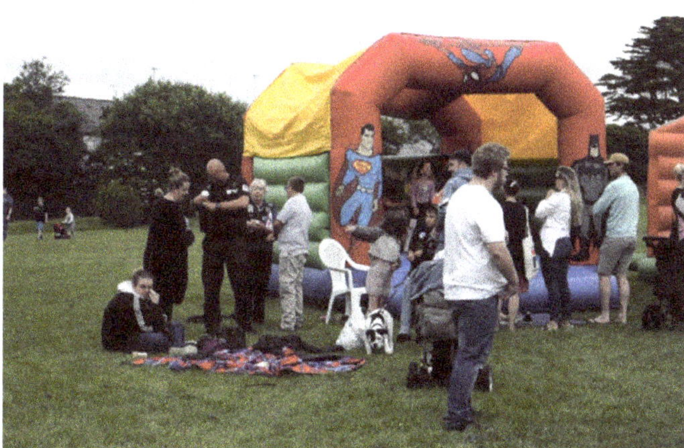

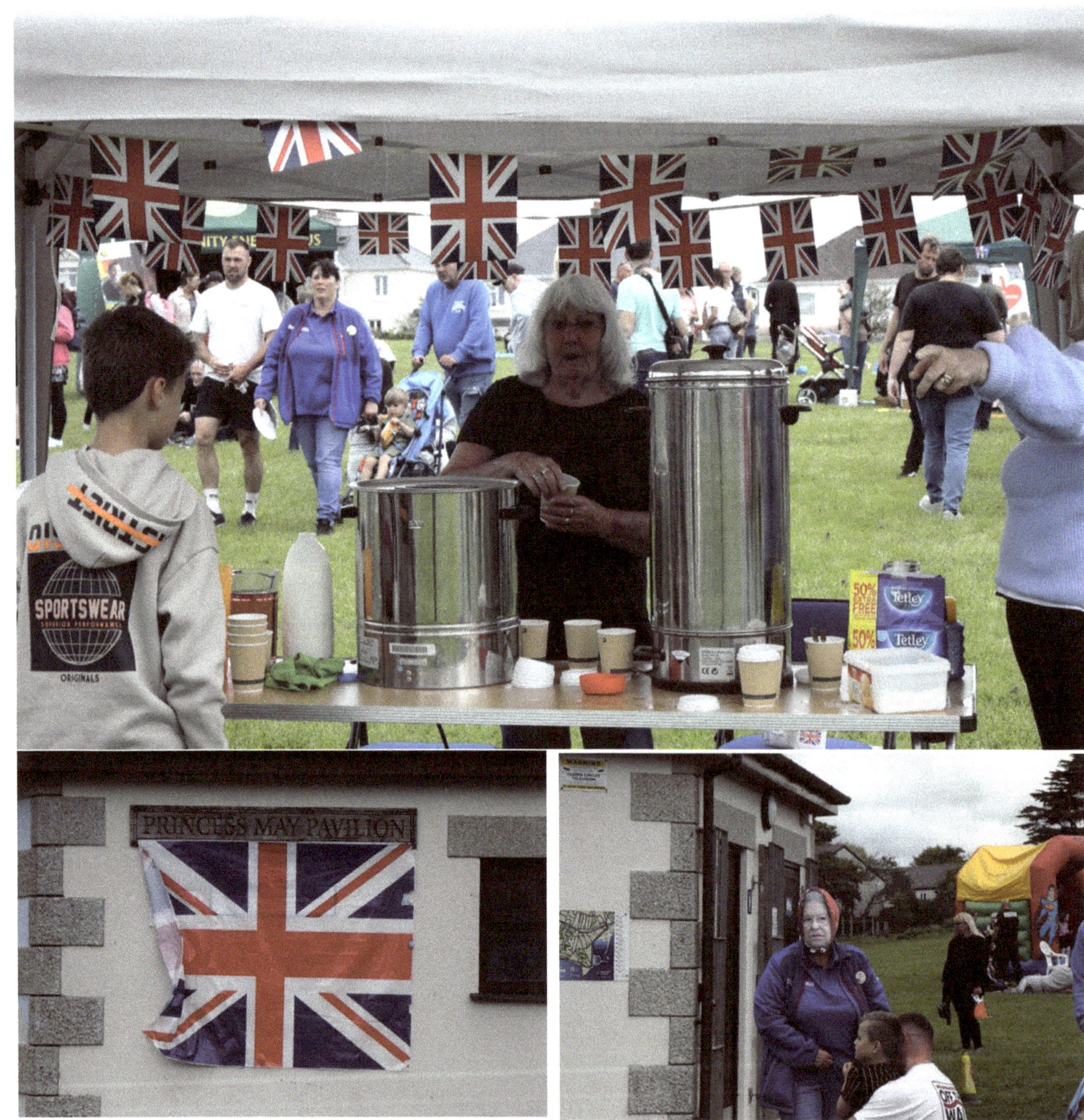
SPORTSWEAR
ORIGINALS
Tetley
Tetley
PRINCESS MAY PAVILION

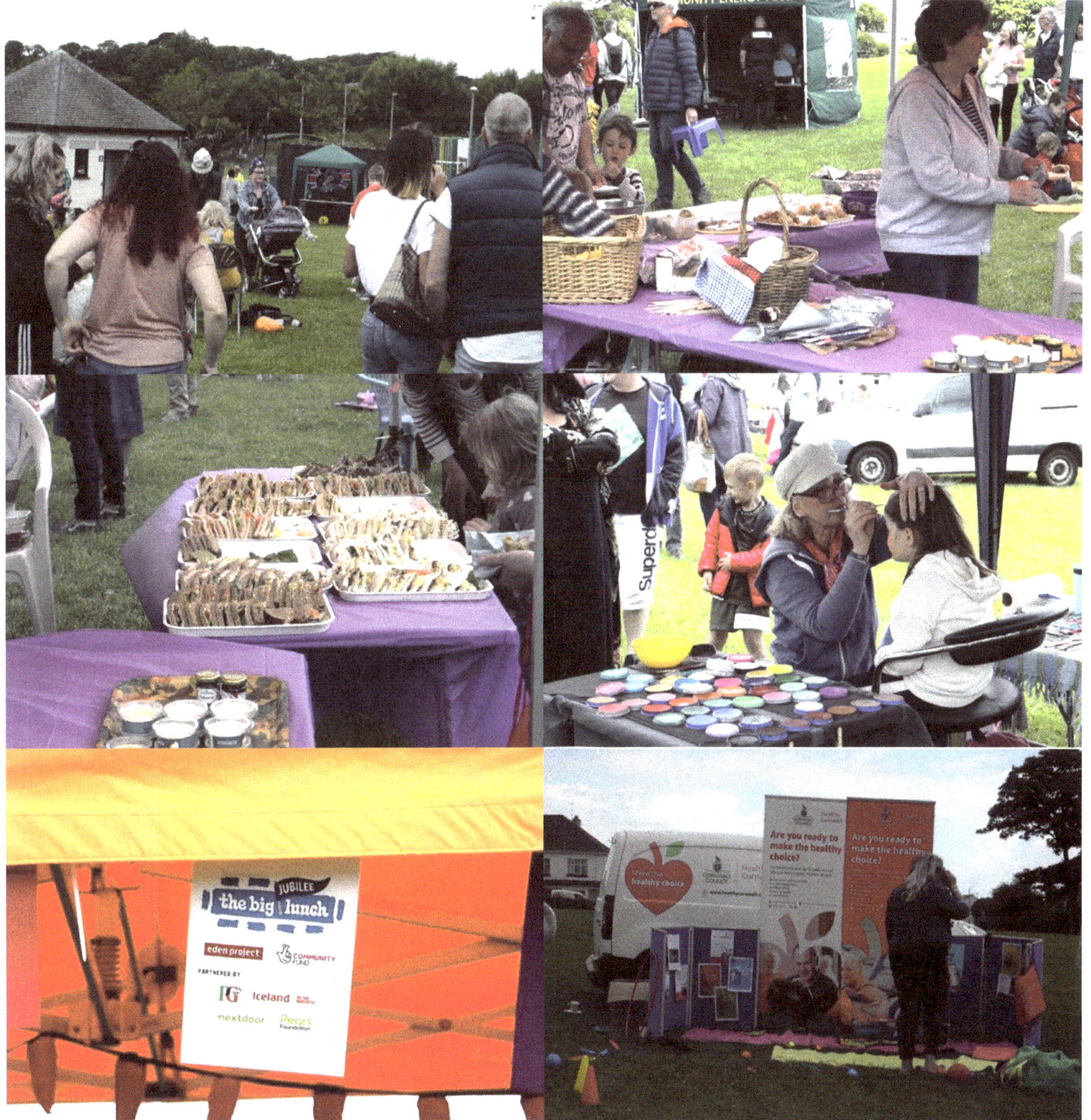
JUBILEE
the big lunch
eden project
COMMUNITY FUND
PARTNERED BY
Iceland
nextdoor
Pears Foundation
Are you ready to make the healthy choice?
Are you ready to make the healthy choice?

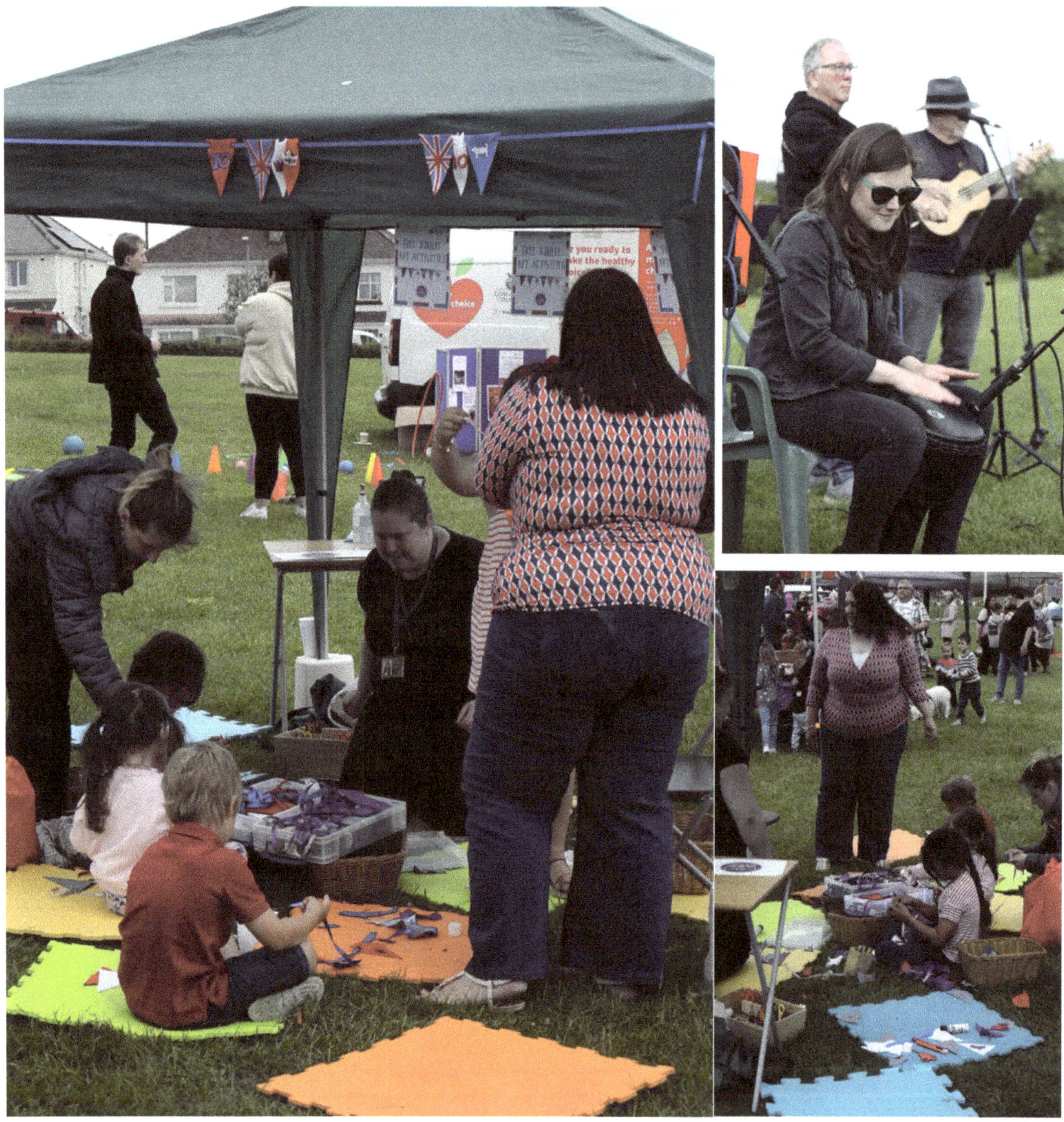
choice

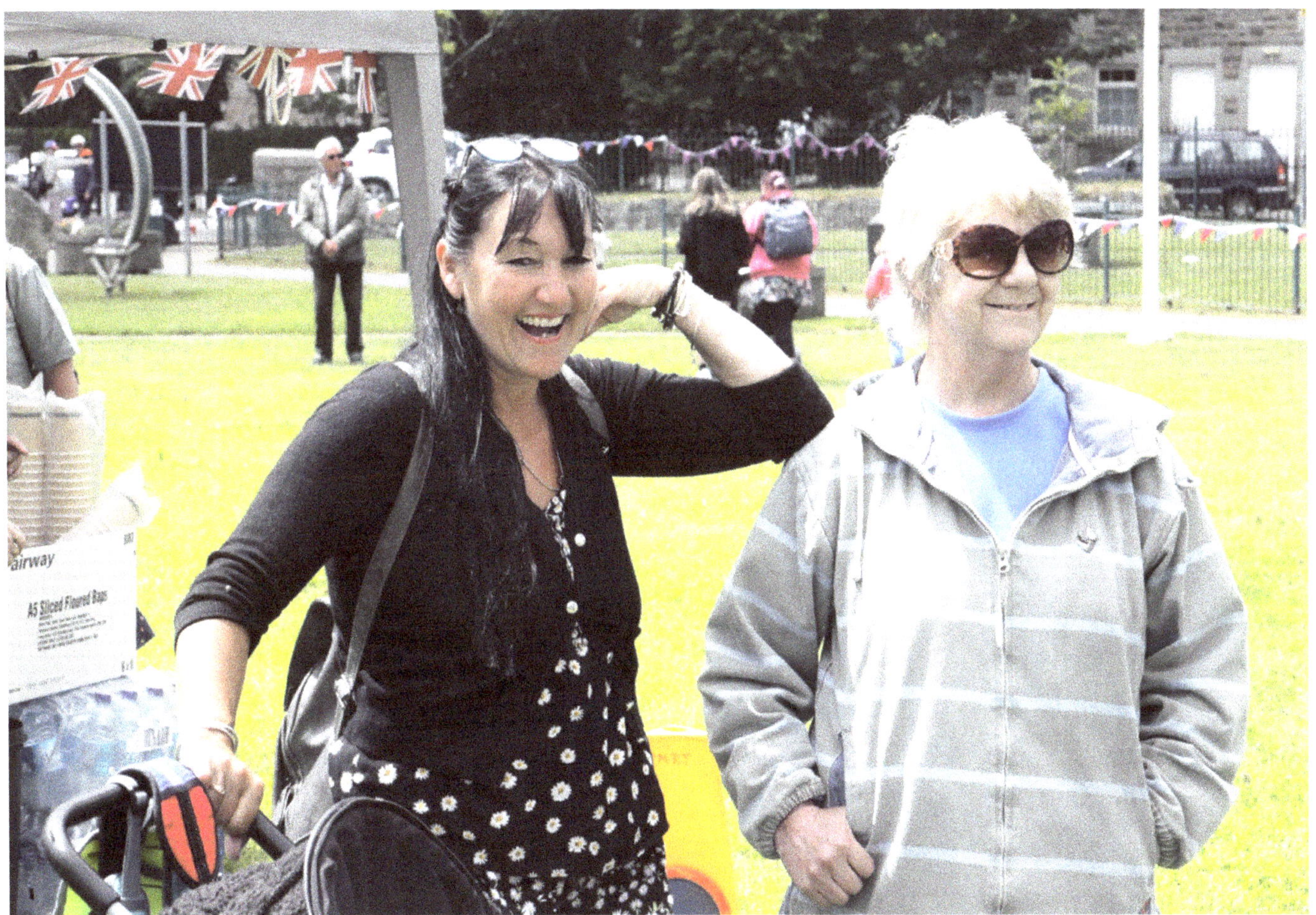
airway
A5 Sliced Floured Baps

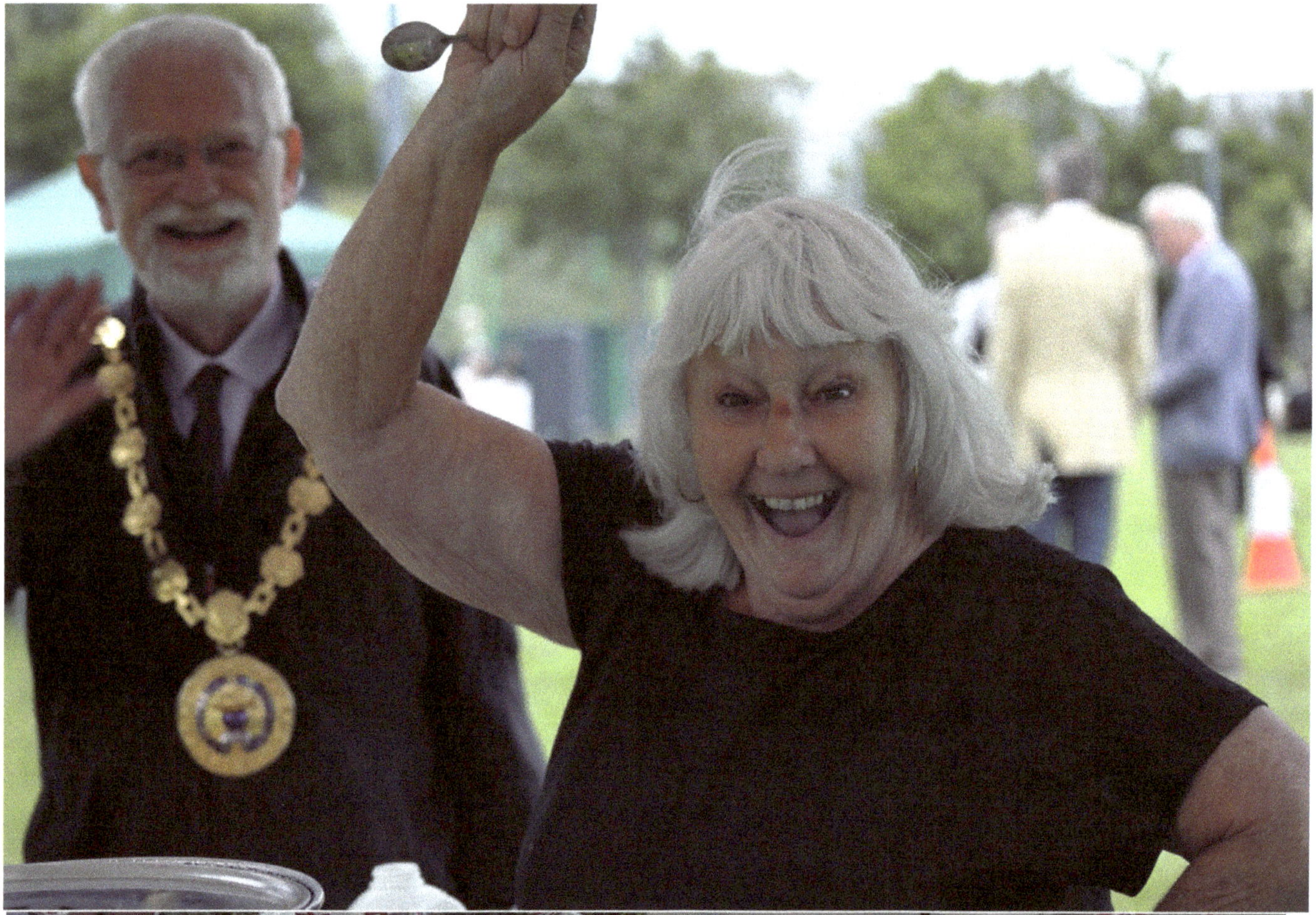

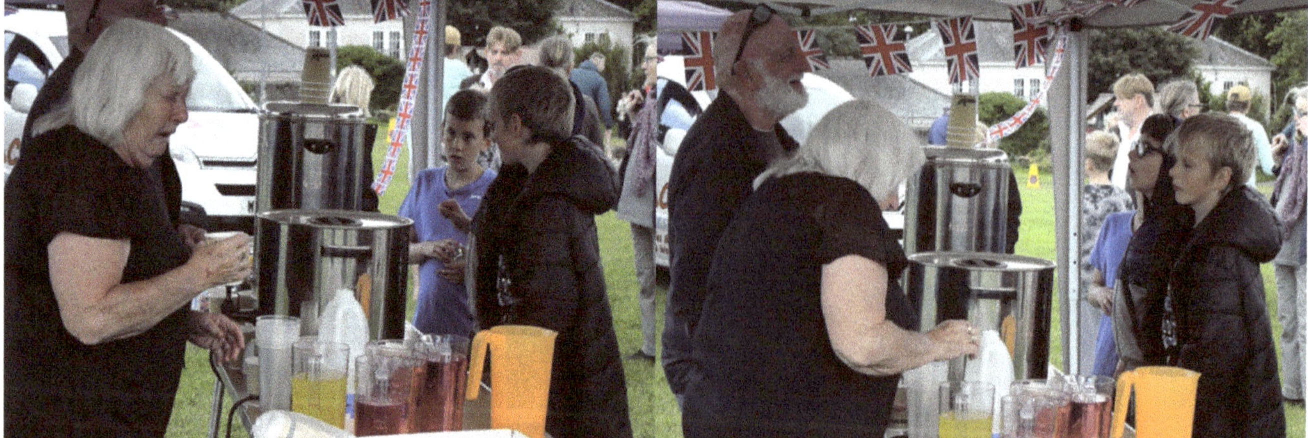

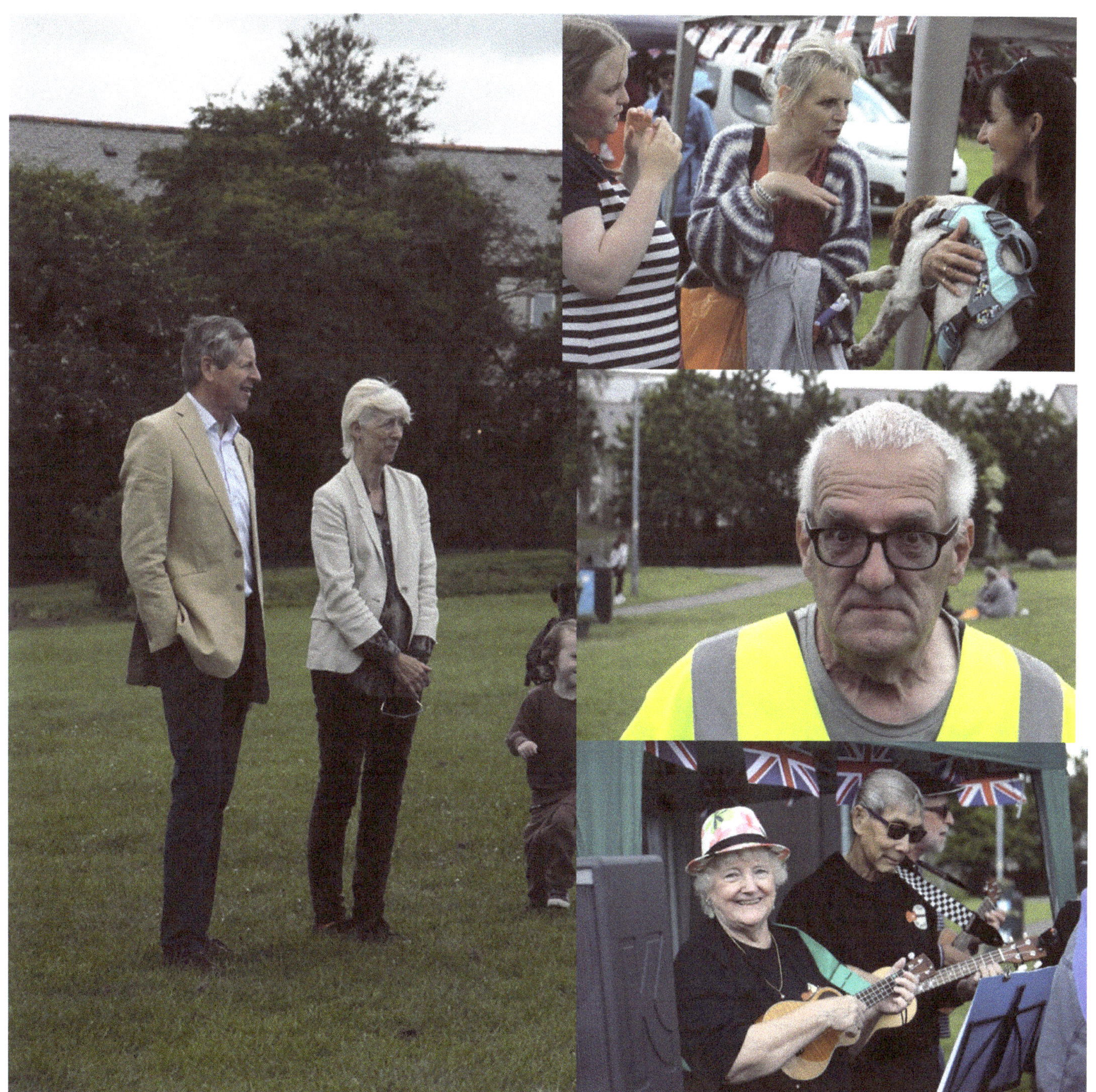

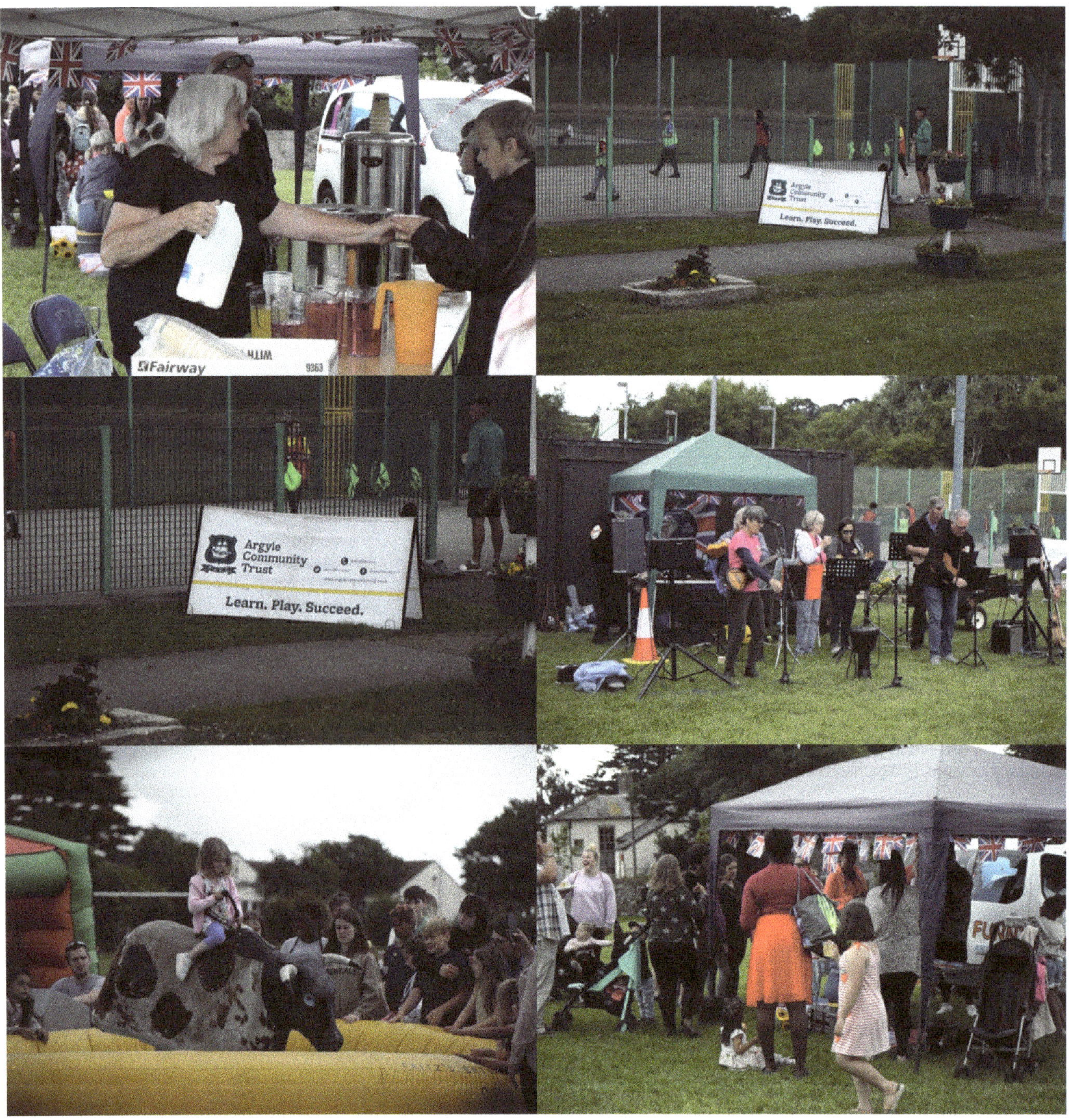
Fairway
Argyle
Community
Trust
Learn. Play. Succeed.

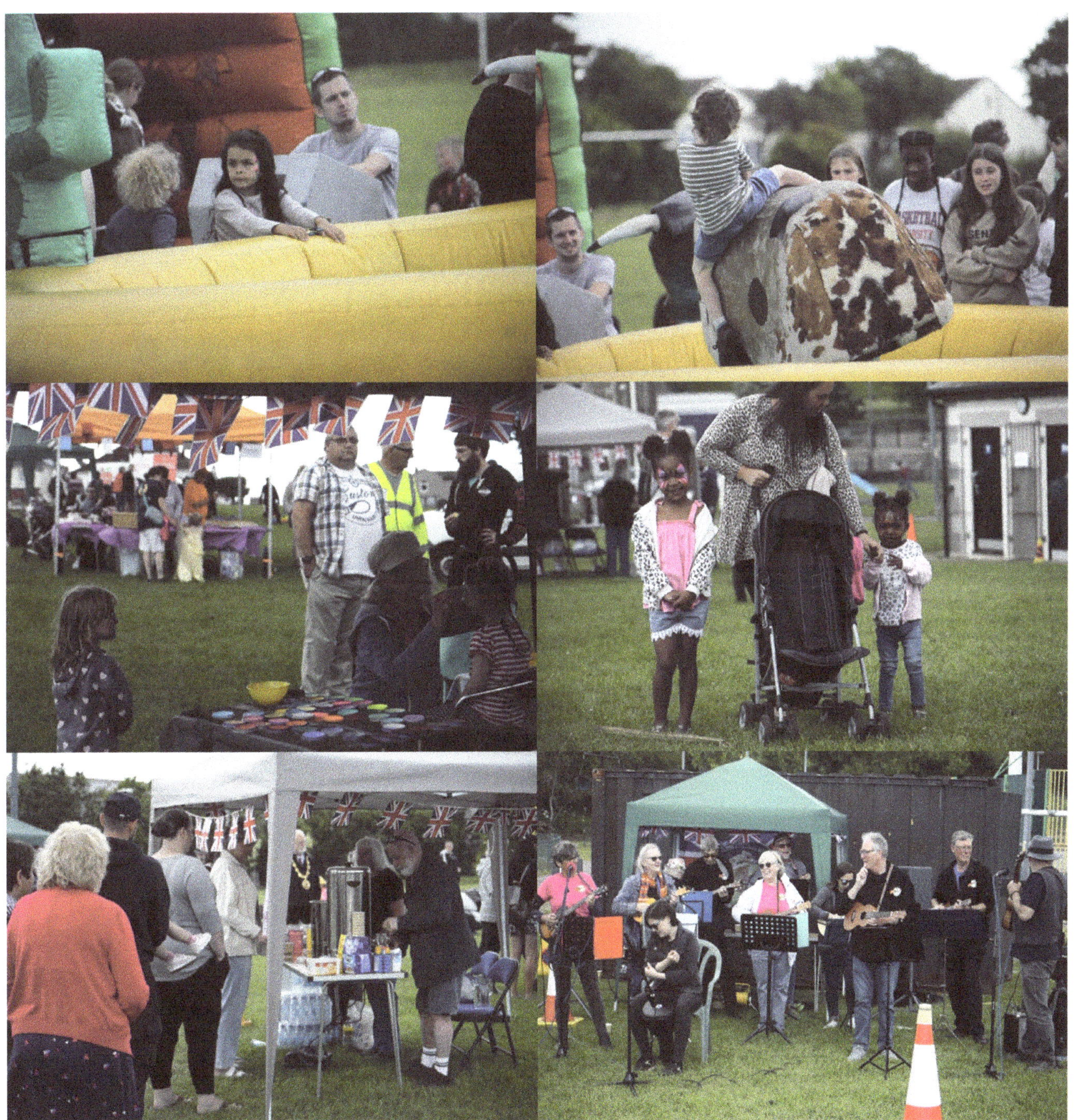

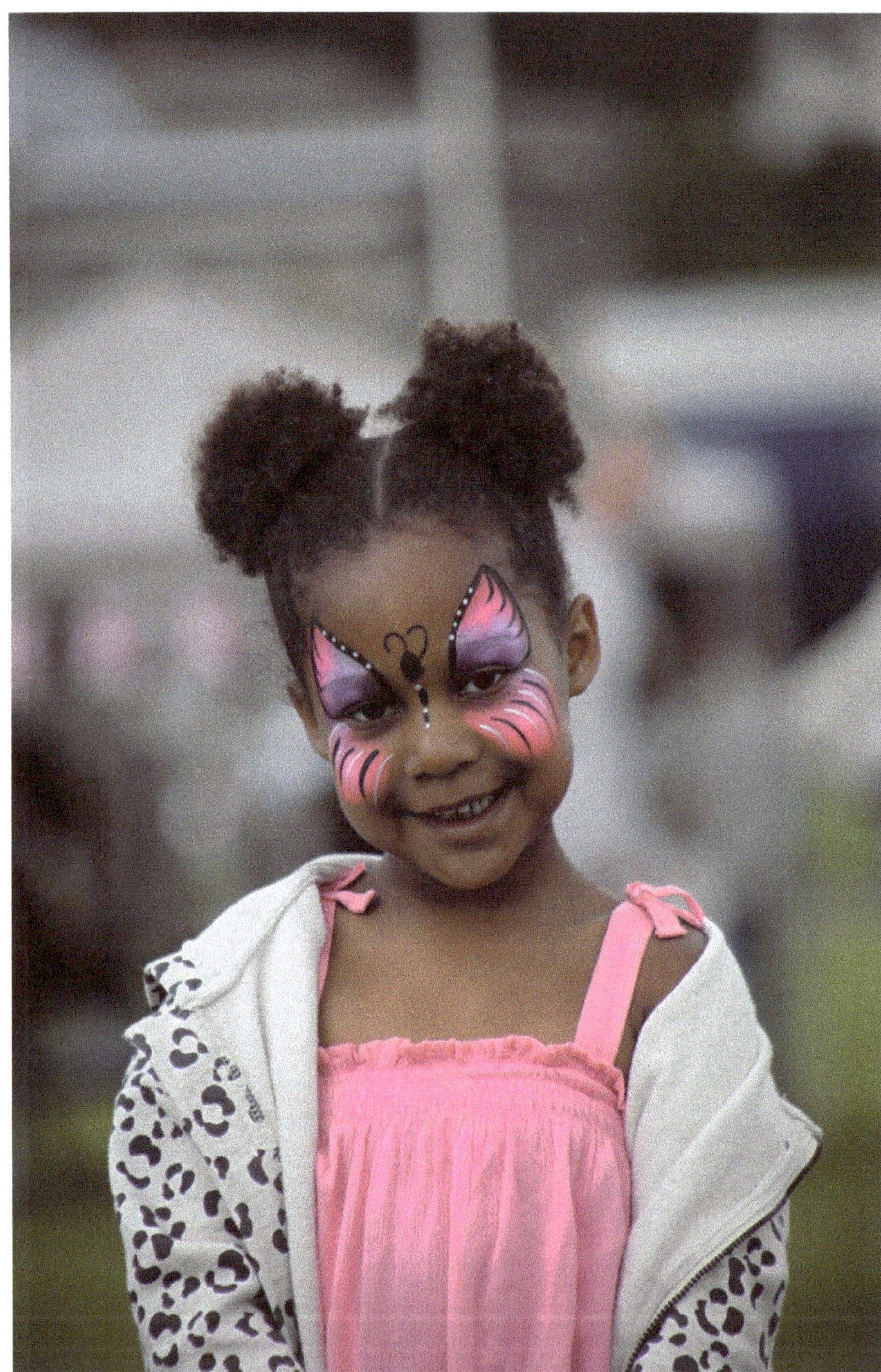

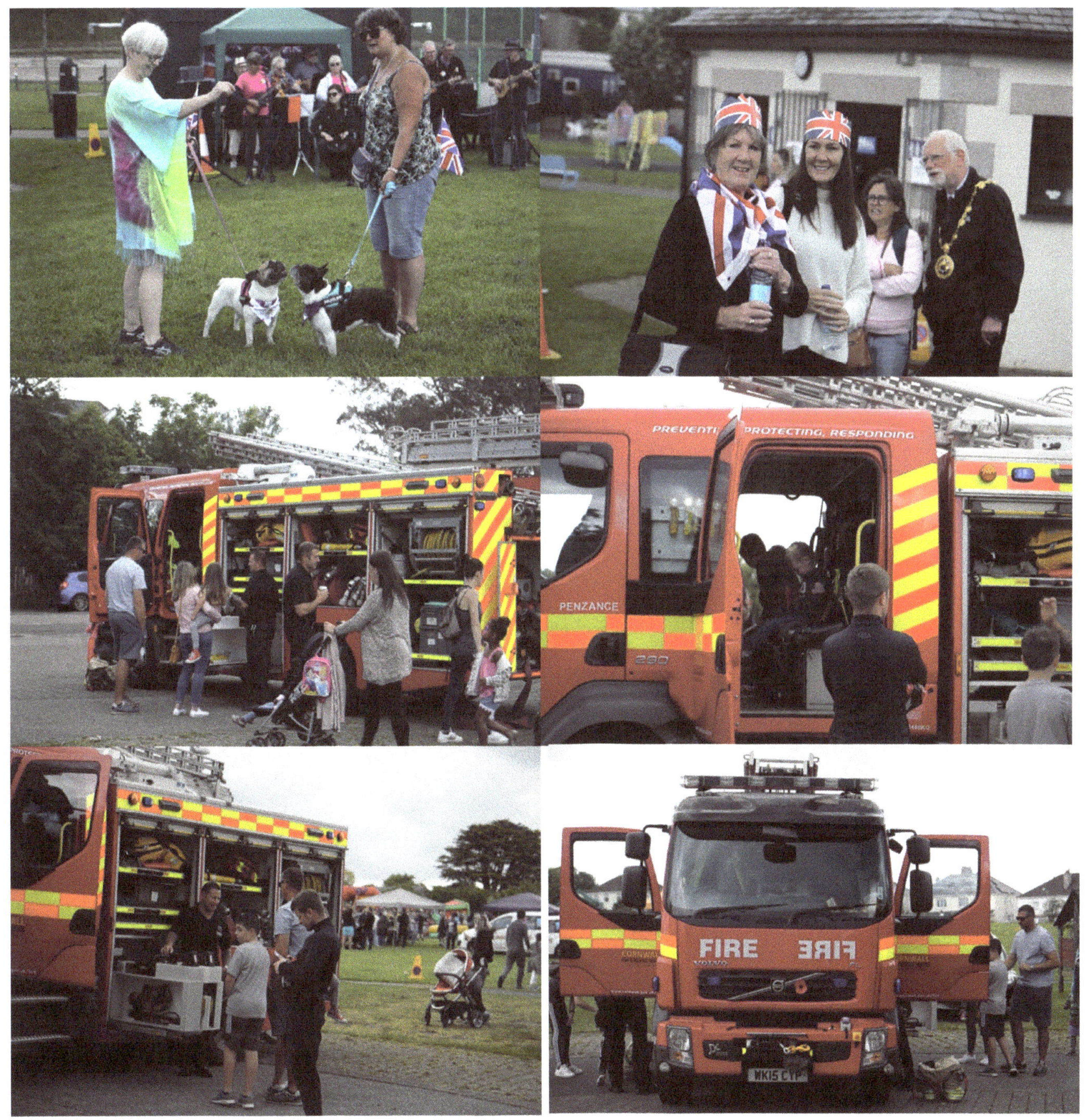
PROTECTING, RESPONDING
PENZANCE
FIRE
WK15 CYP

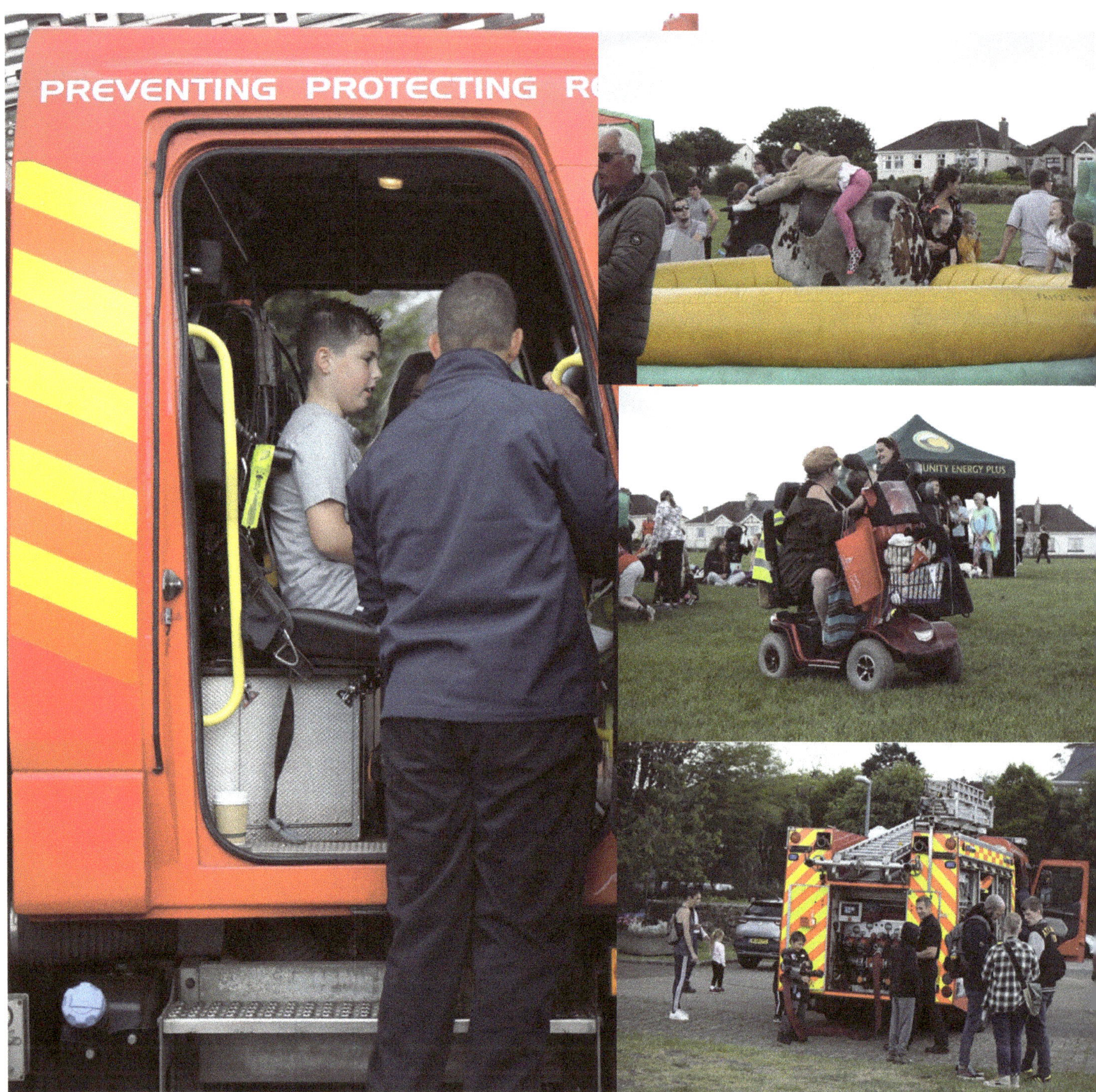
PREVENTING PROTECTING
ENERGY PLUS

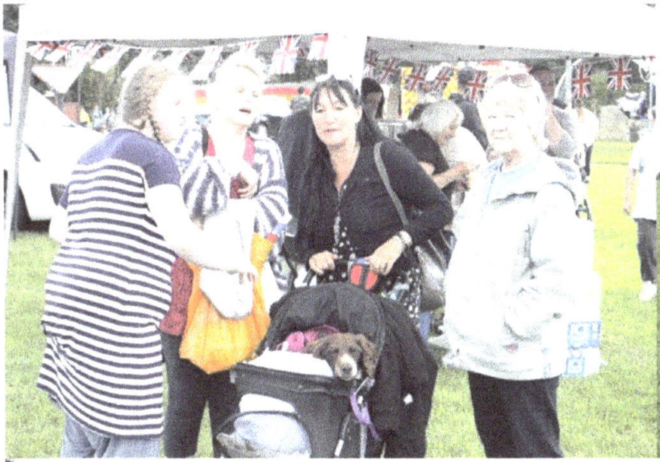

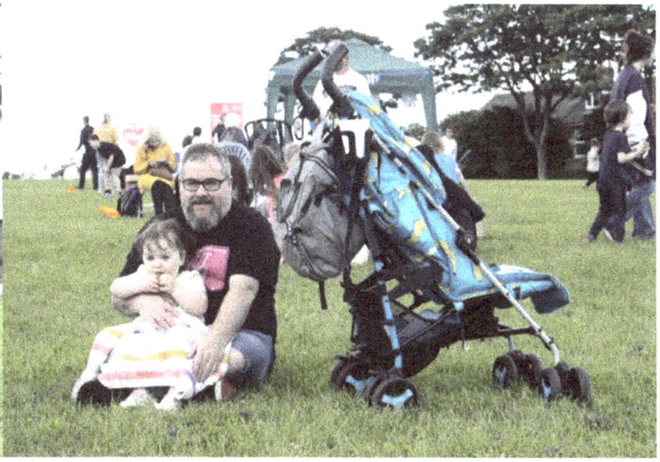

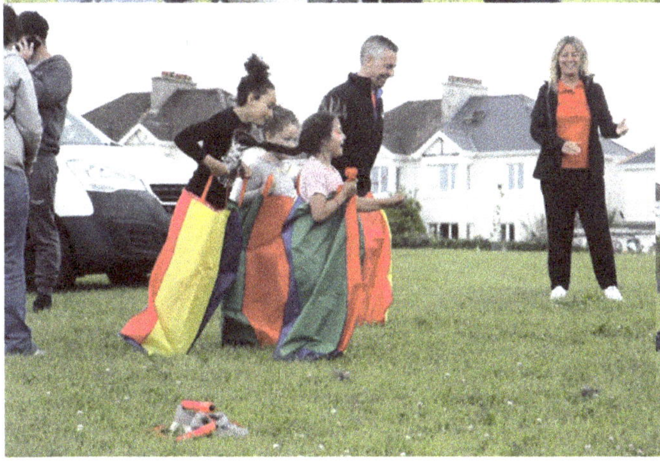

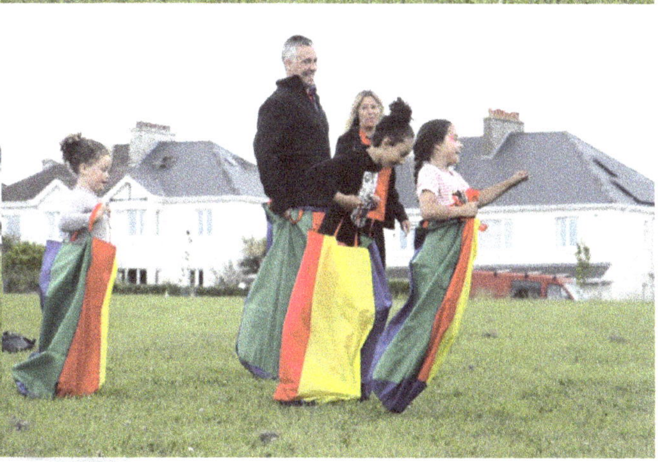

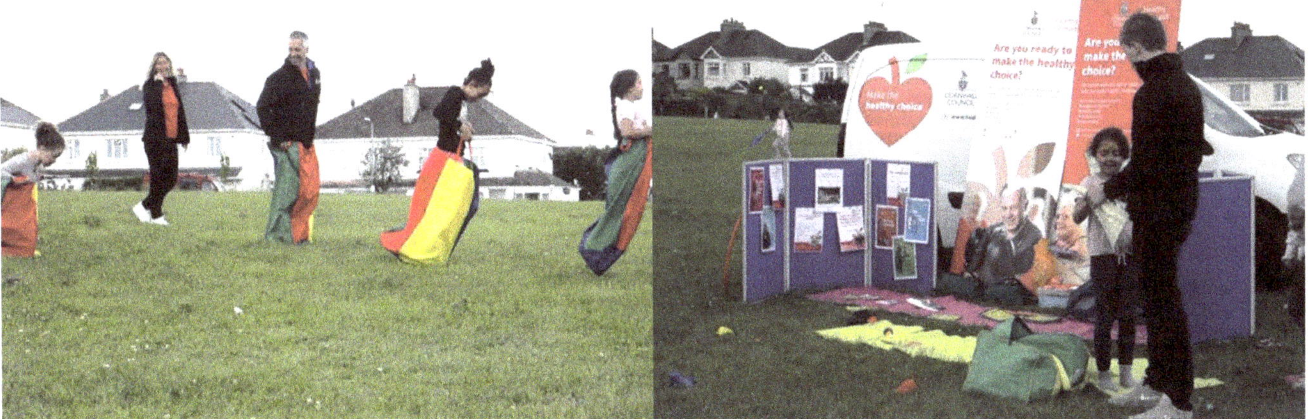
Make the
healthy choice
Are you ready to
make the health
choice?
CORNWALL COUNCIL

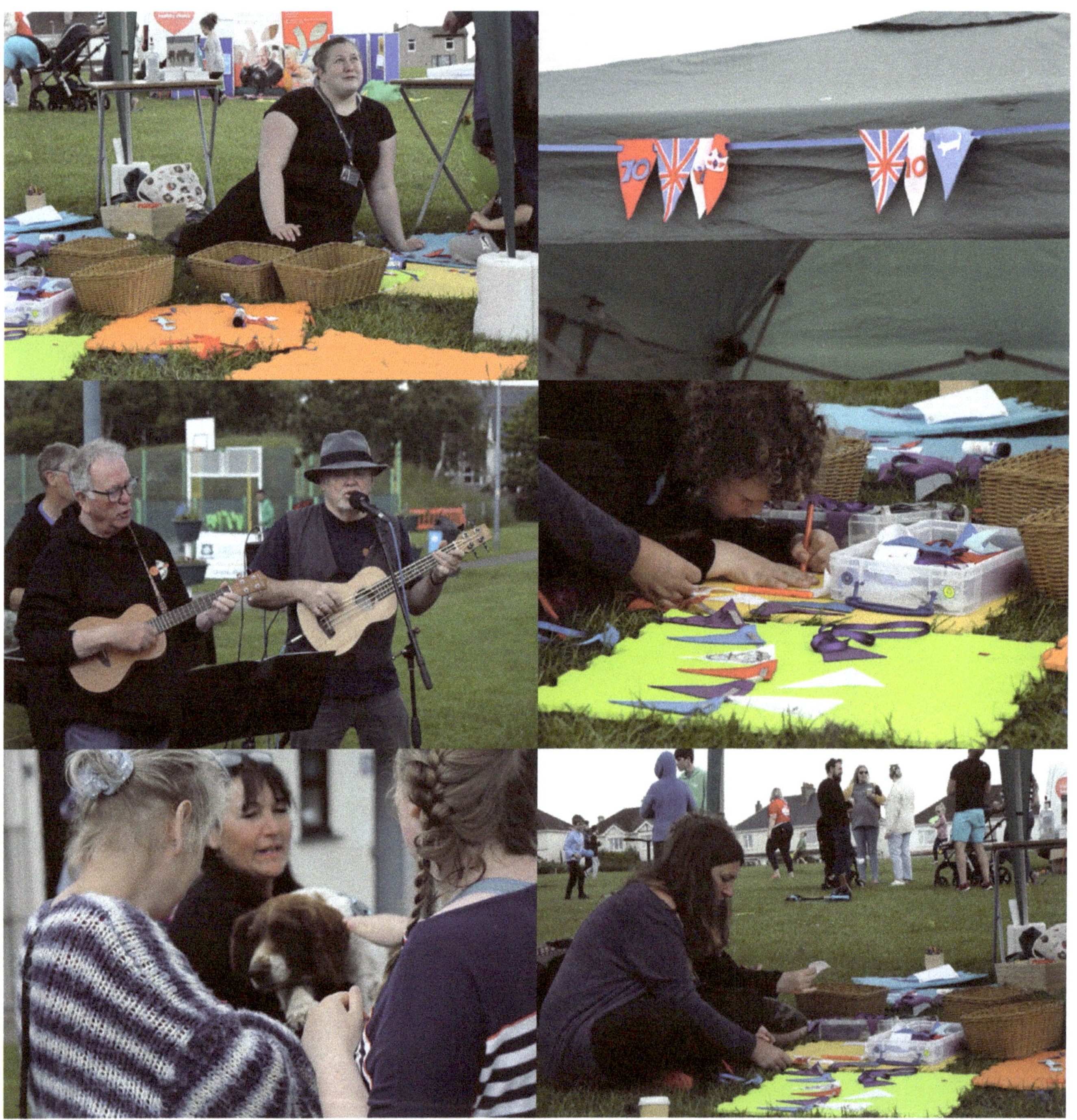

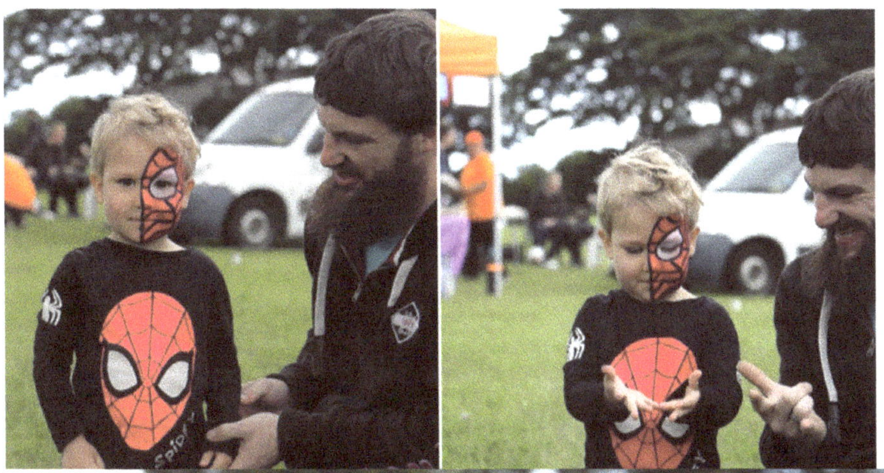

Super Cool Dude!

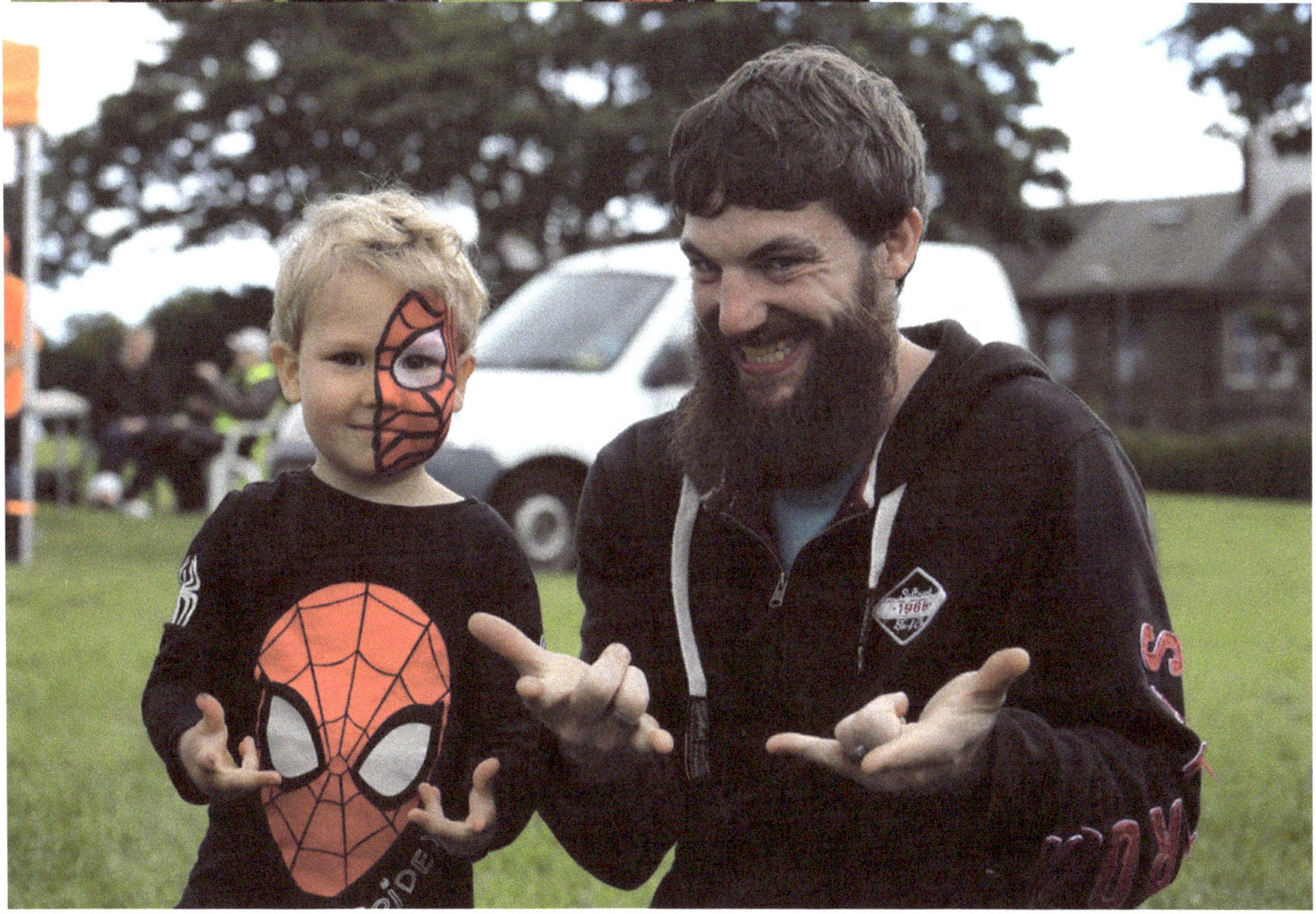

Super Cool Dudette!

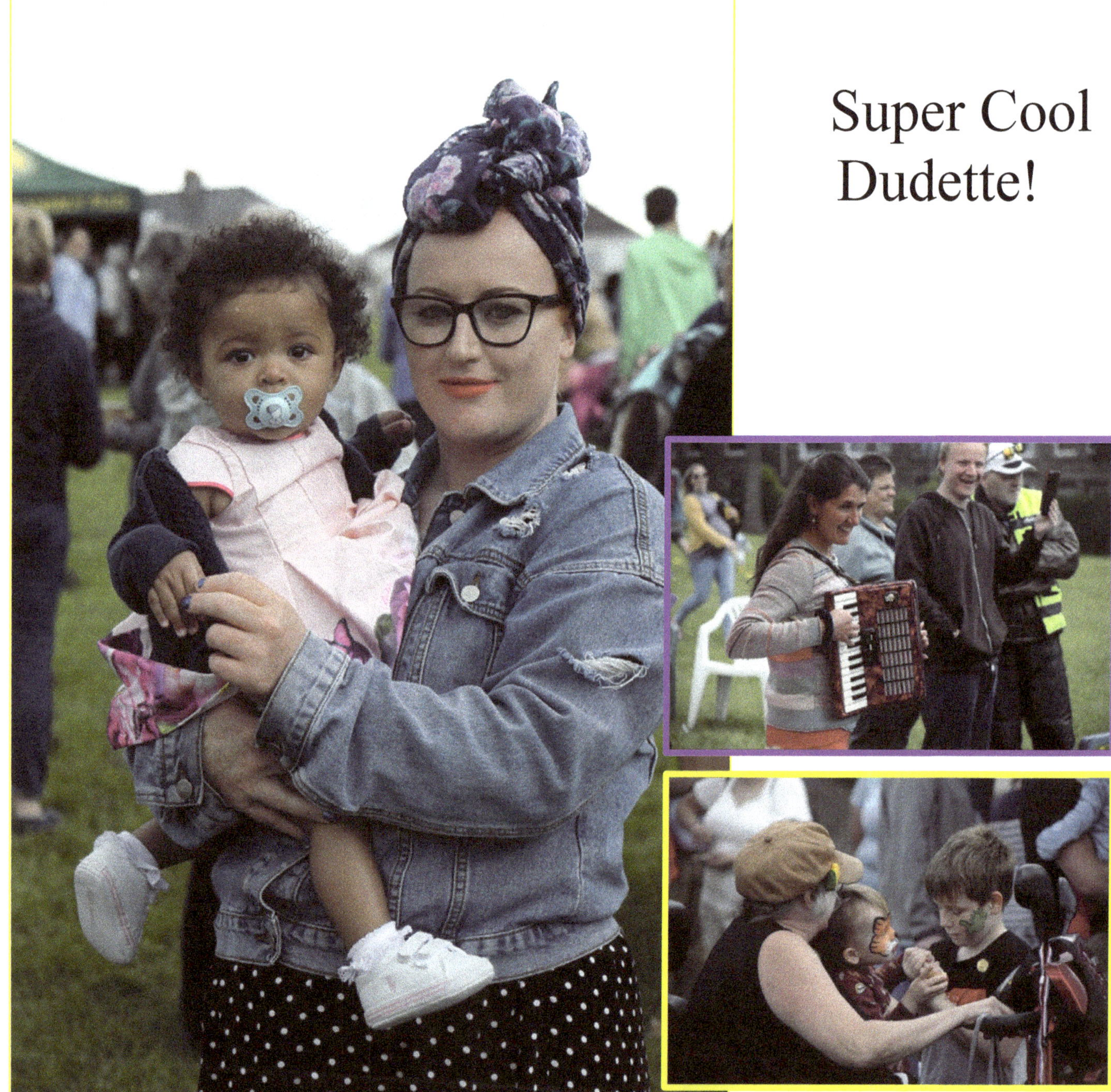

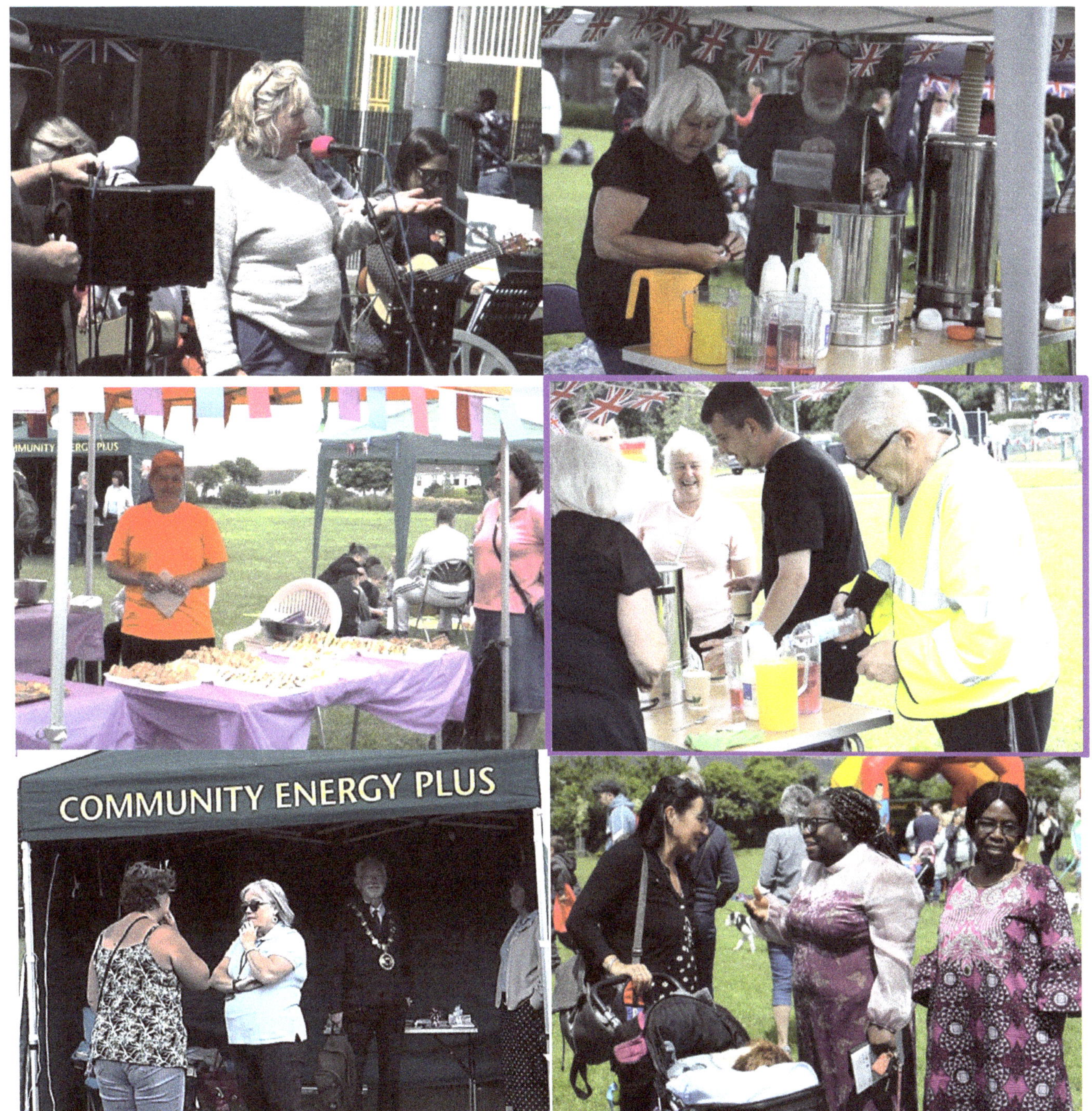
COMMUNITY ENERGY PLUS

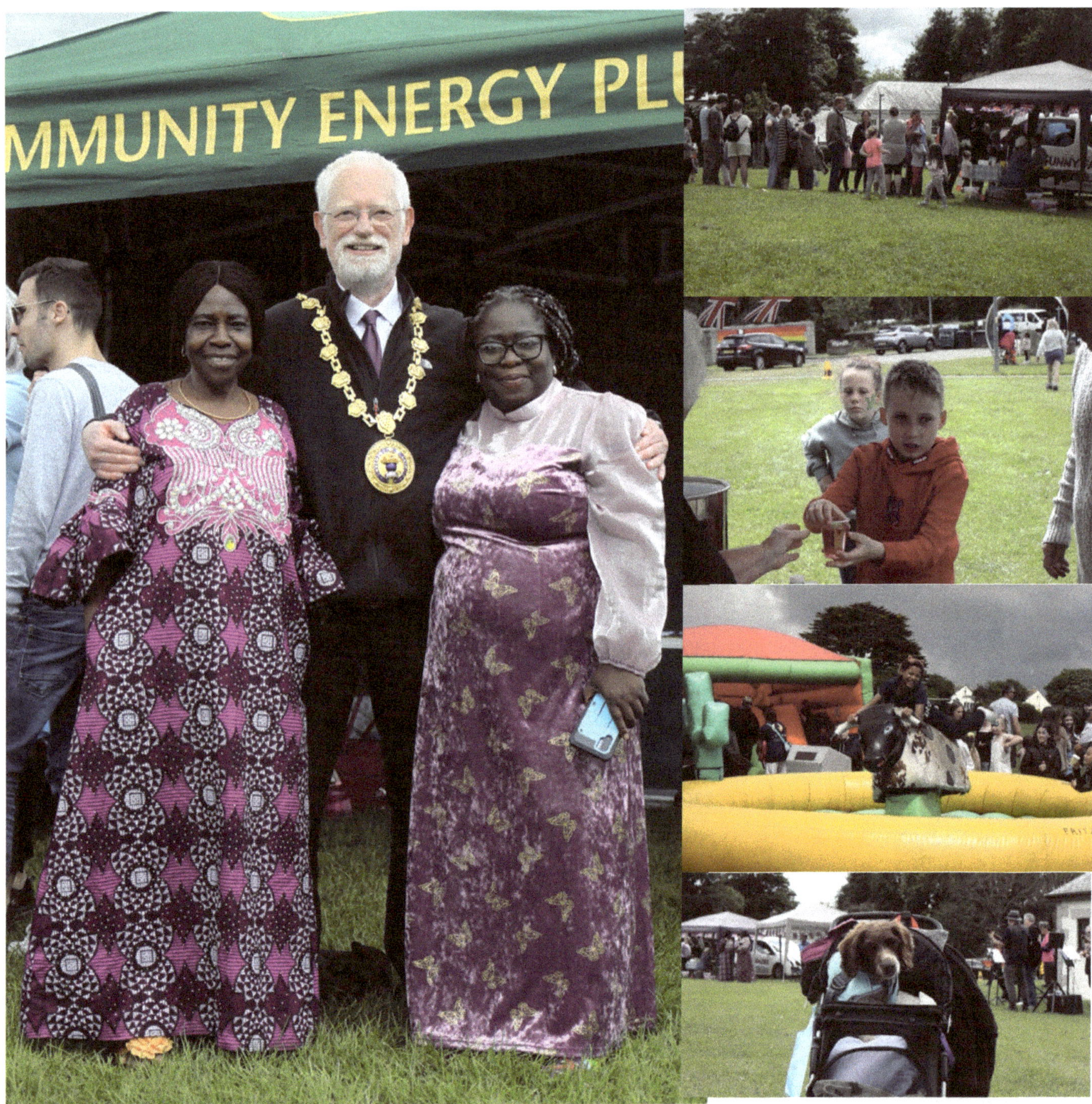
MMUNITY ENERGY PL

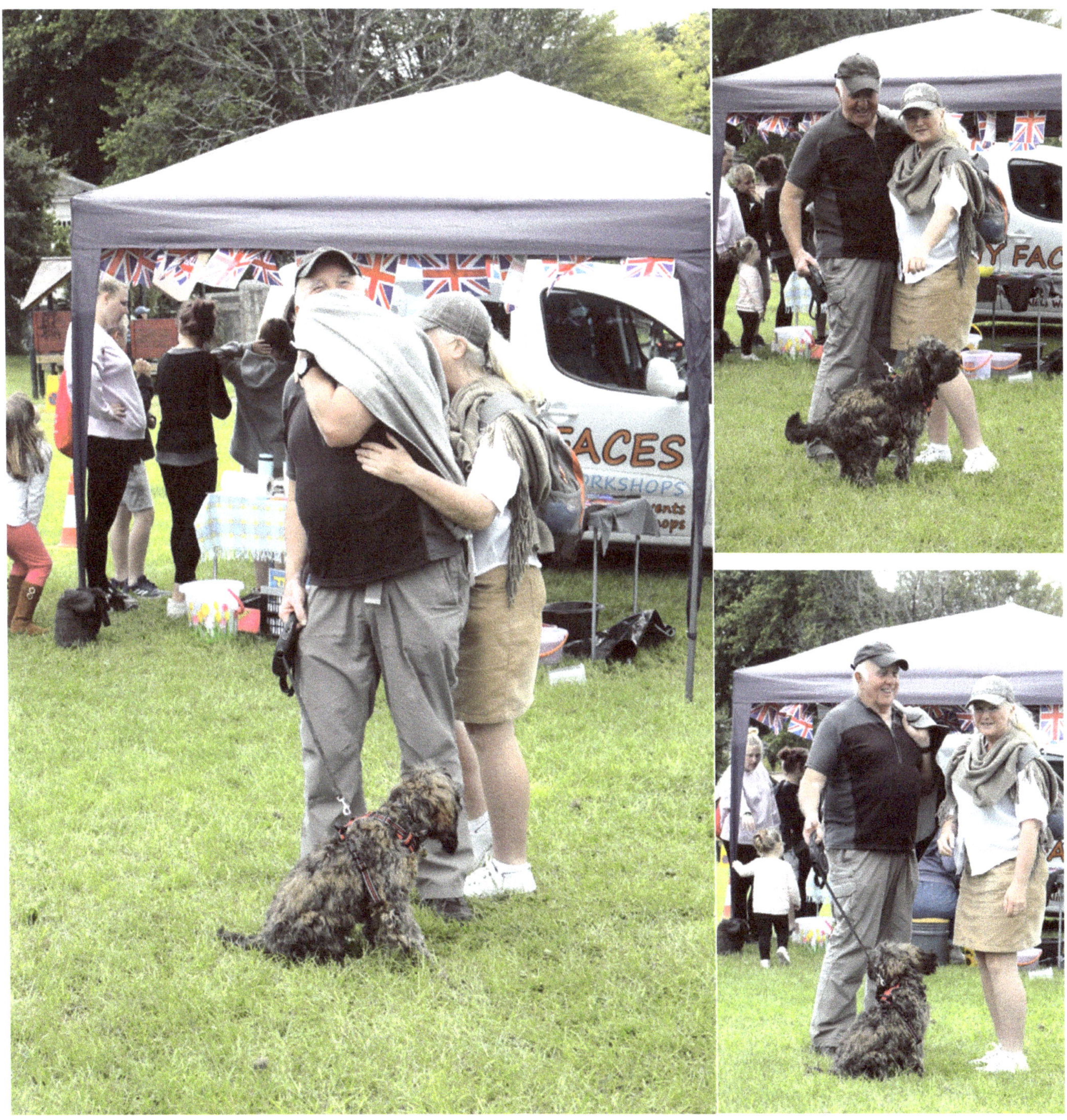

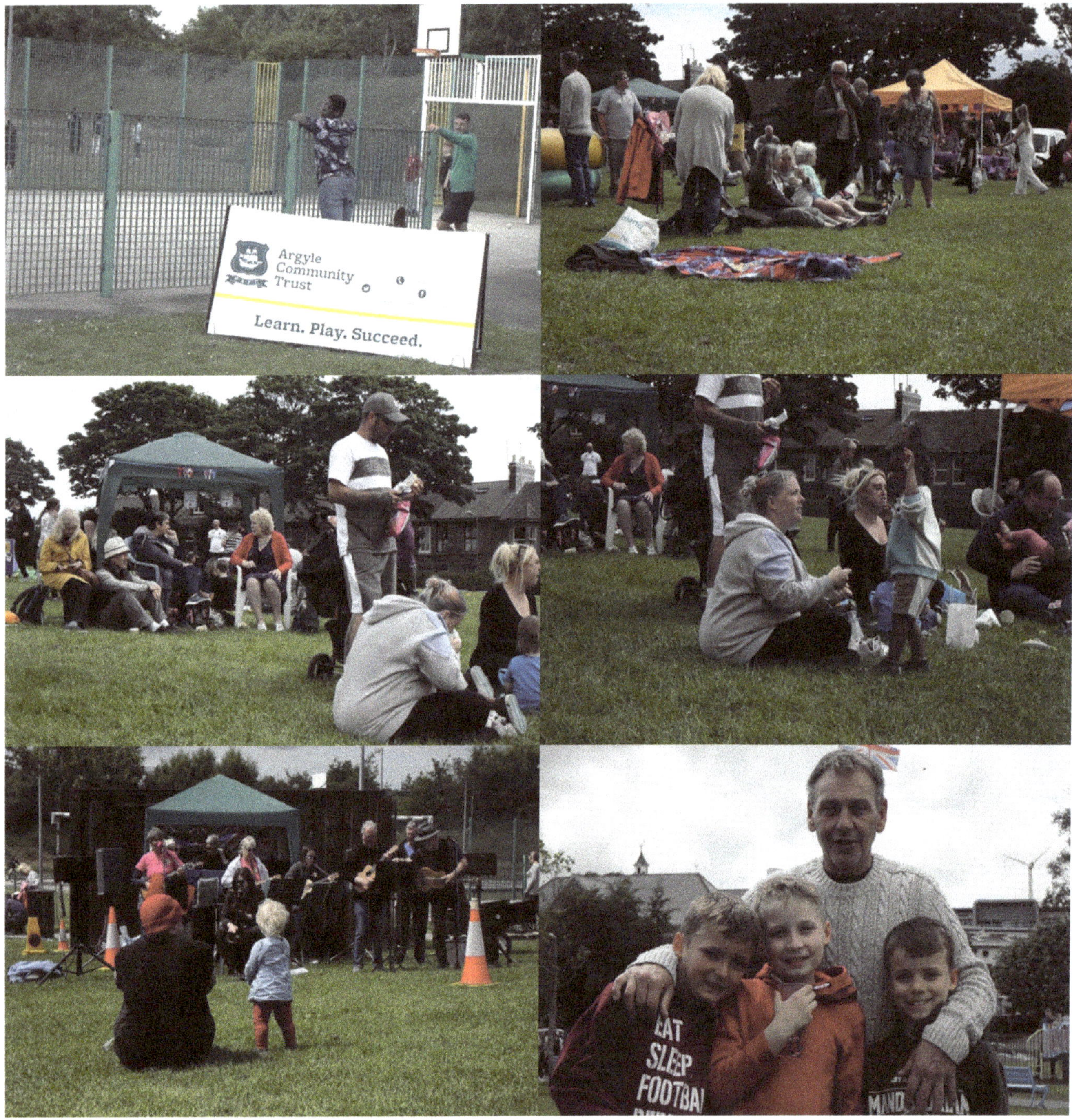
Argyle
Community
Trust
Learn. Play. Succeed.
EAT
SLEEP
FOOTBA

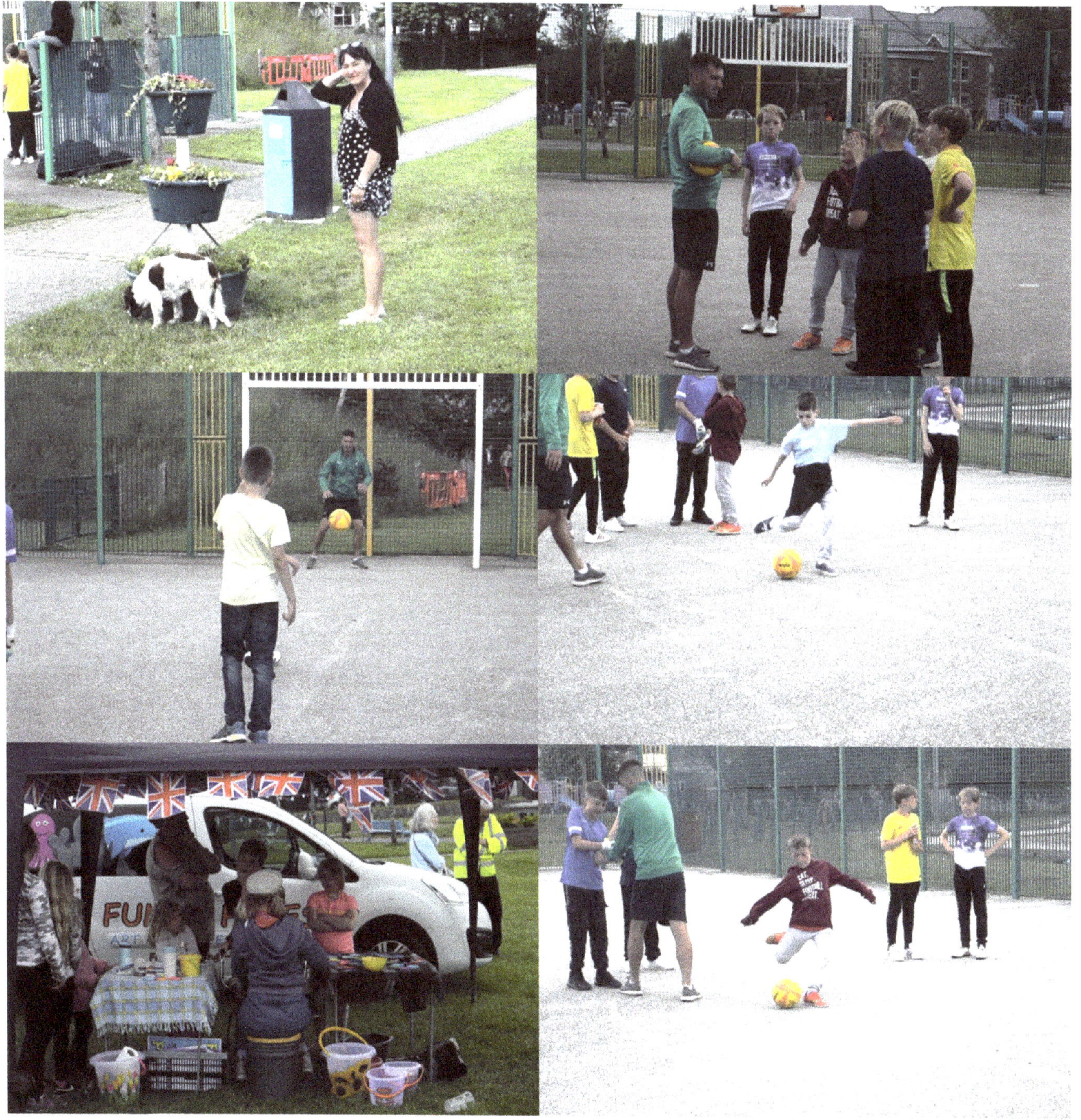

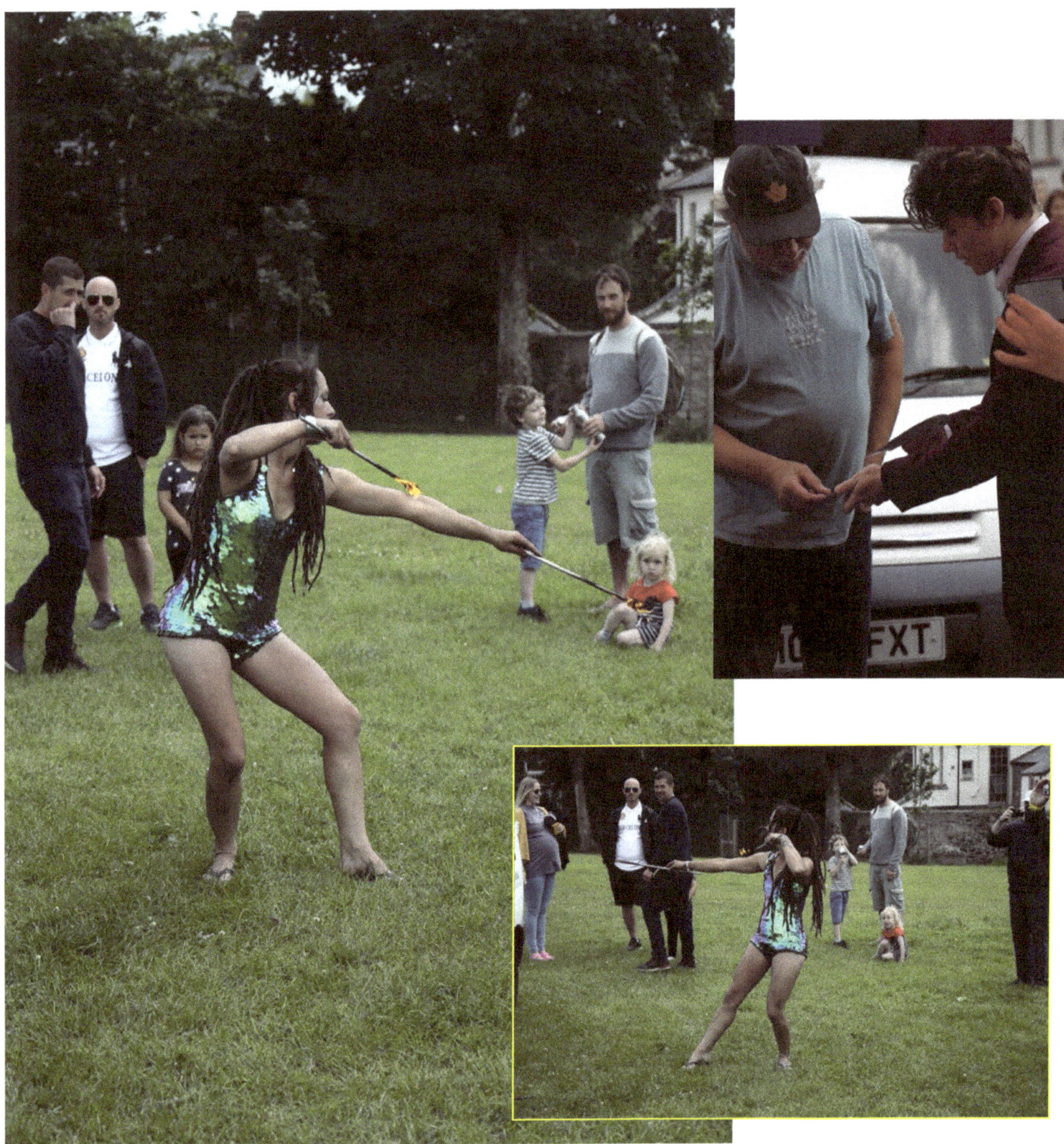

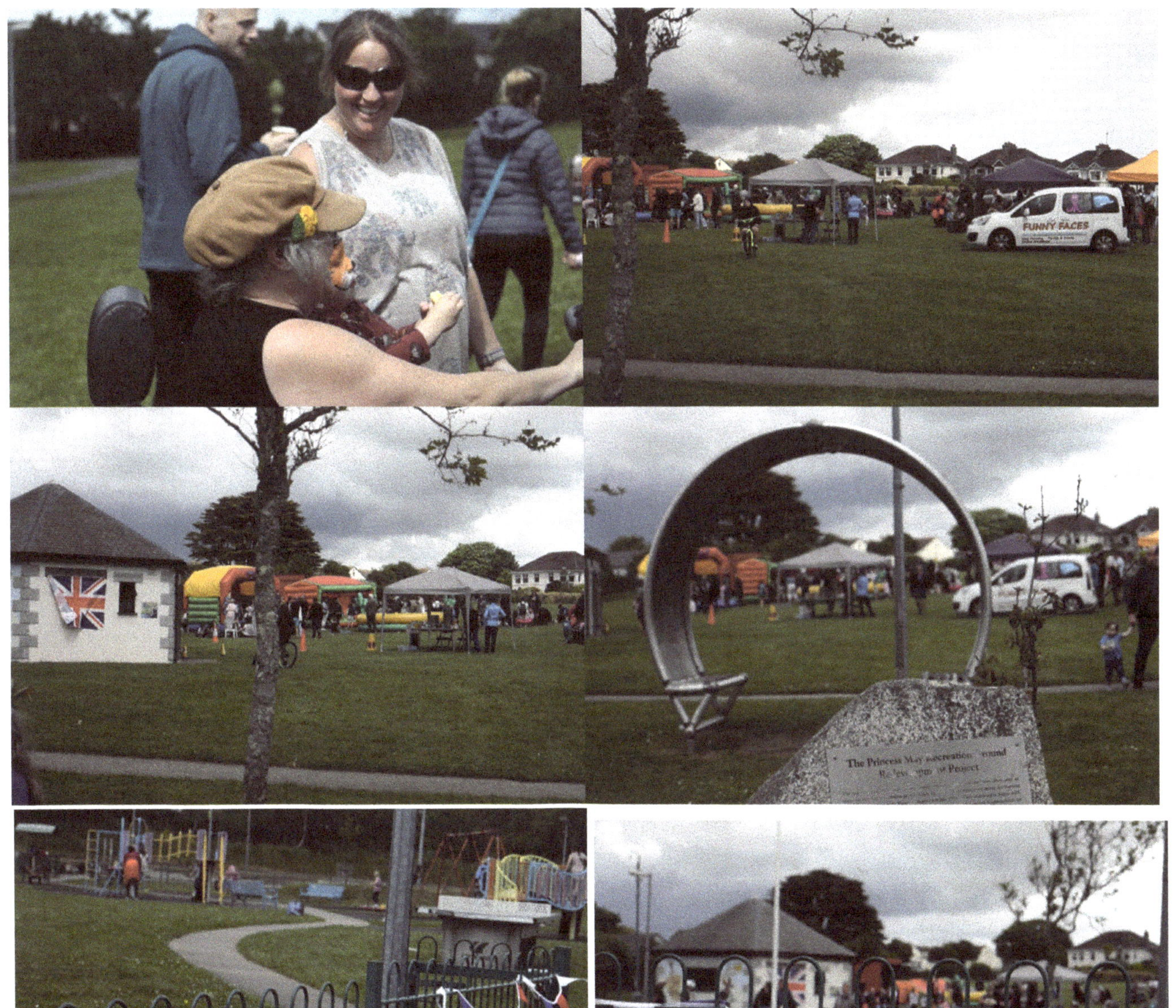
FUNNY FACES

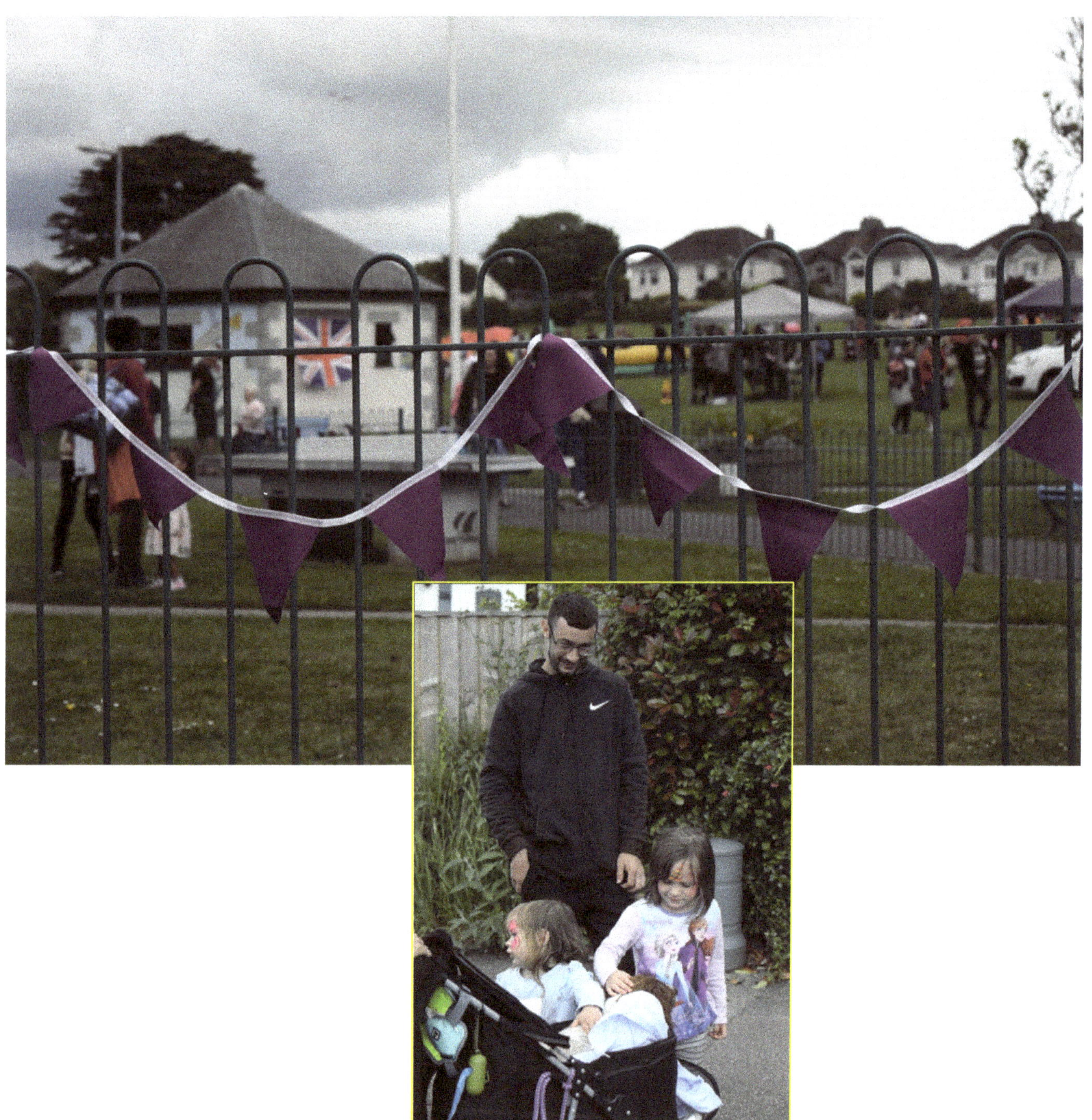

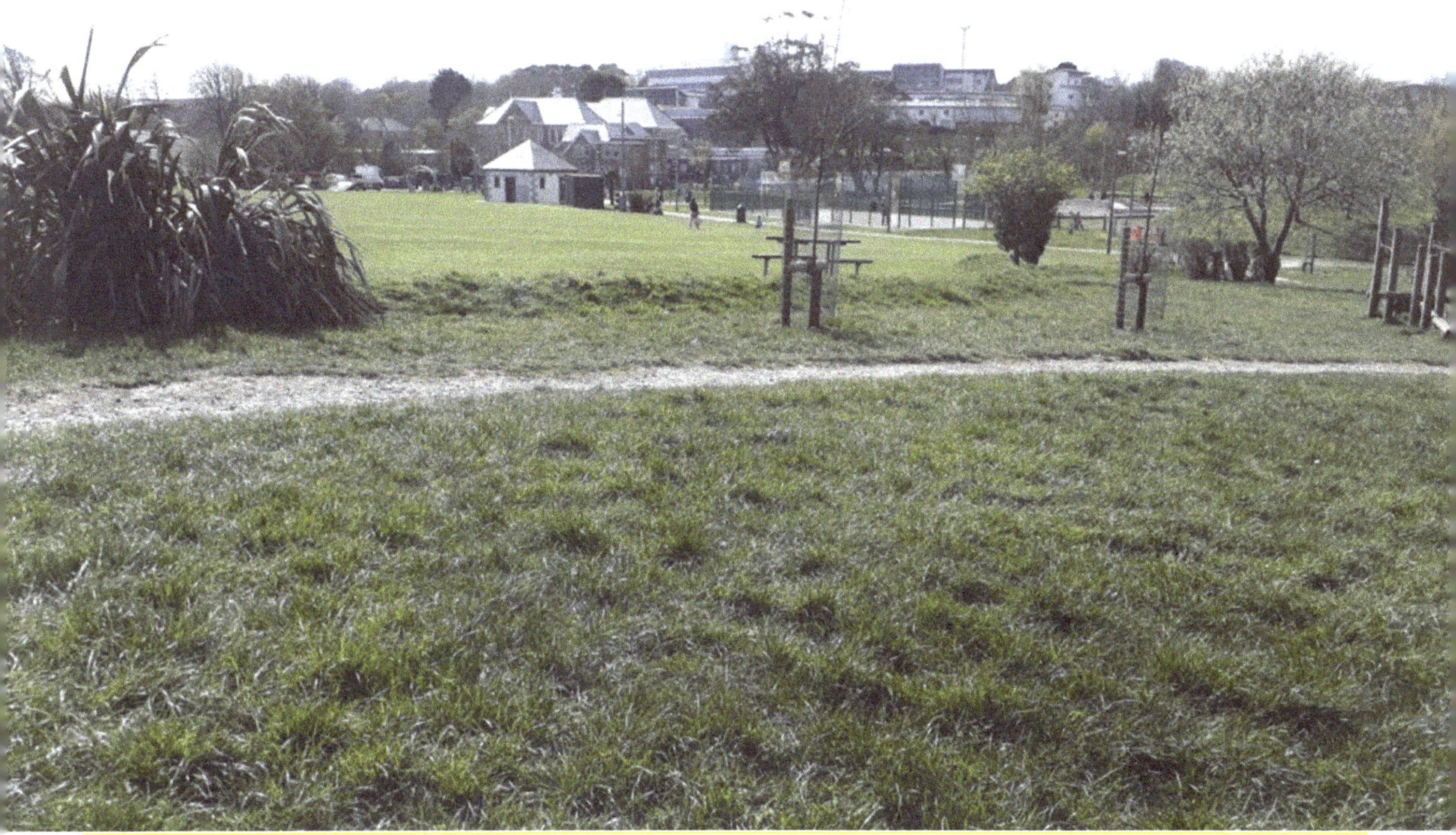

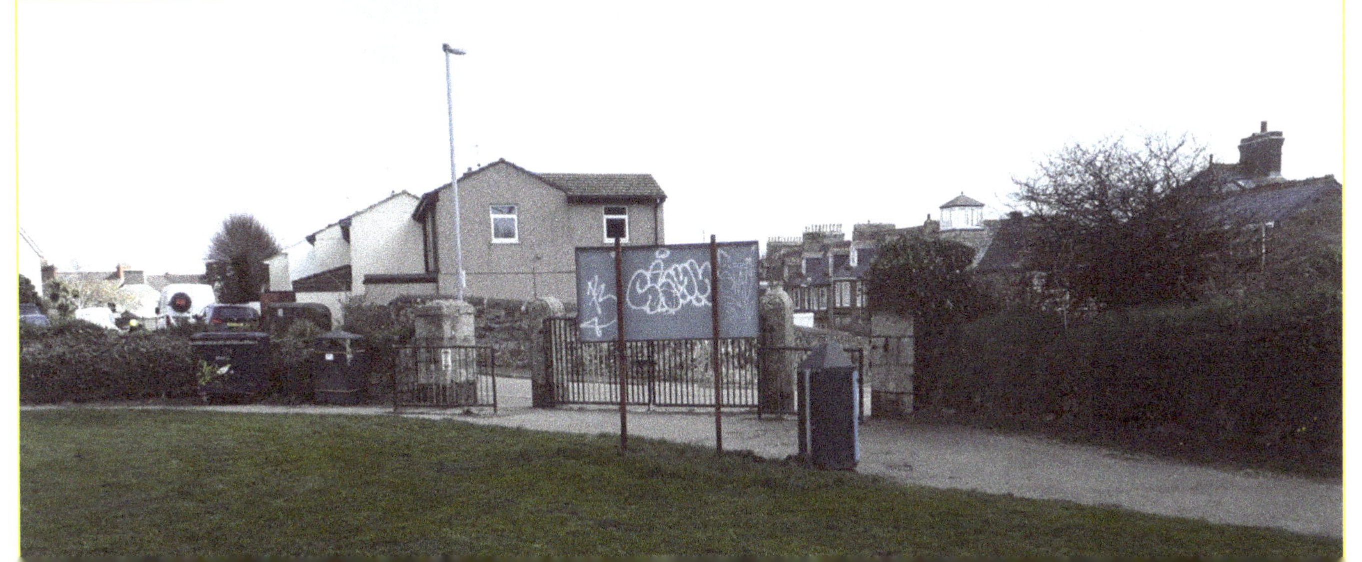

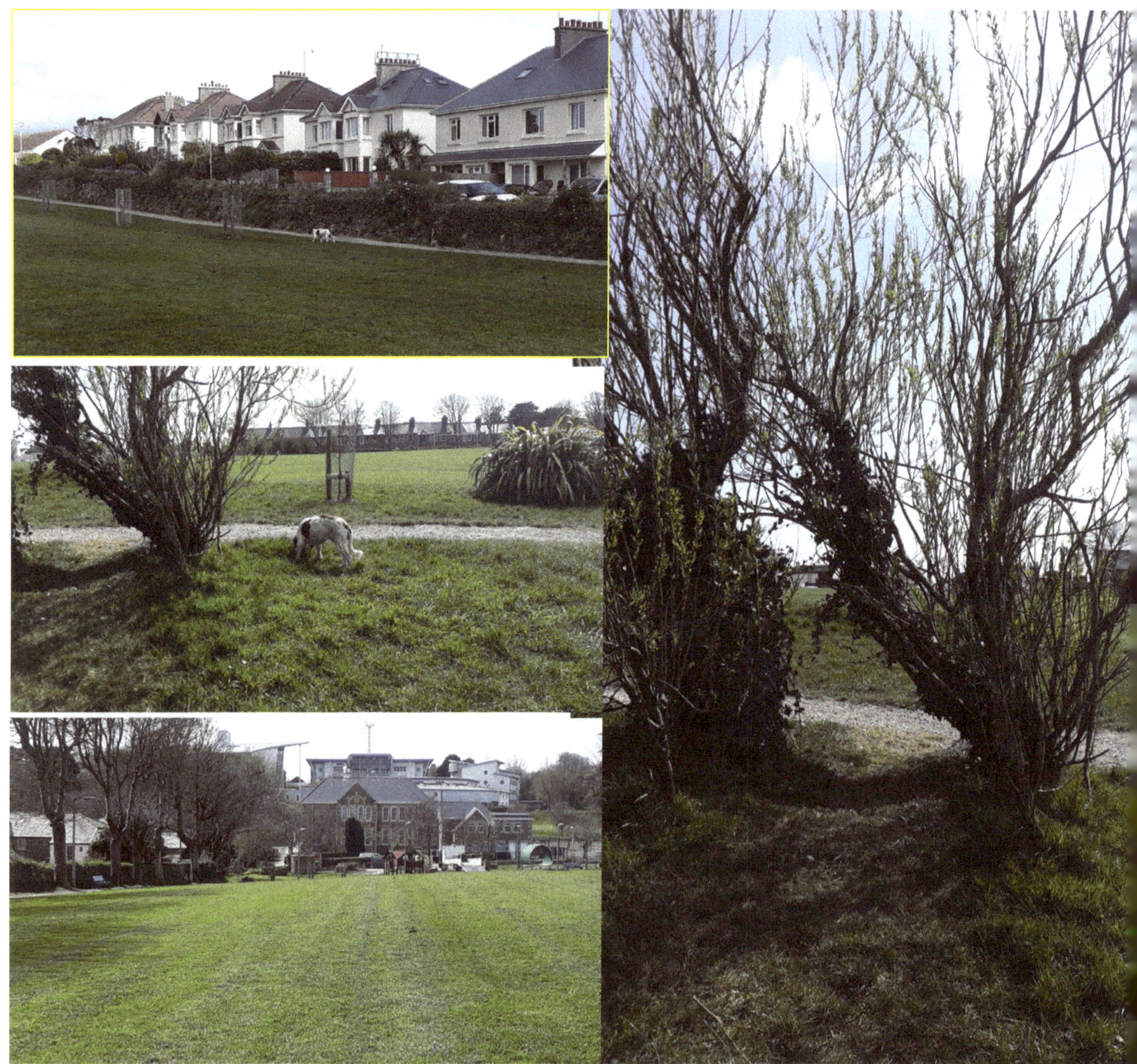

Winter Solstice, Montol

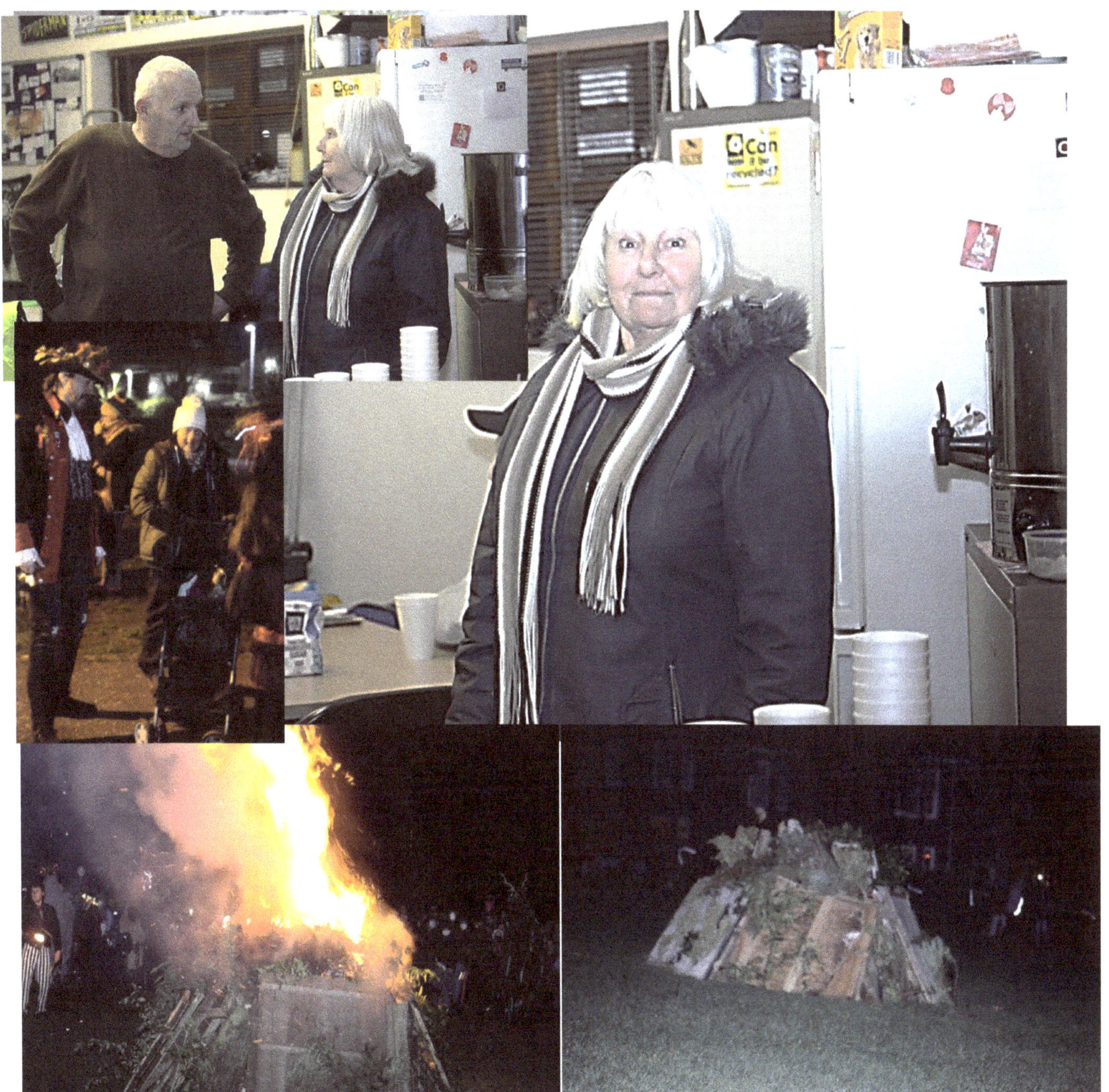

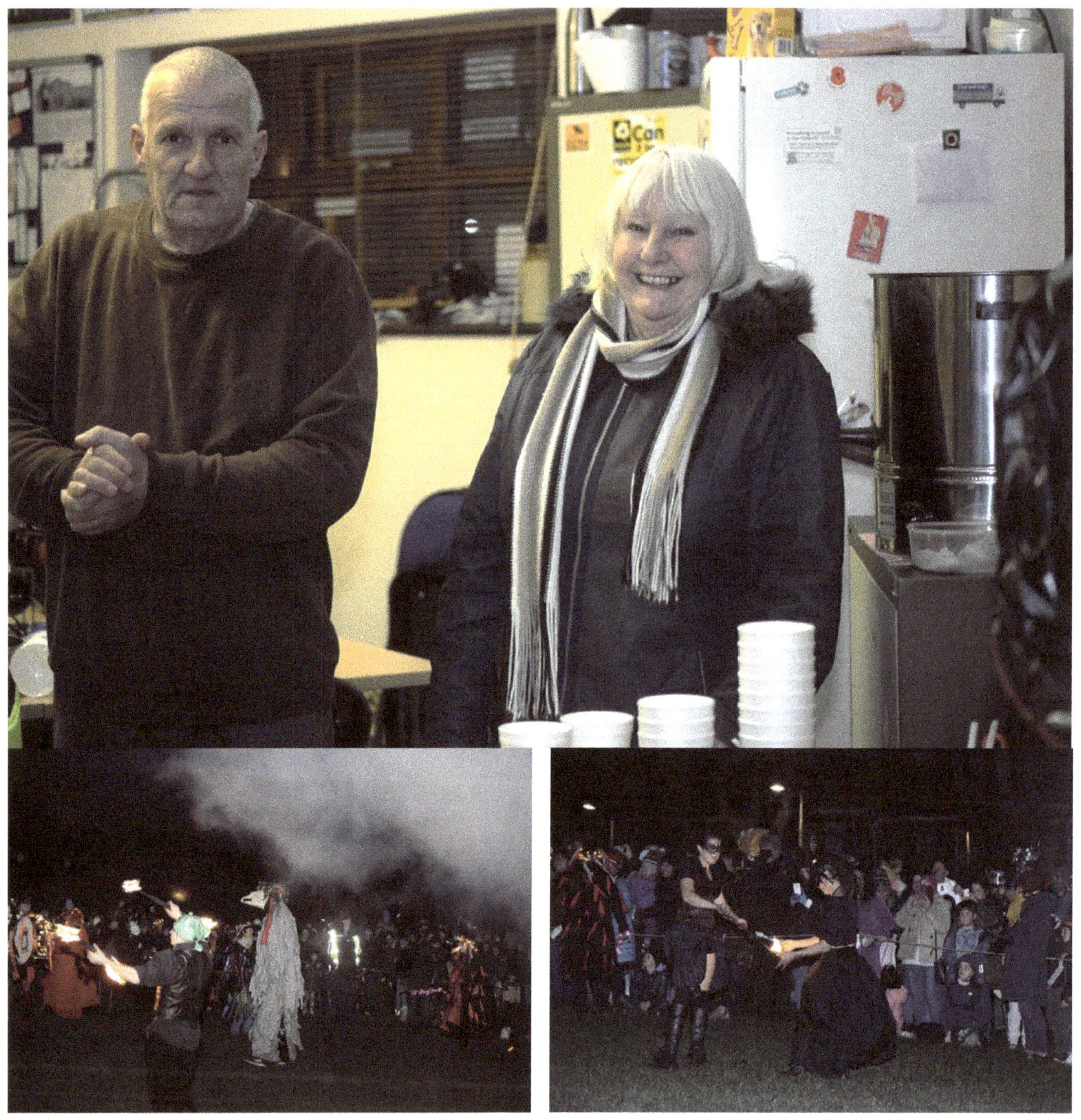

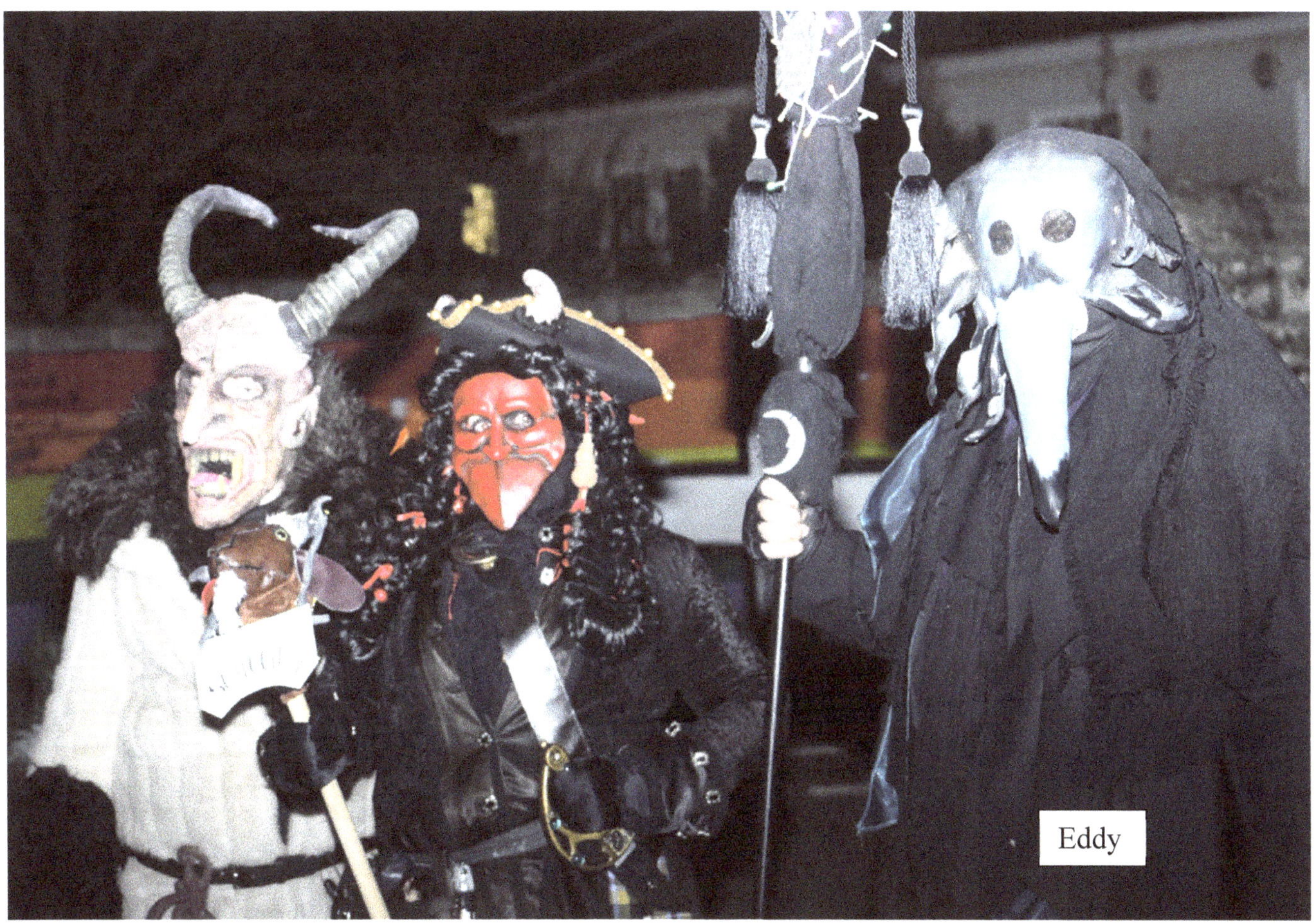

Nightmare on legs…

2022

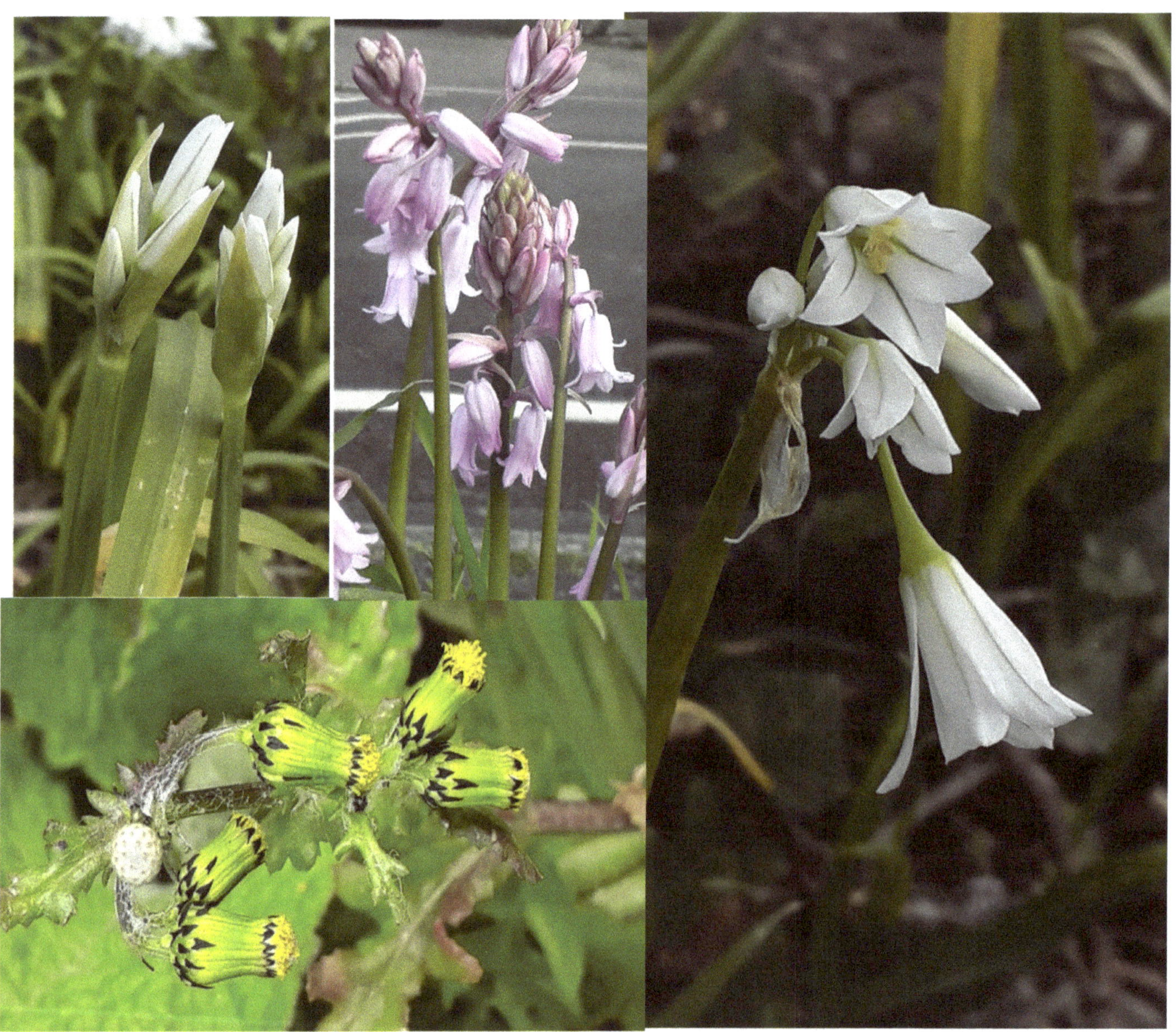

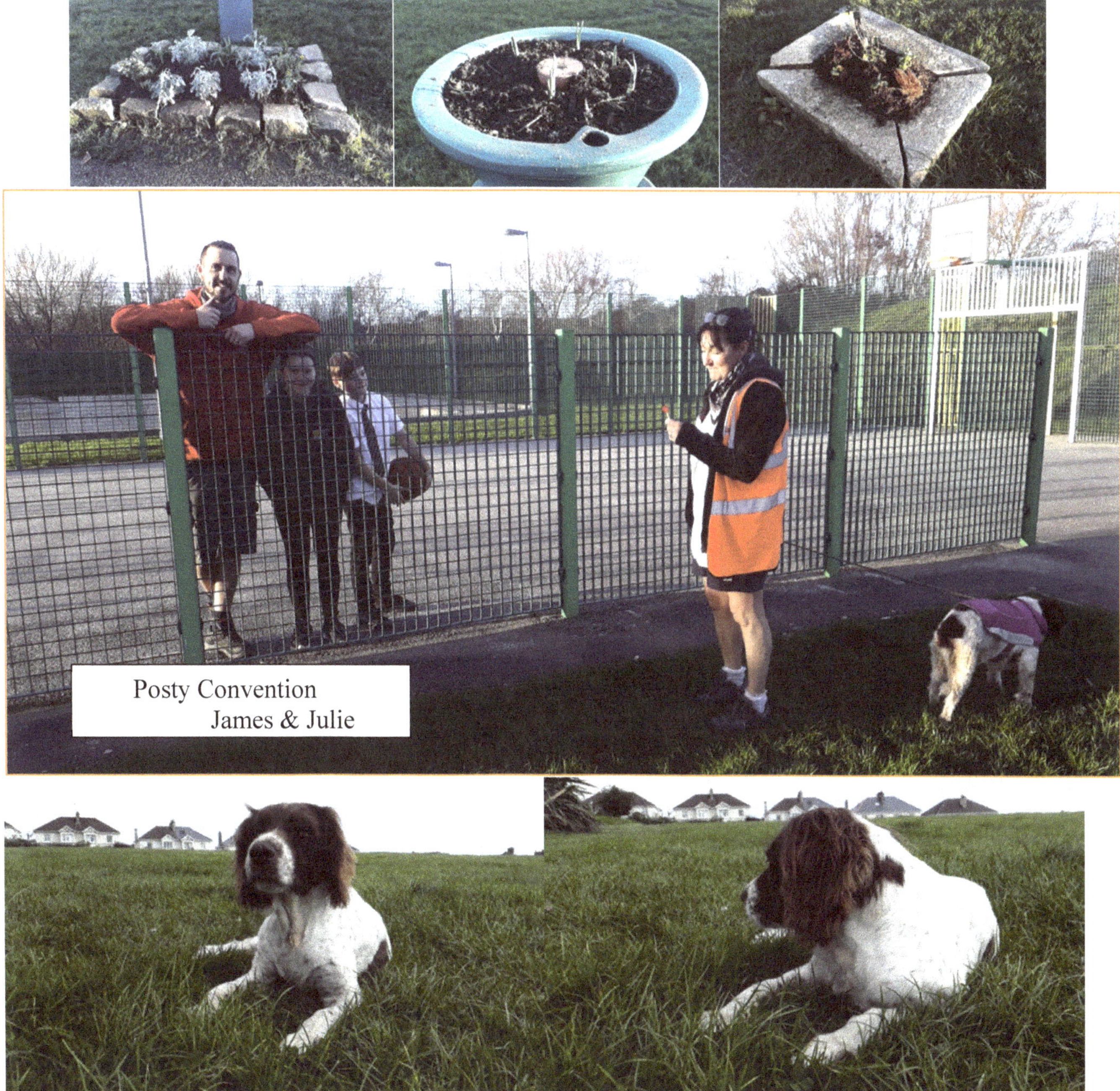
Posty Convention
James & Julie

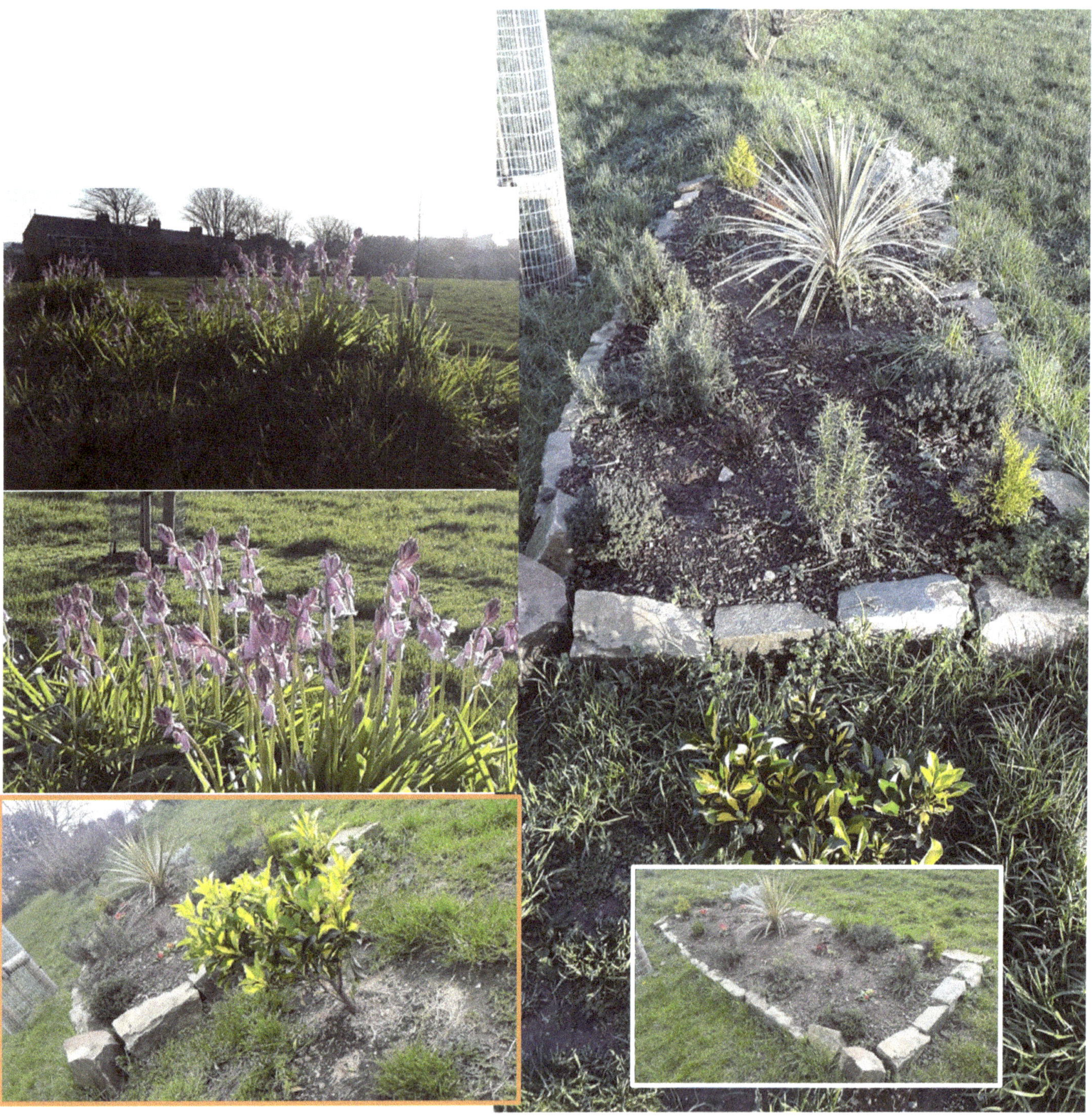

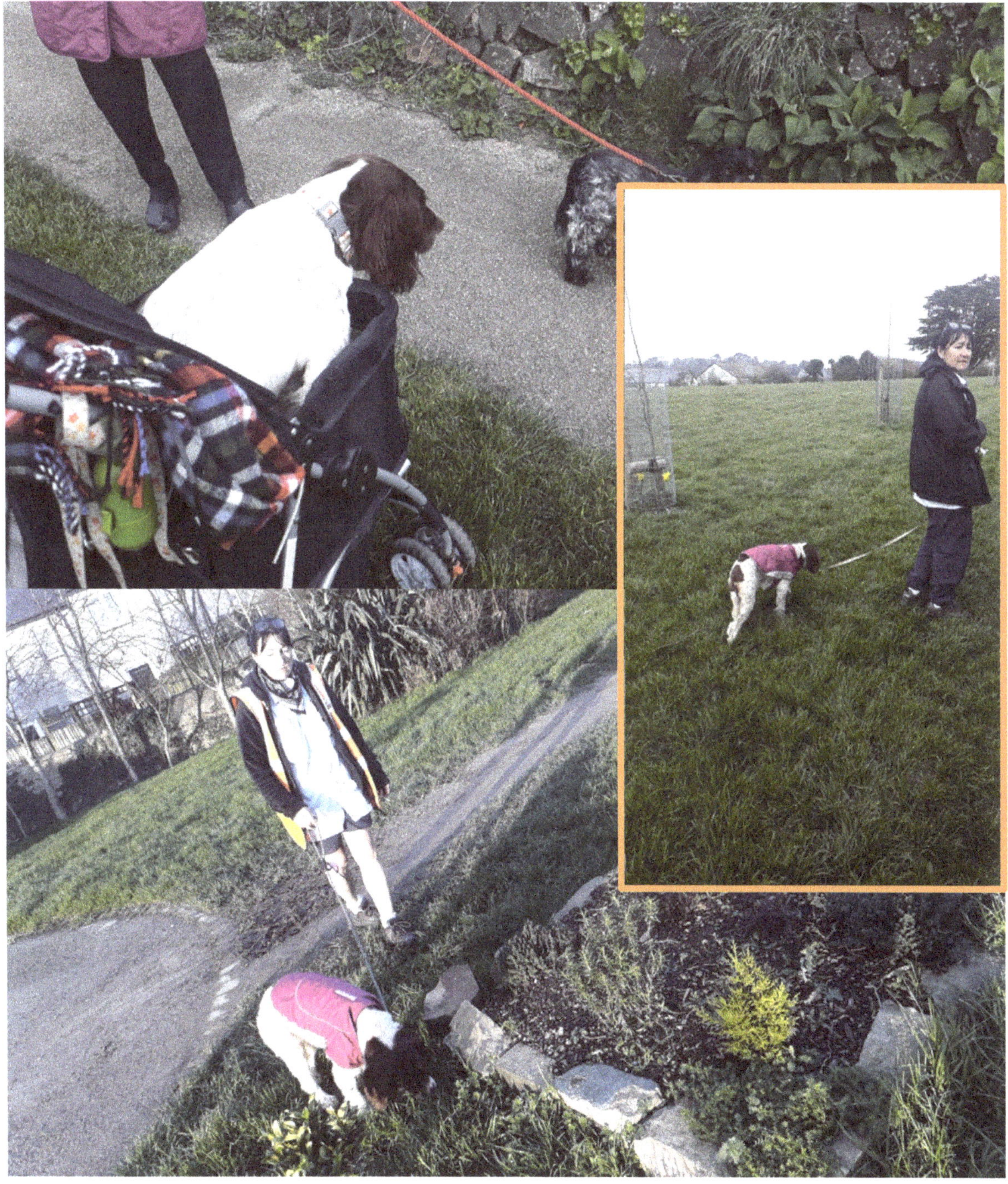

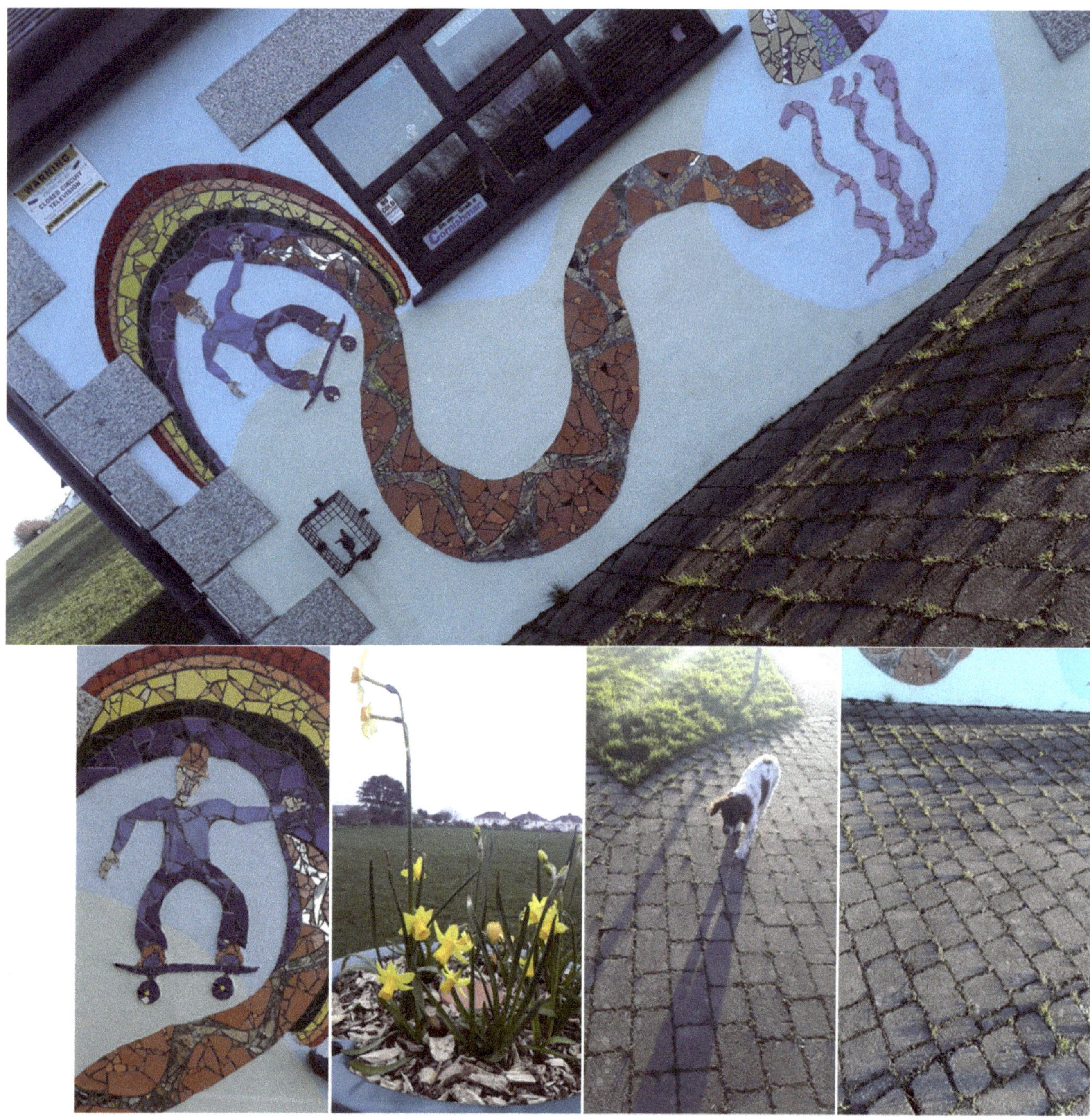
WARNING
CLOSED CIRCUIT TELEVISION
Cornishman

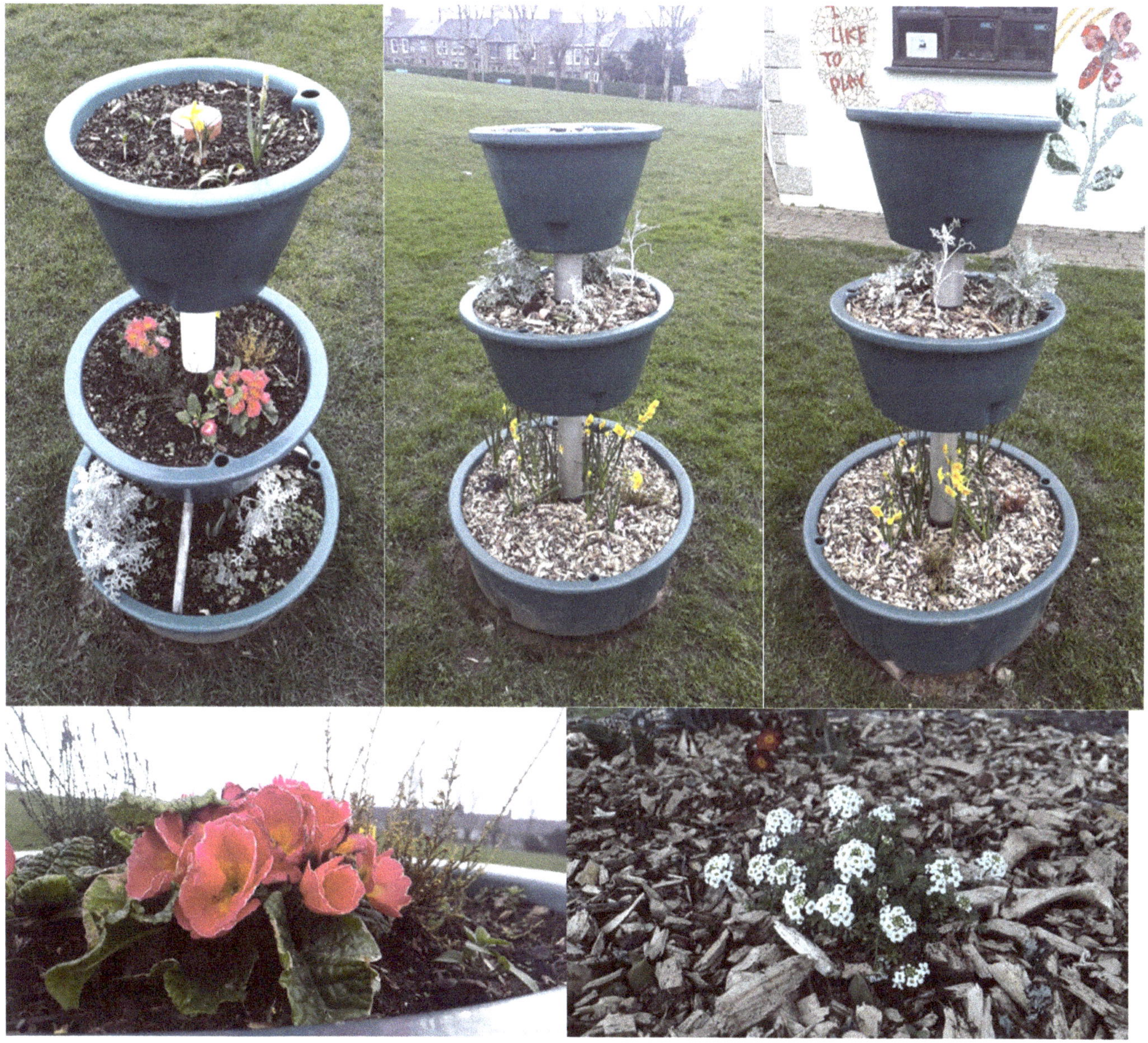
I LIKE TO PLAY

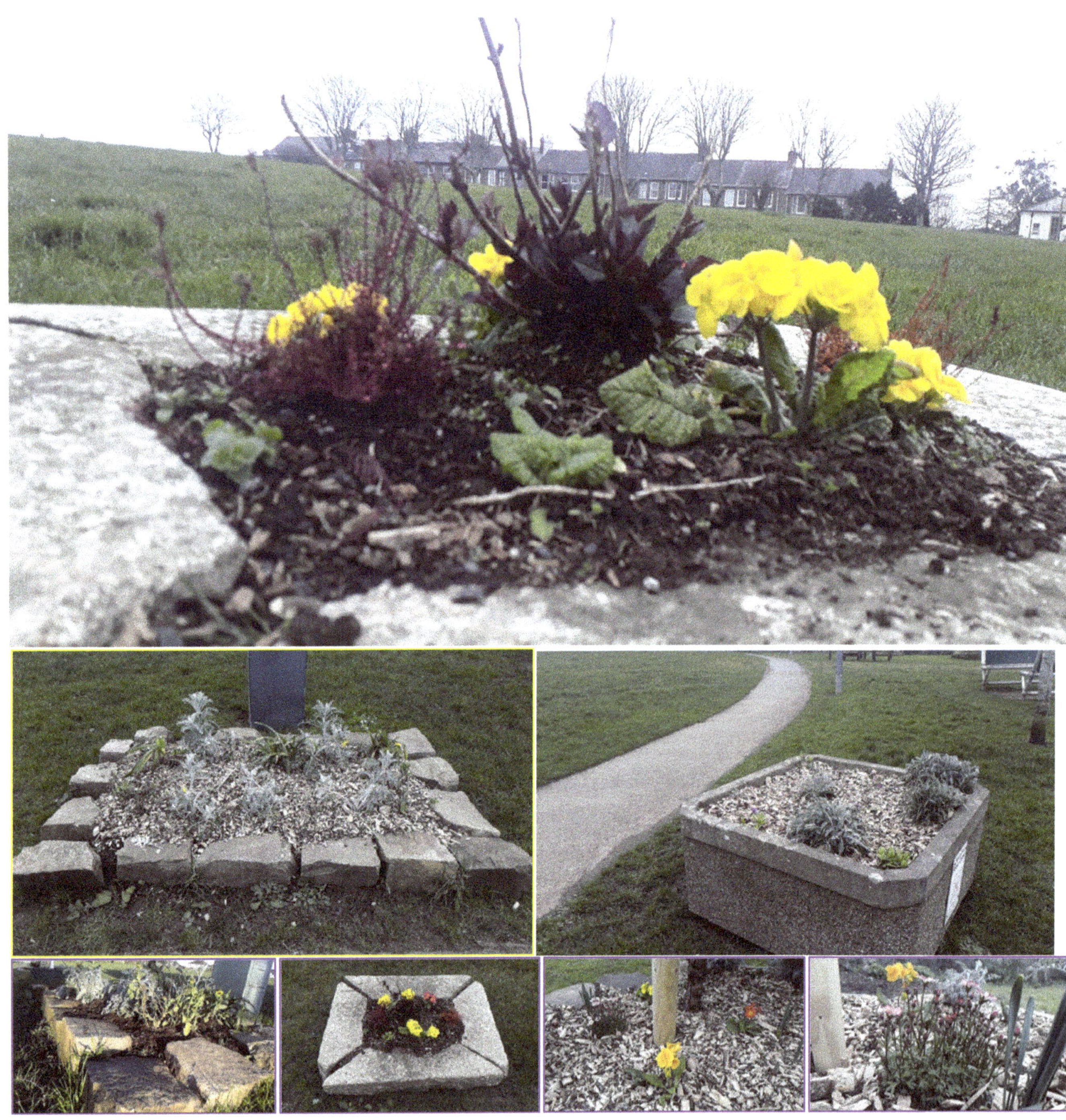

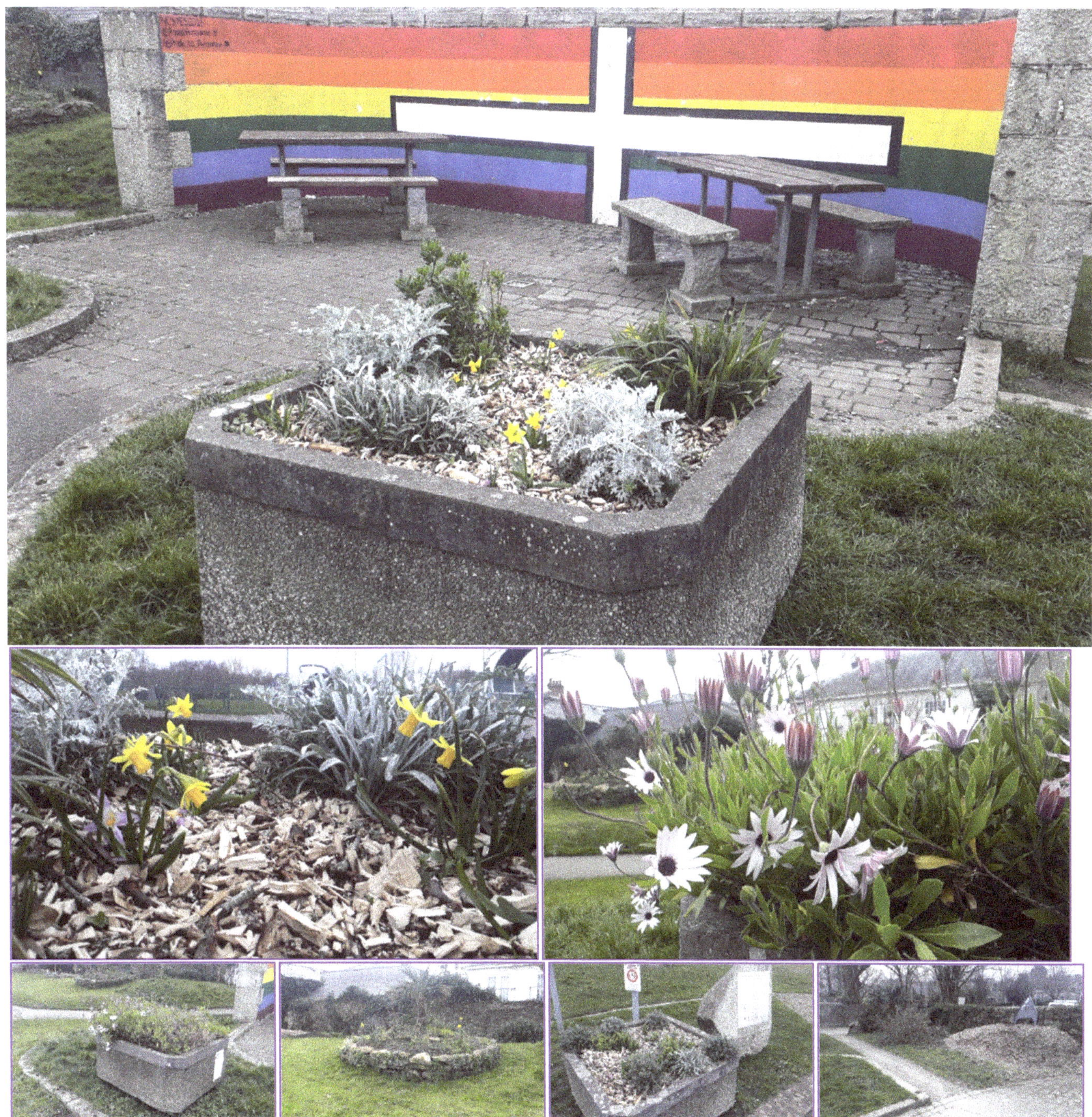

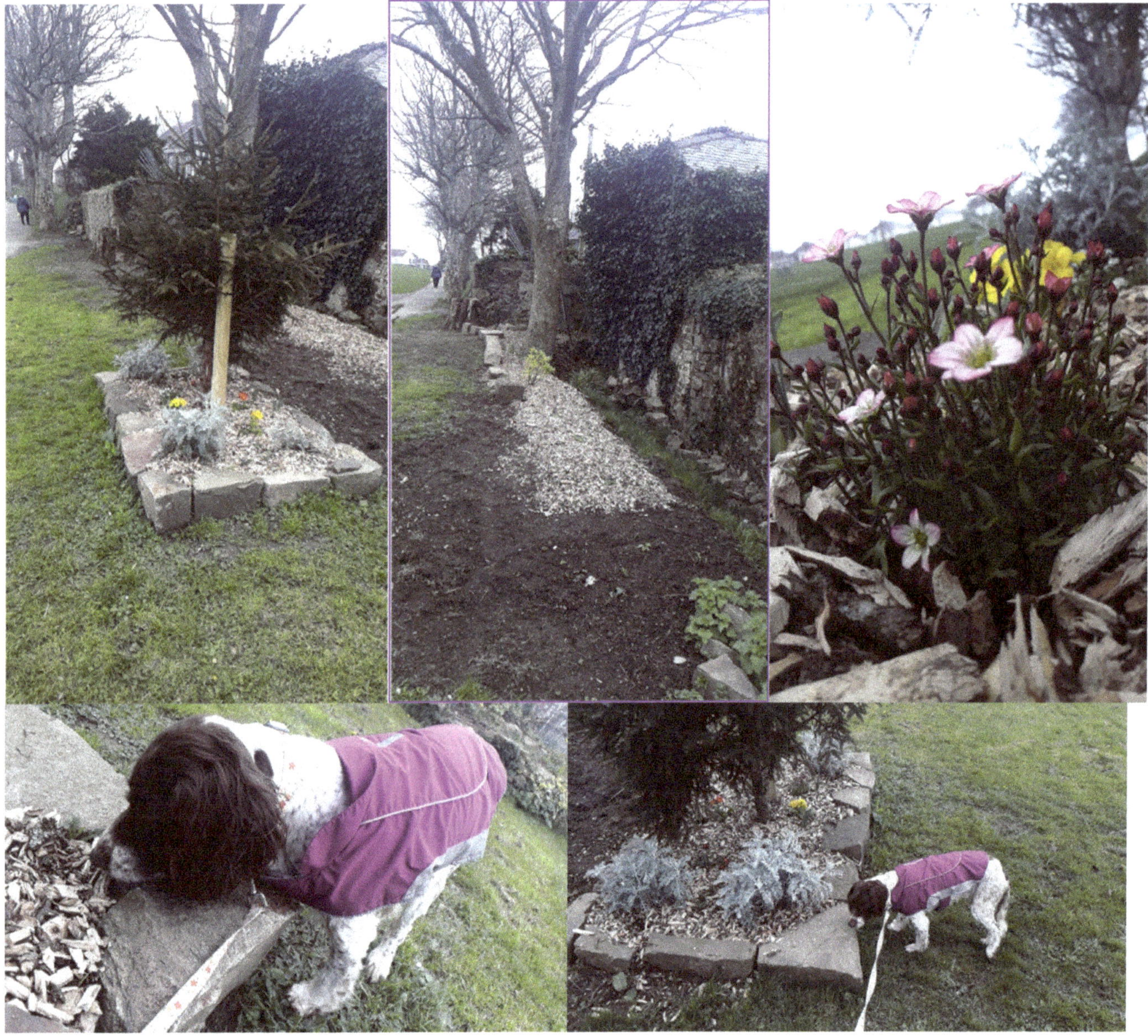

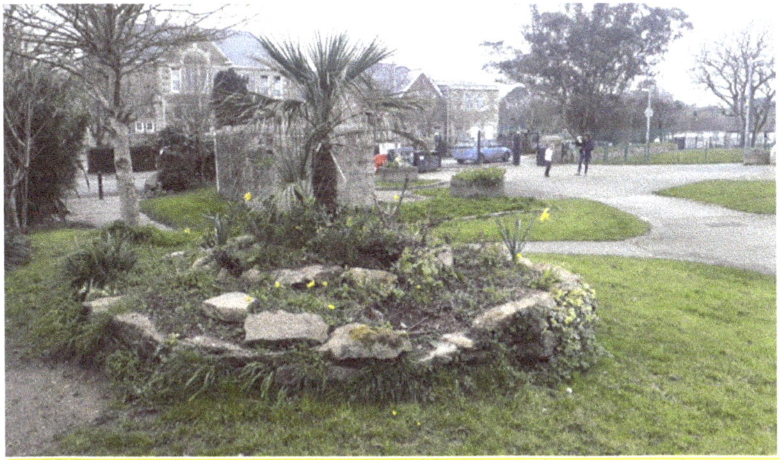

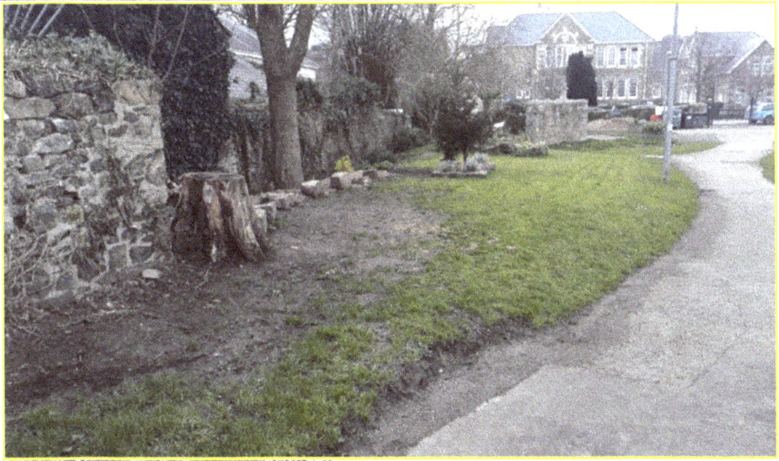

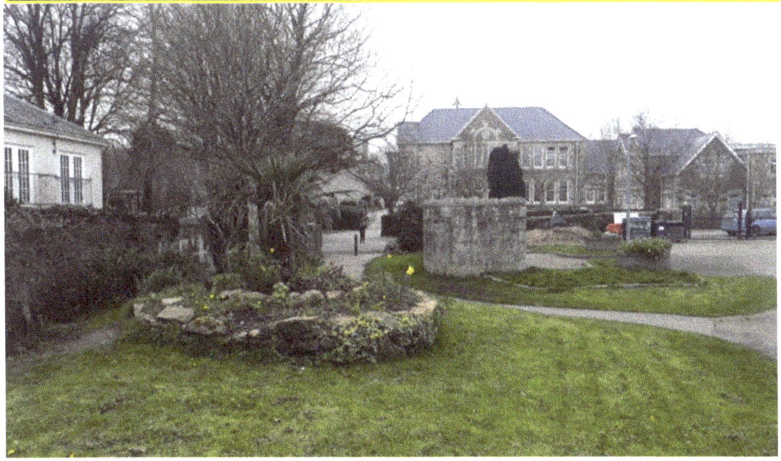

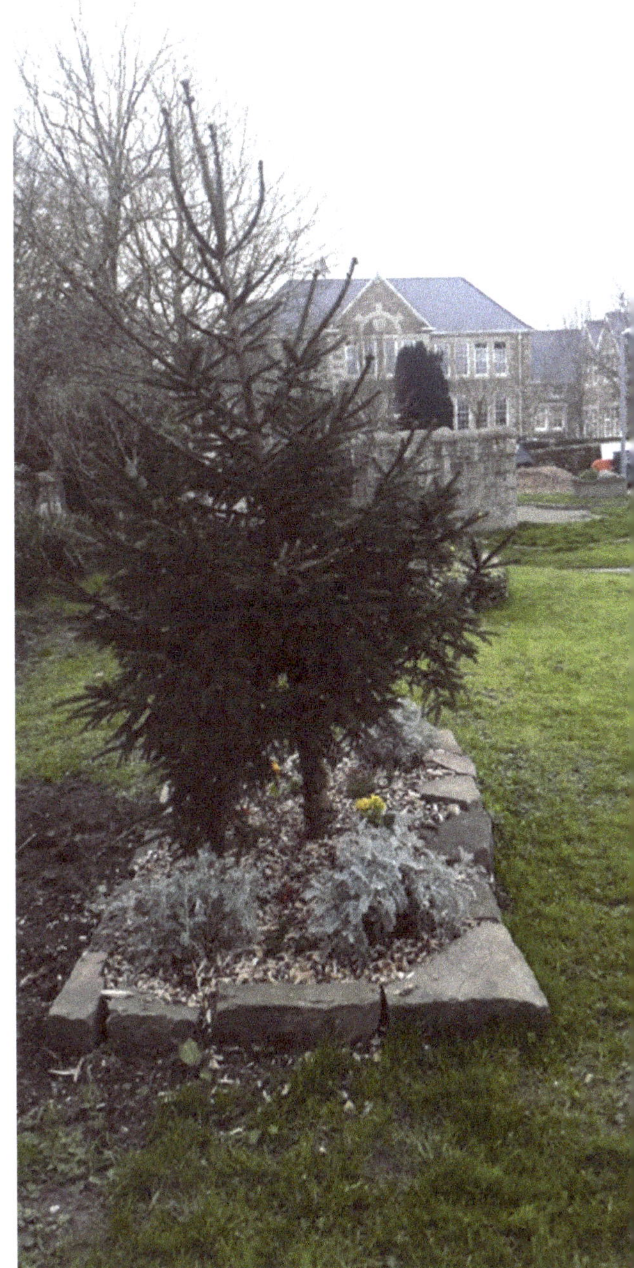

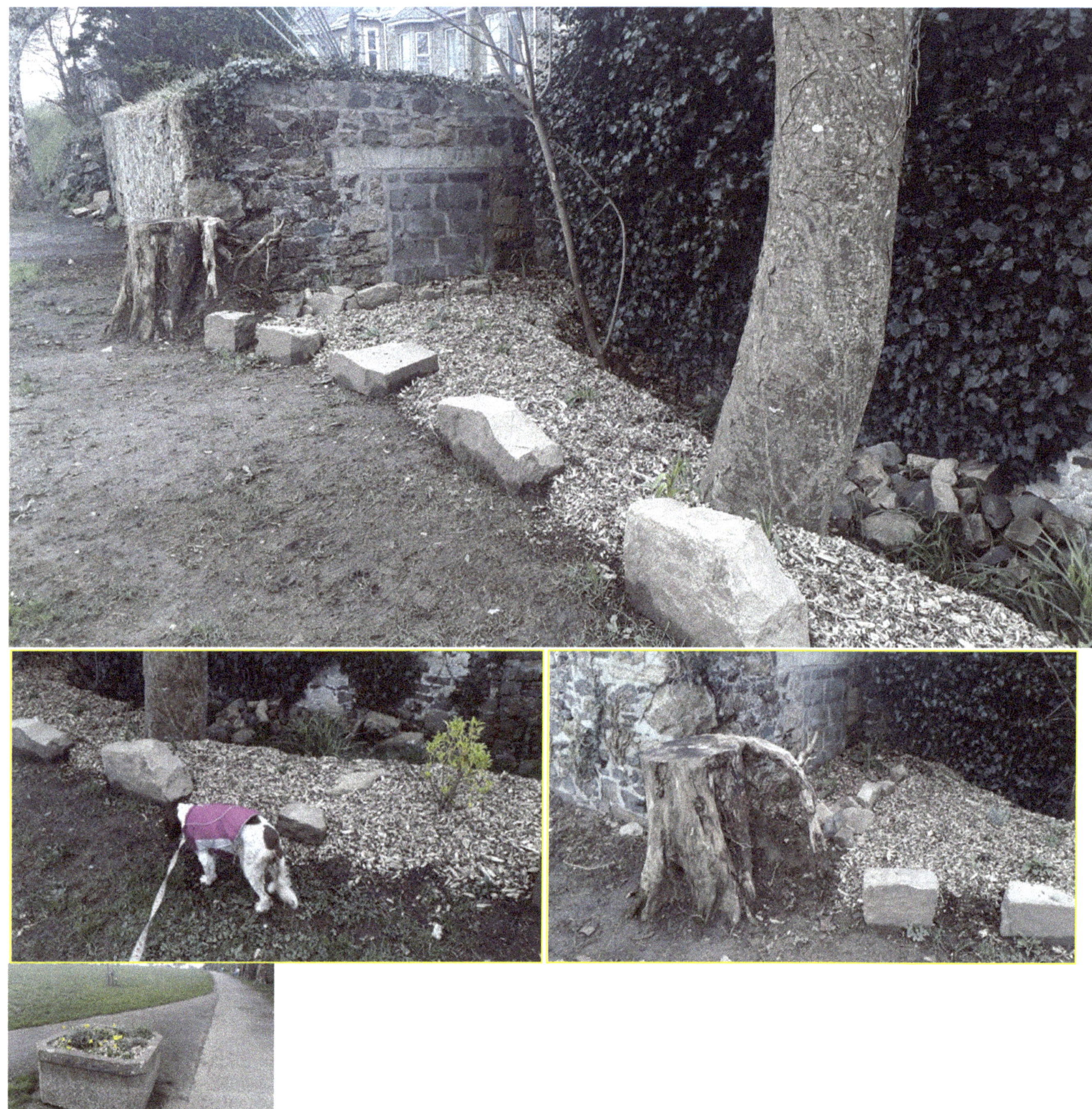

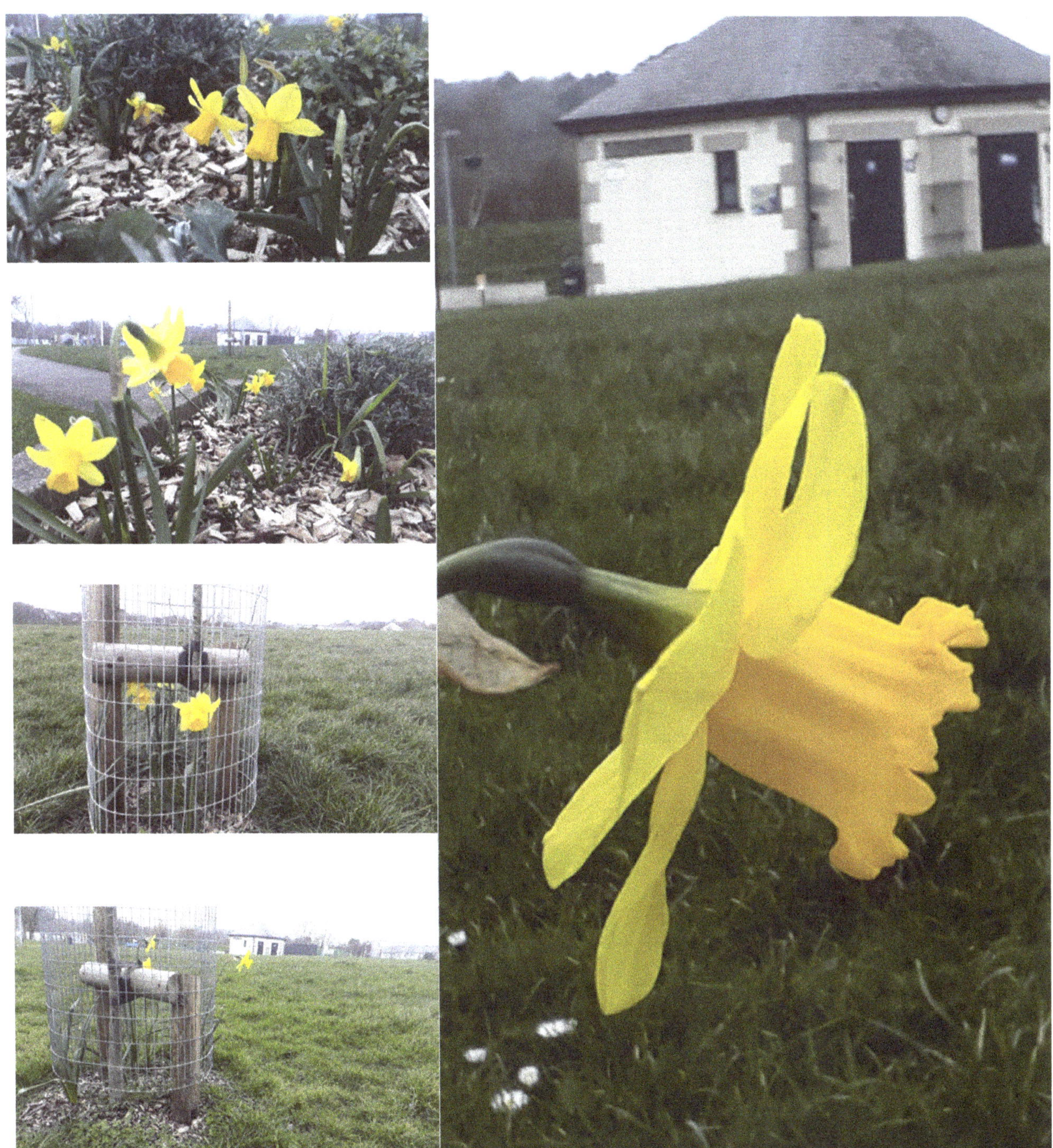

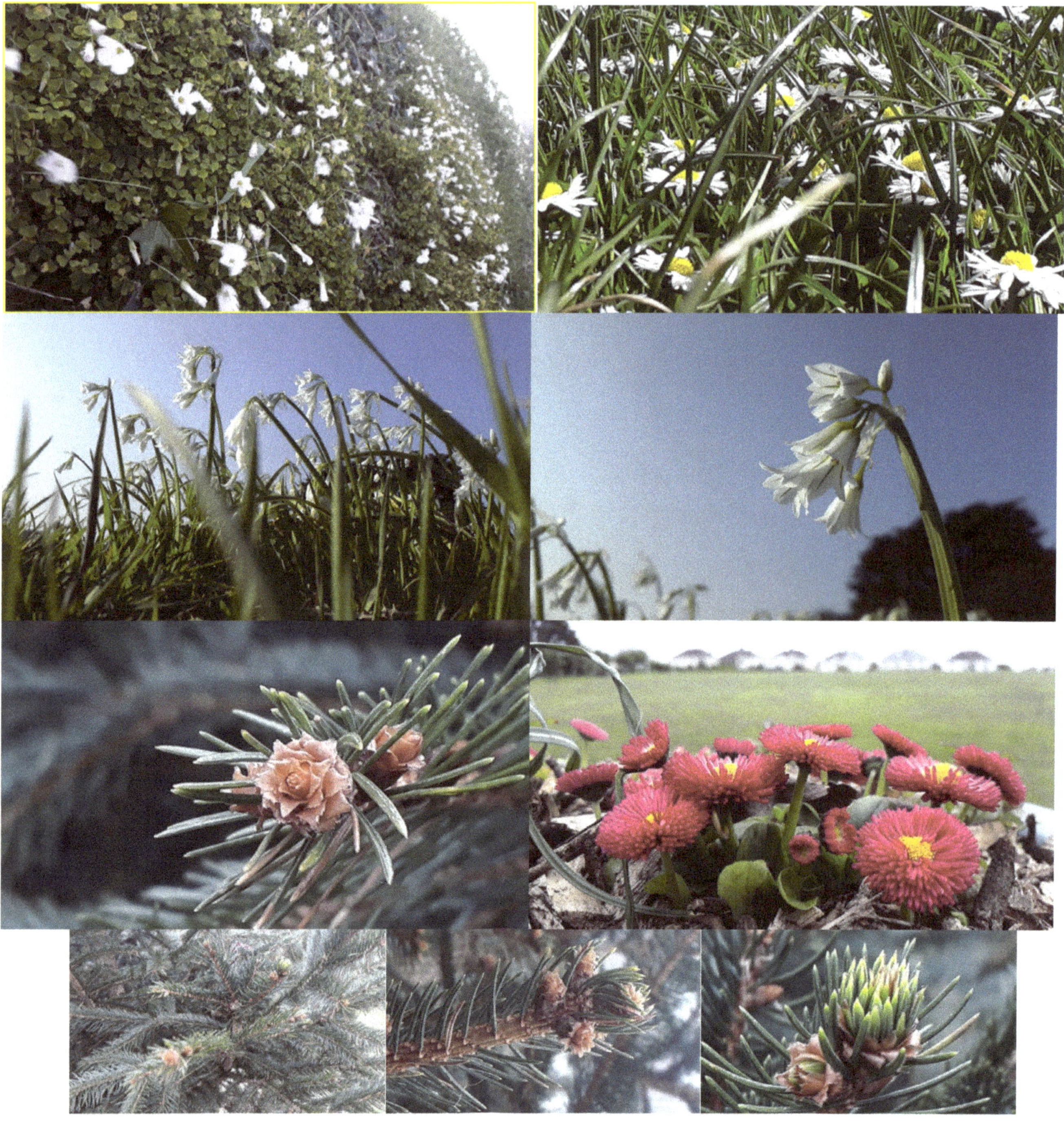

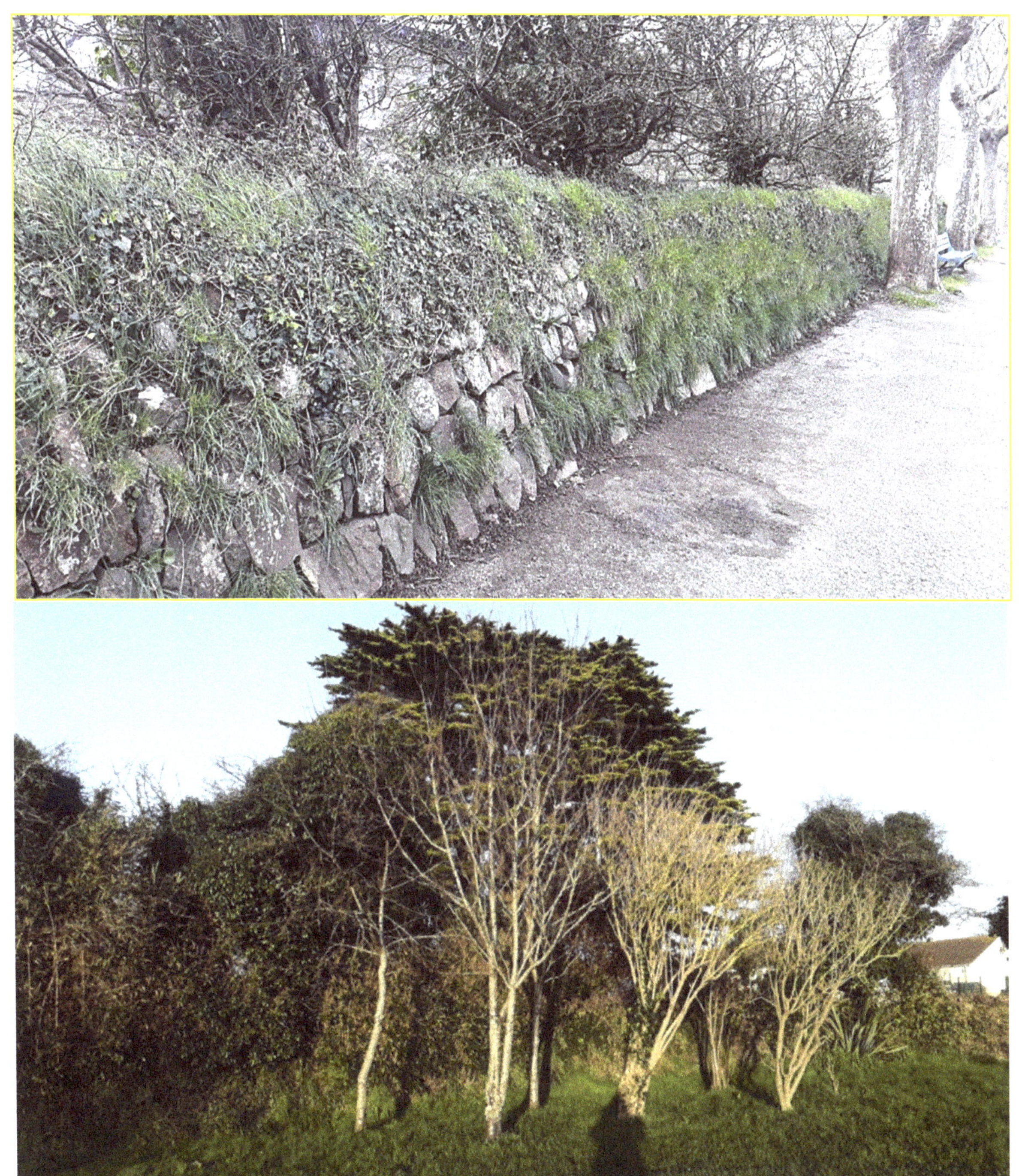

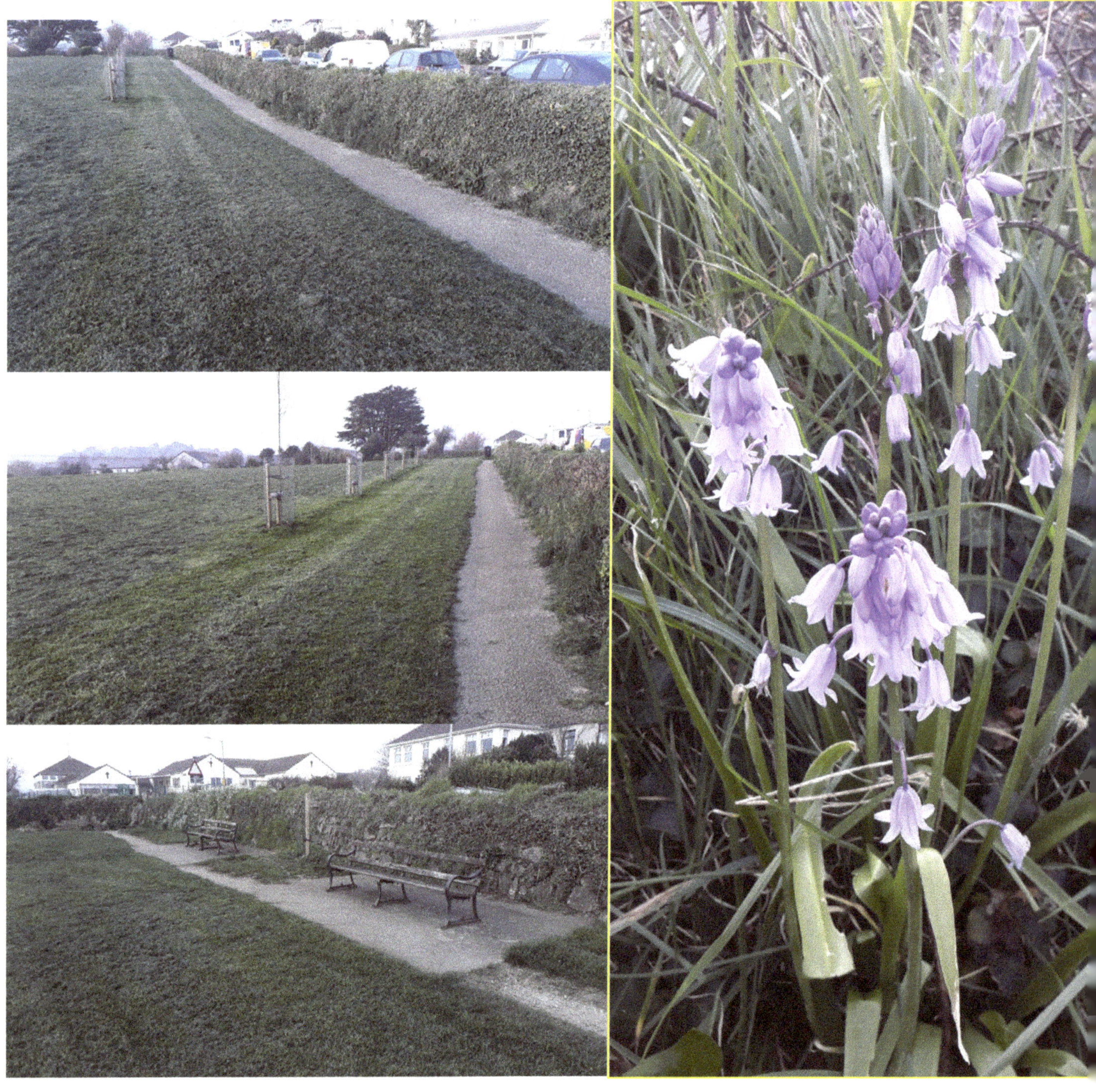

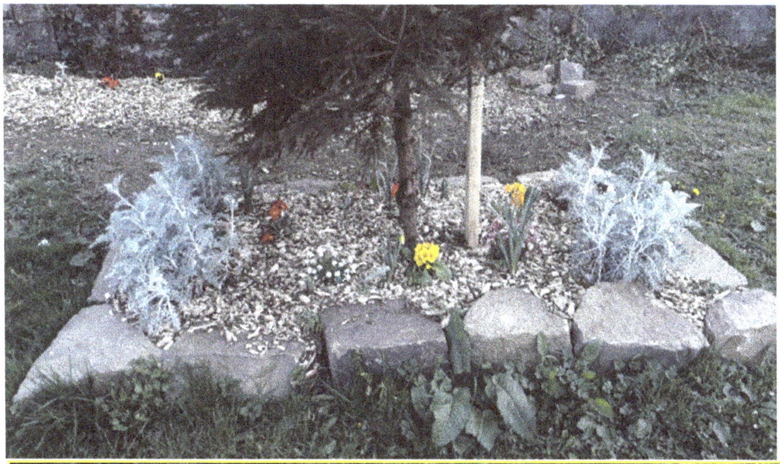

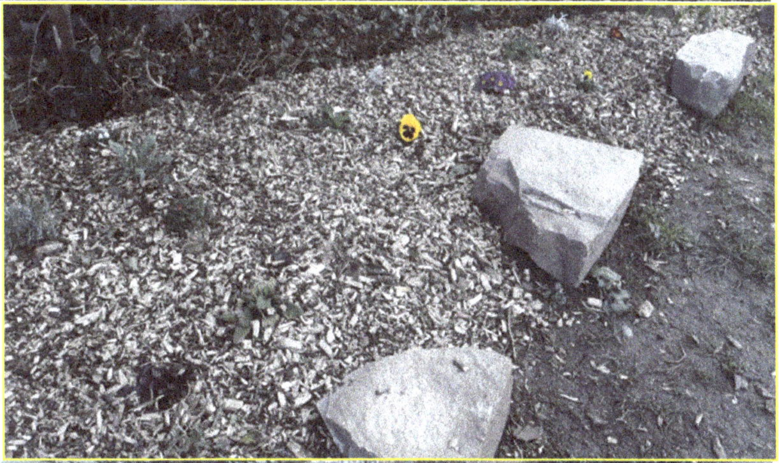

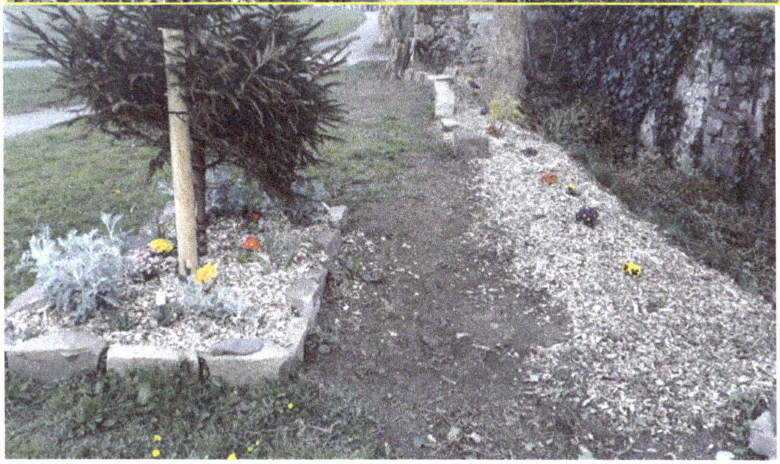

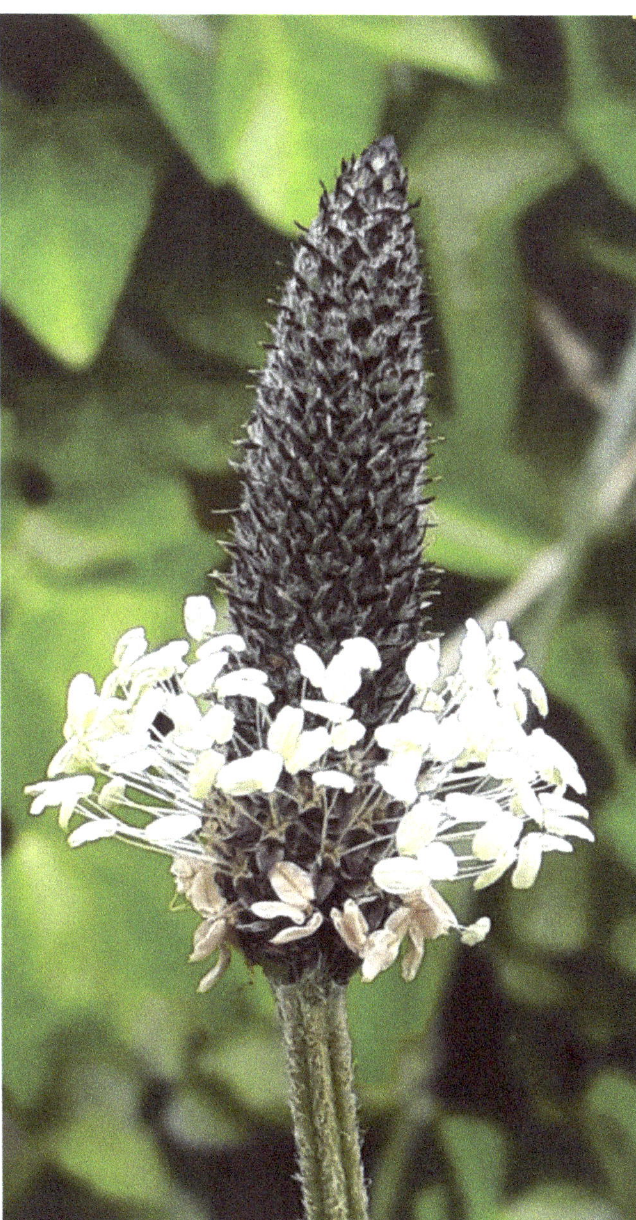

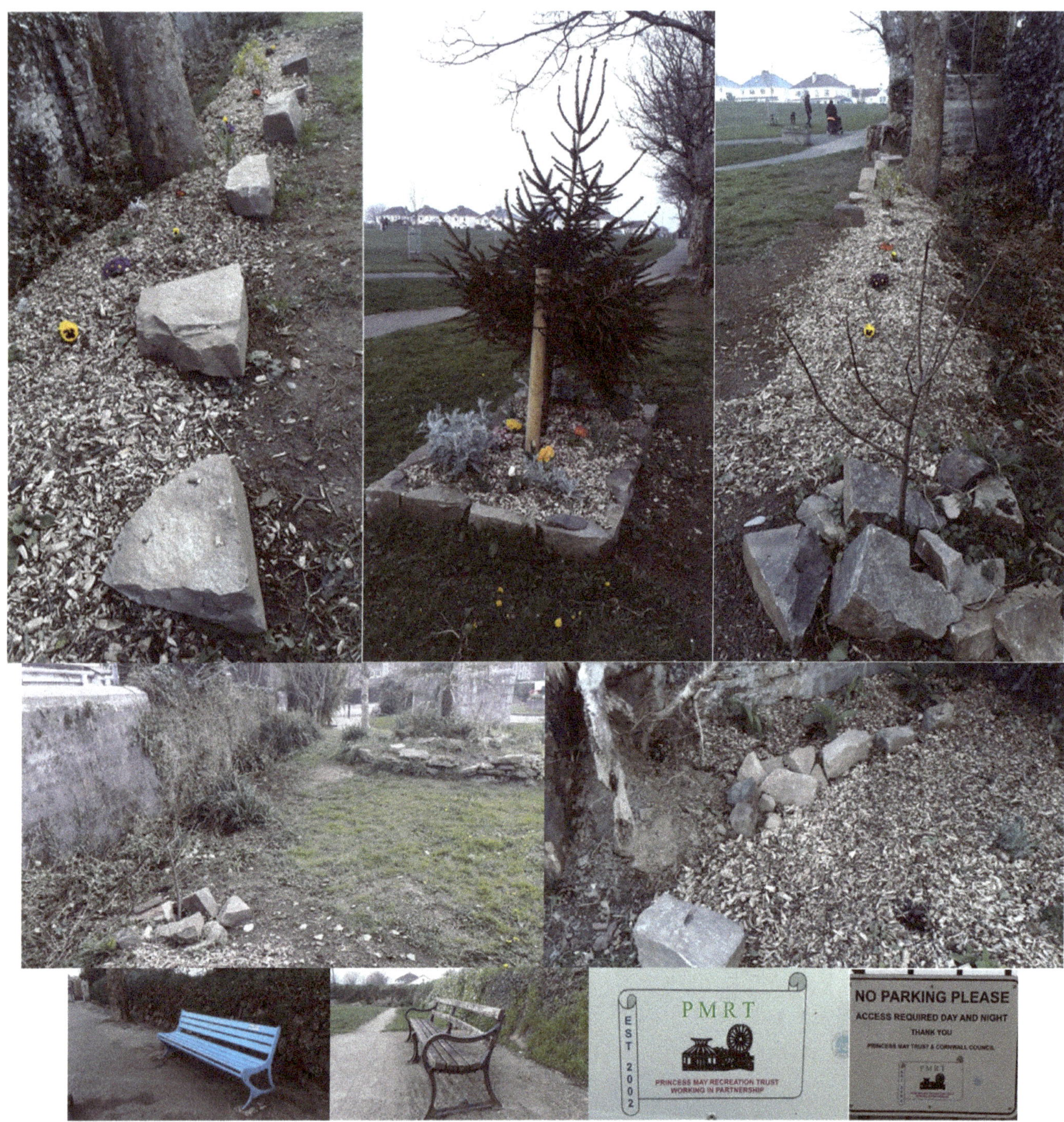
PMRT
EST 2002
PRINCESS MAY RECREATION TRUST
WORKING IN PARTNERSHIP
NO PARKING PLEASE
ACCESS REQUIRED DAY AND NIGHT
THANK YOU

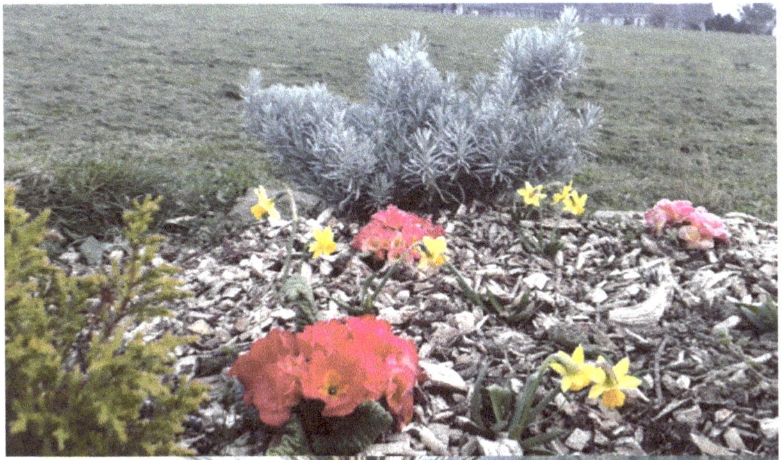

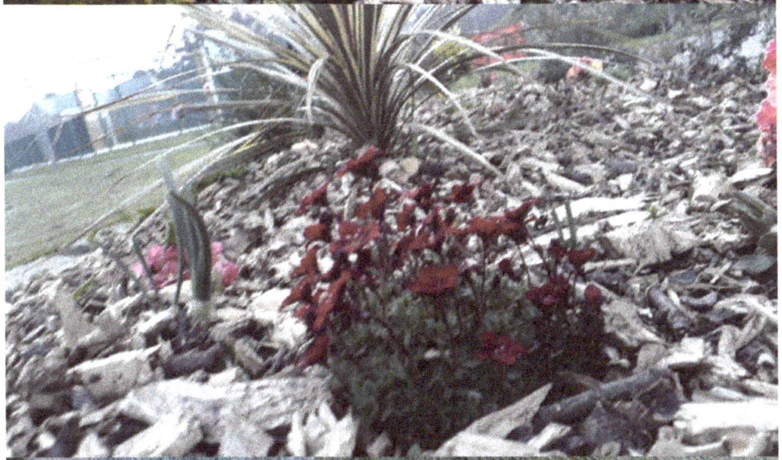

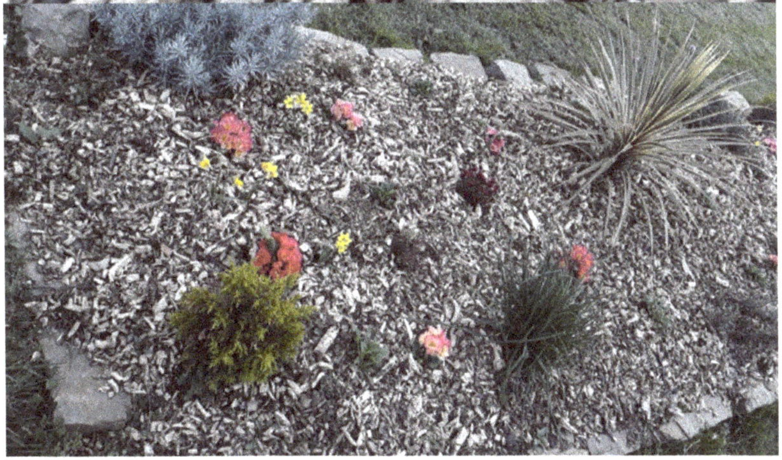

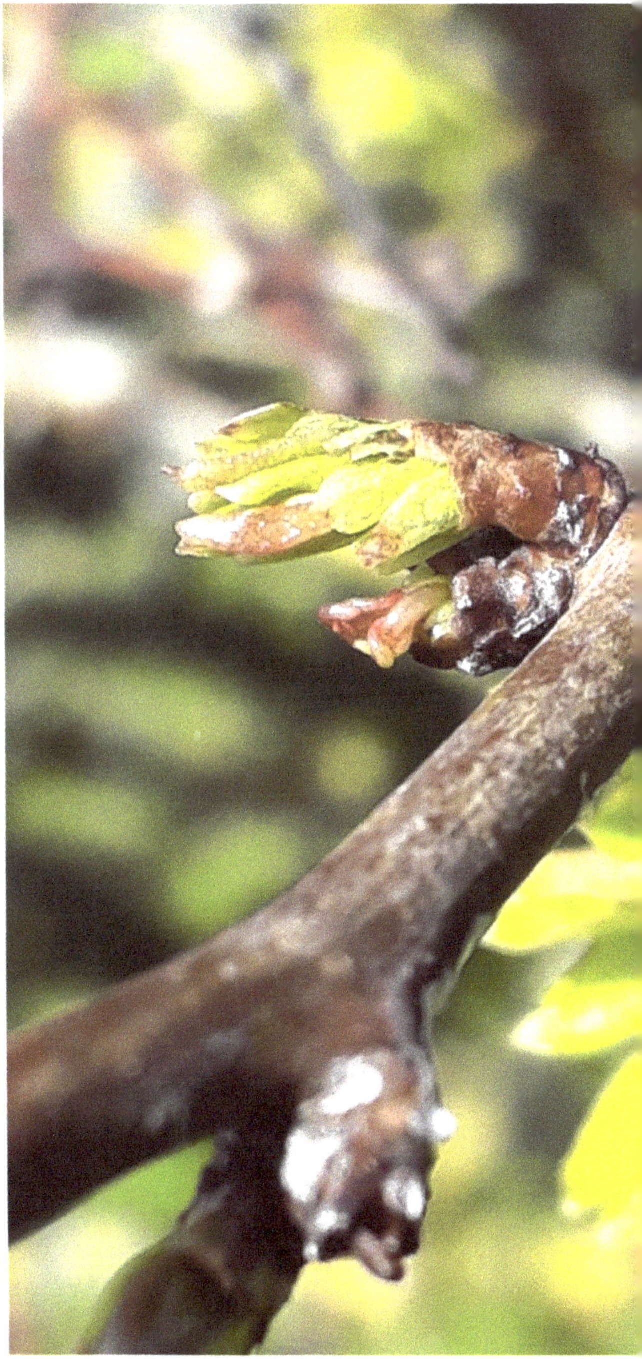

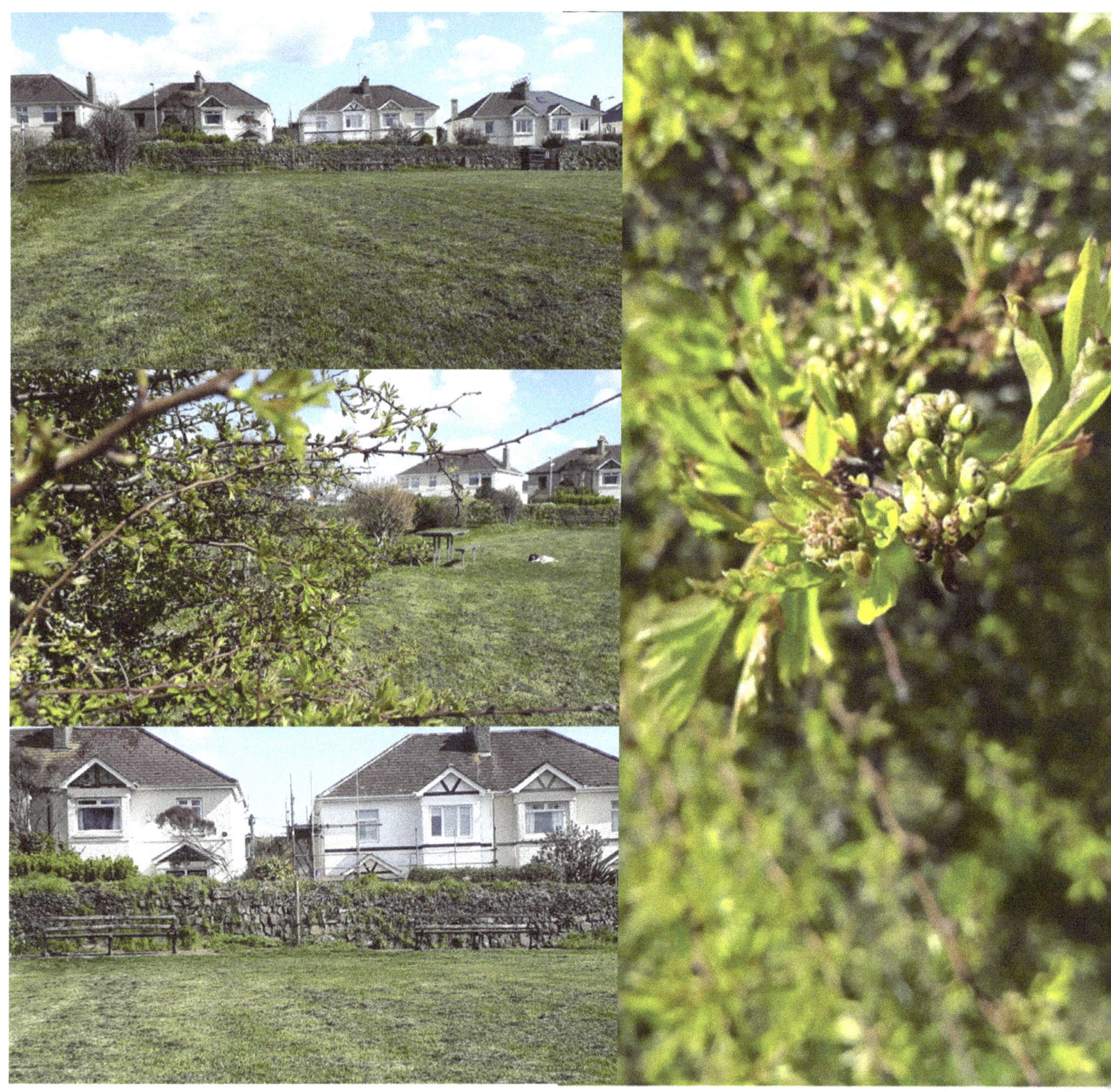

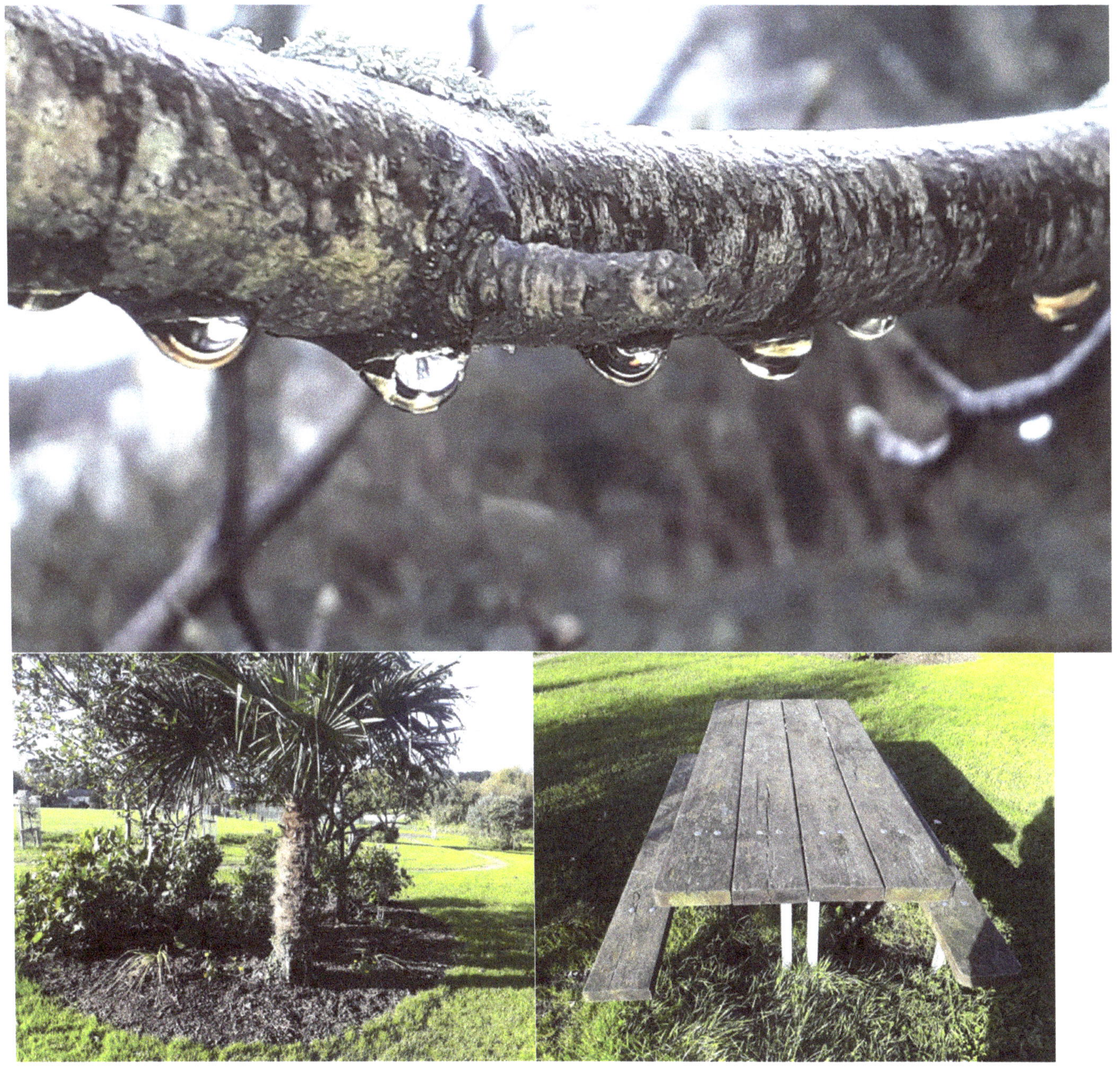

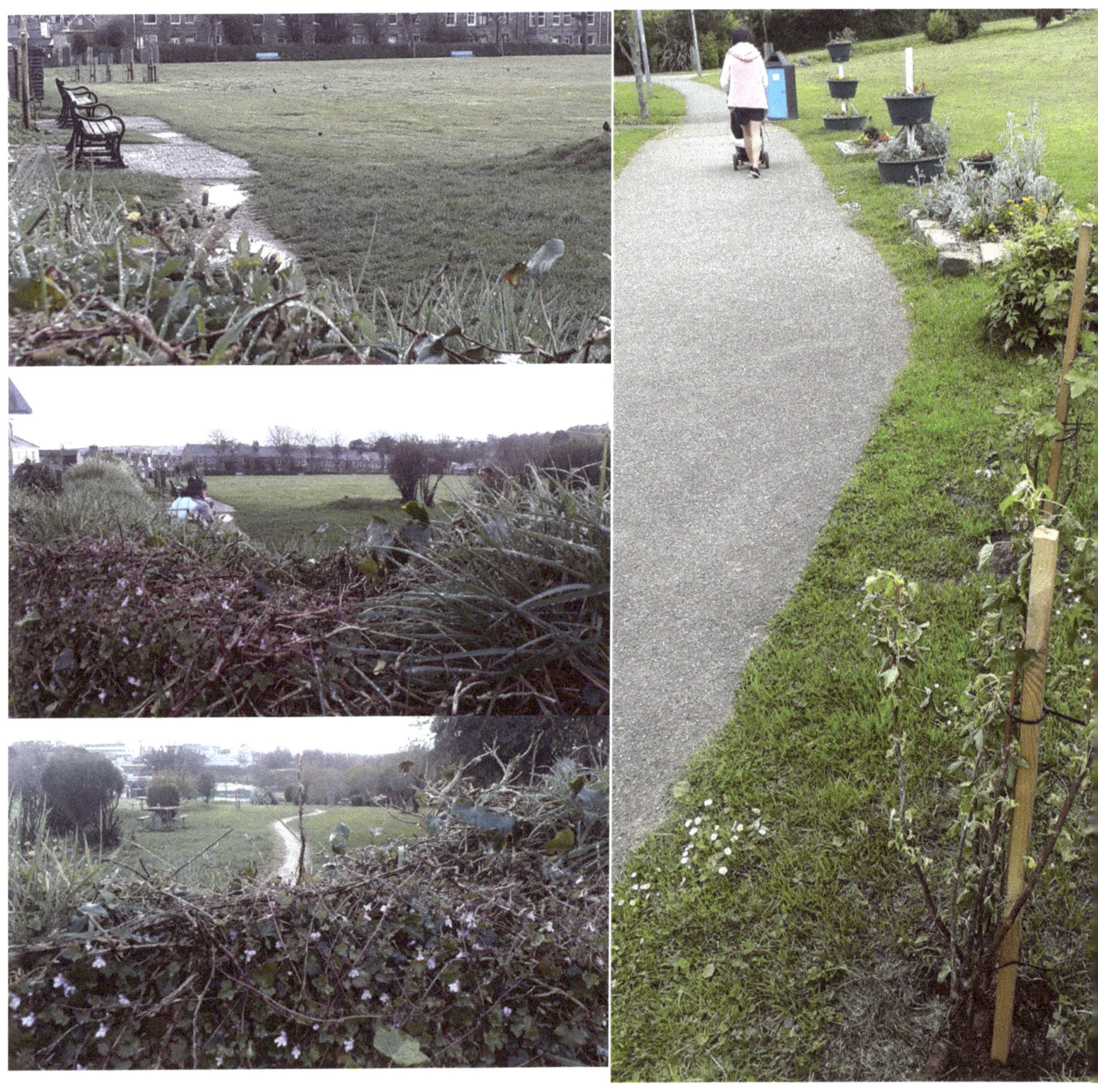

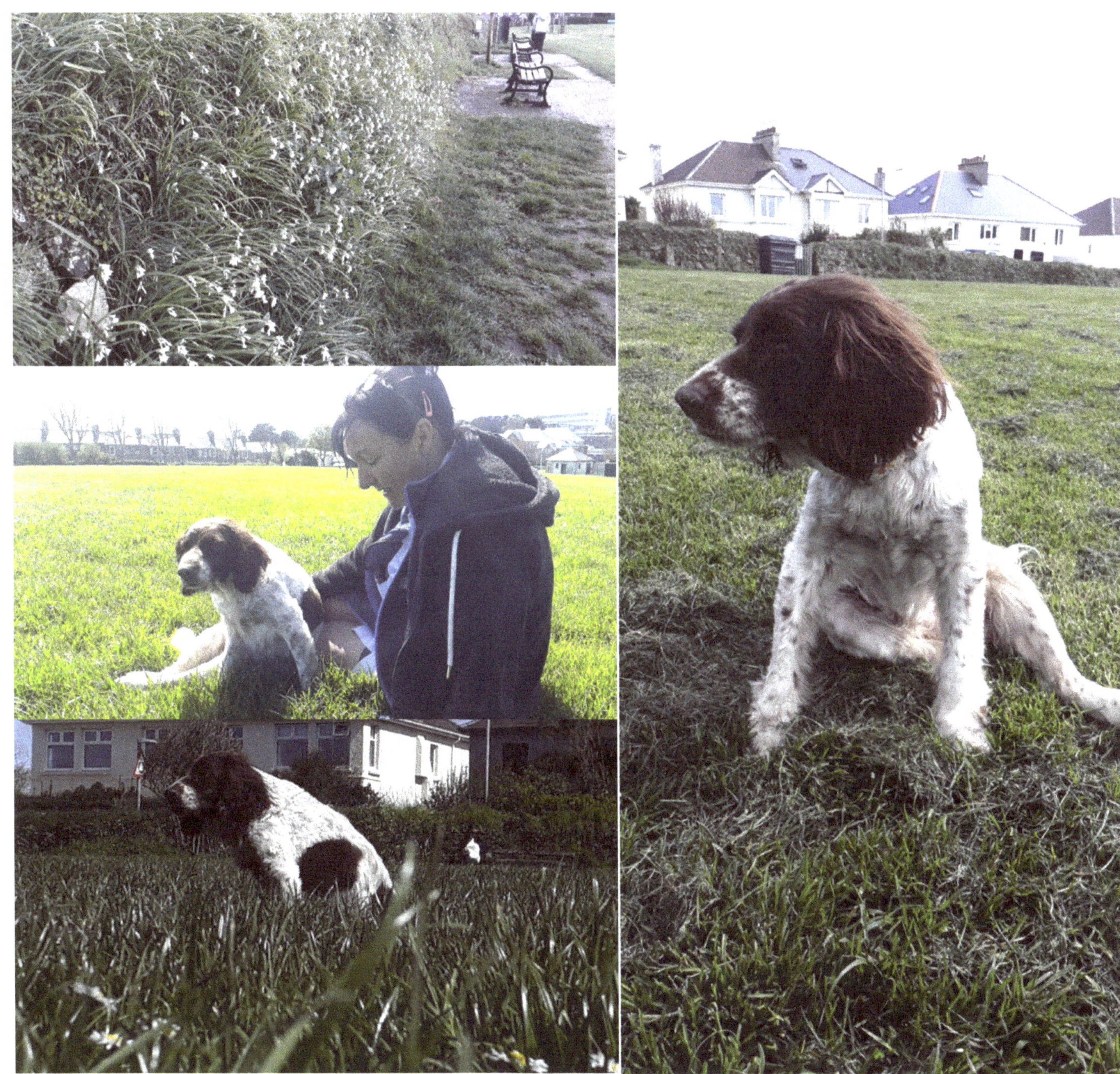

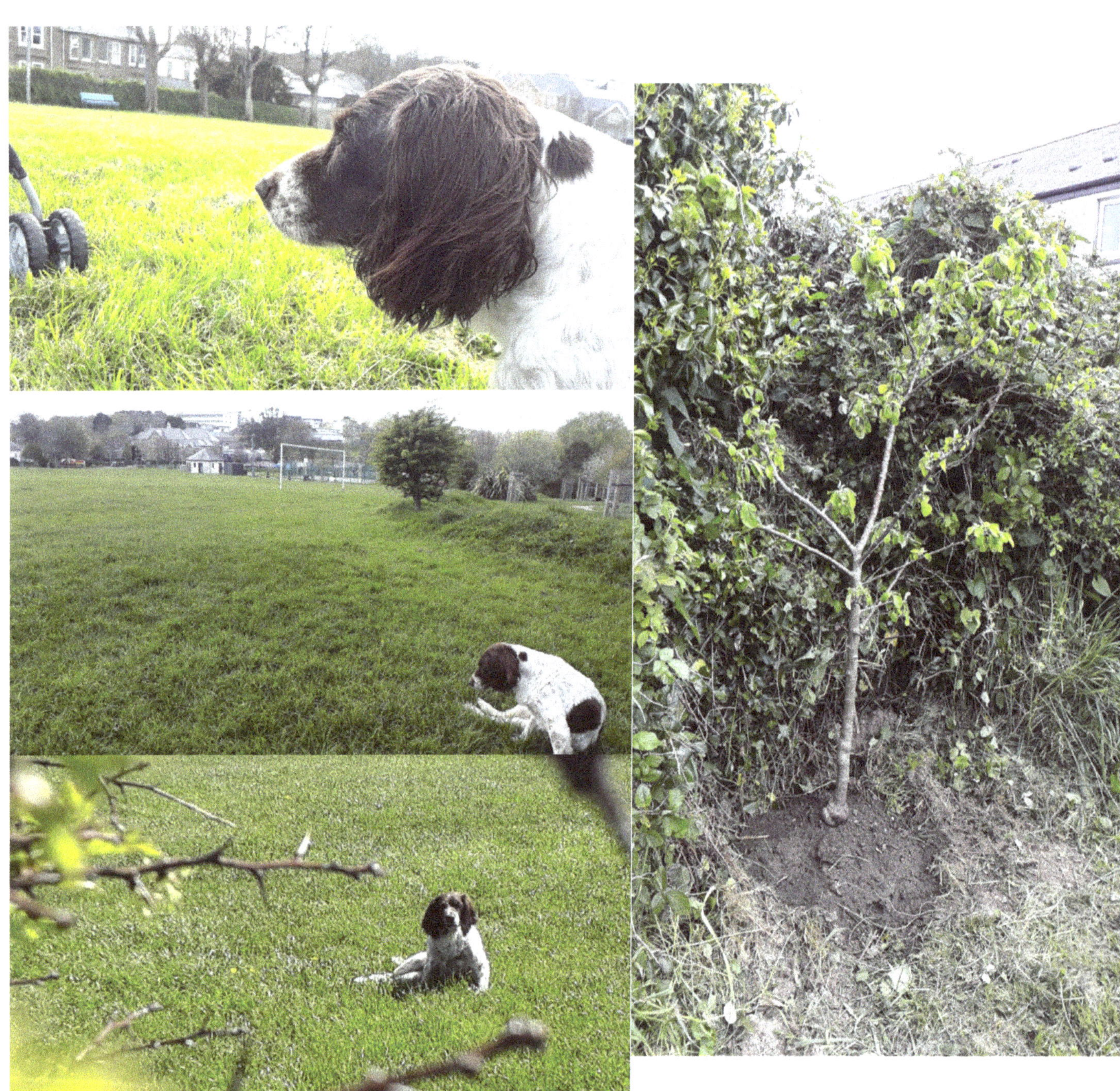

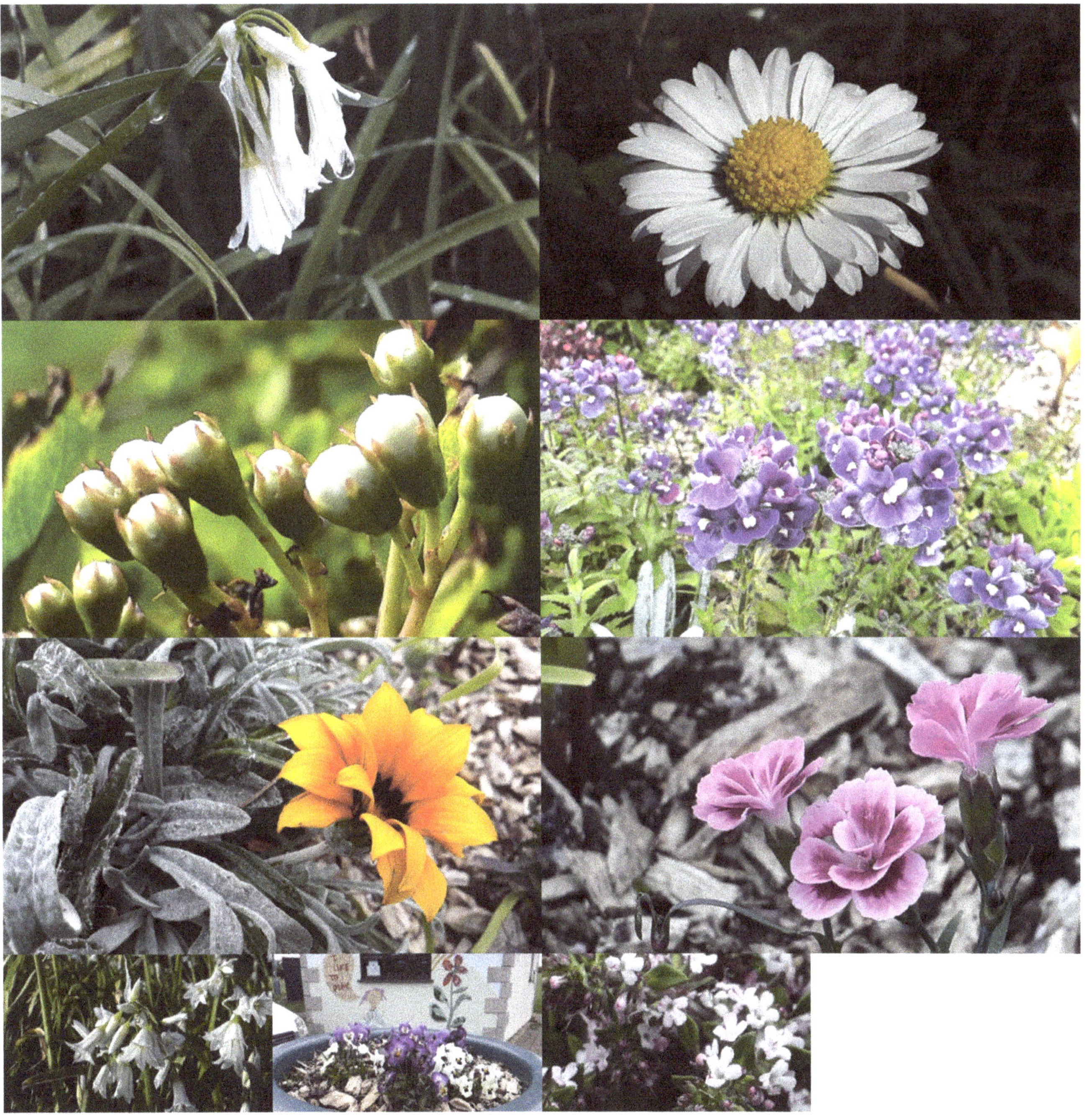

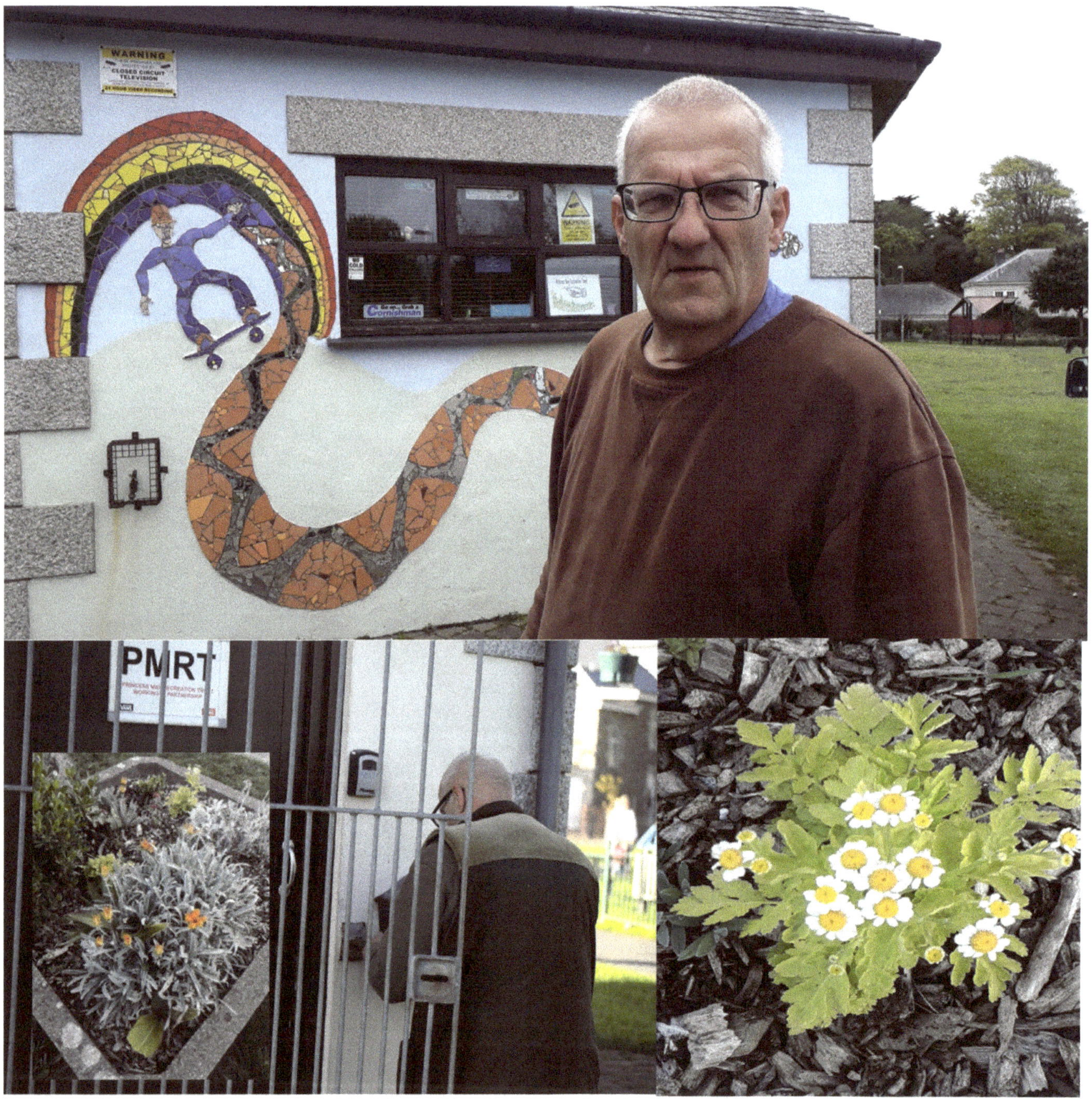
WARNING
PMRT

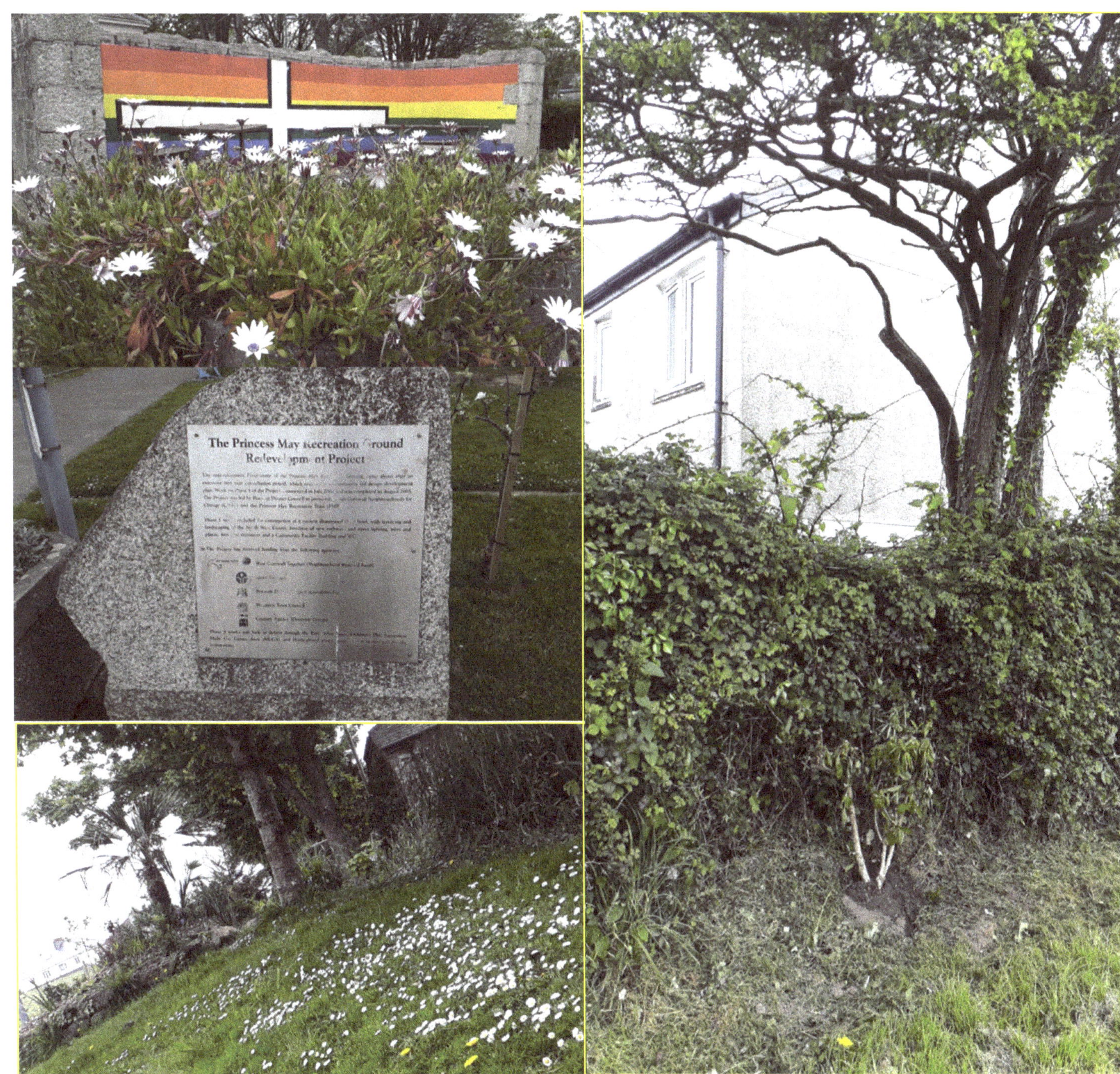
The Princess May Recreation Ground
Redevelopment Project

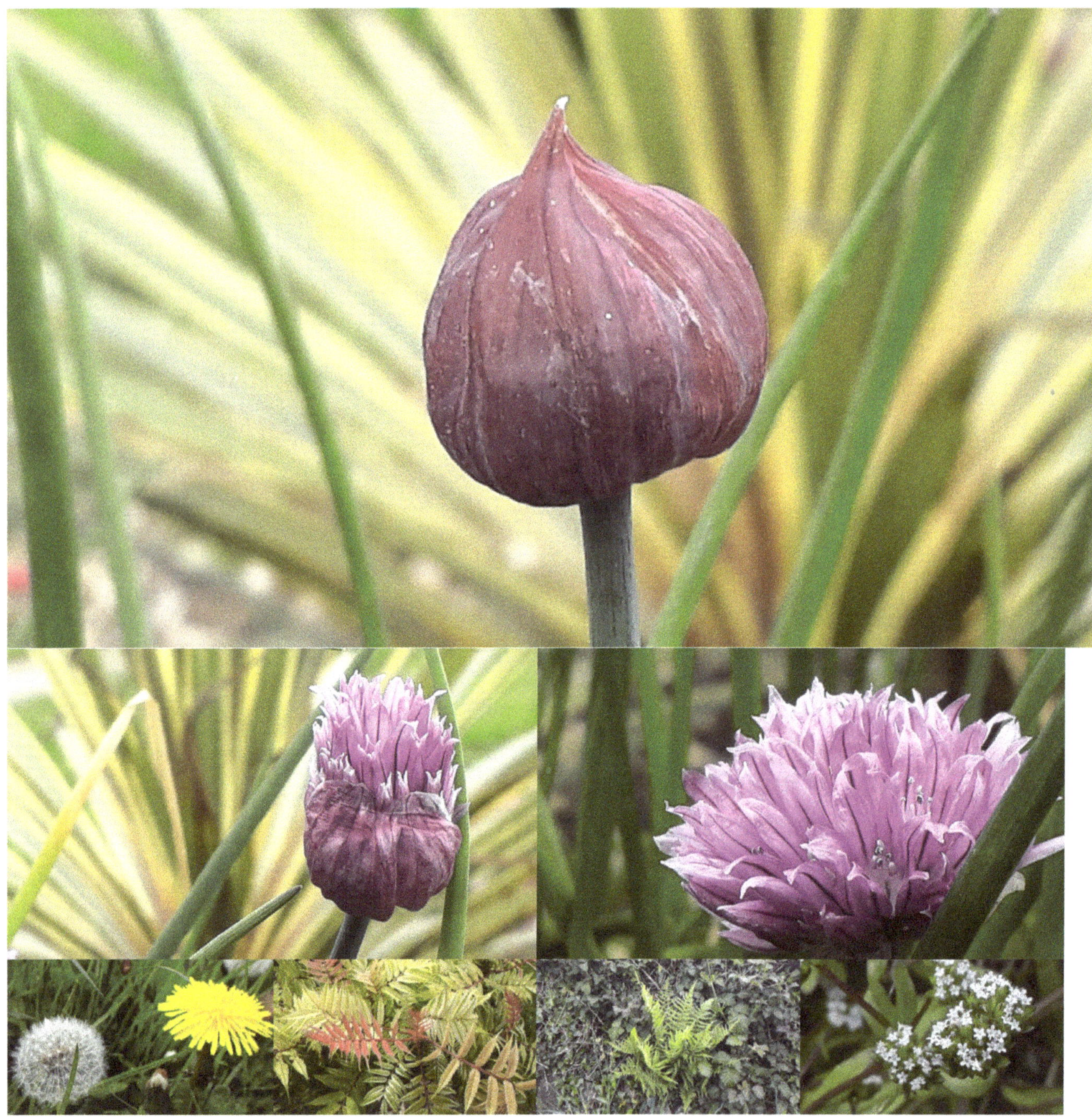

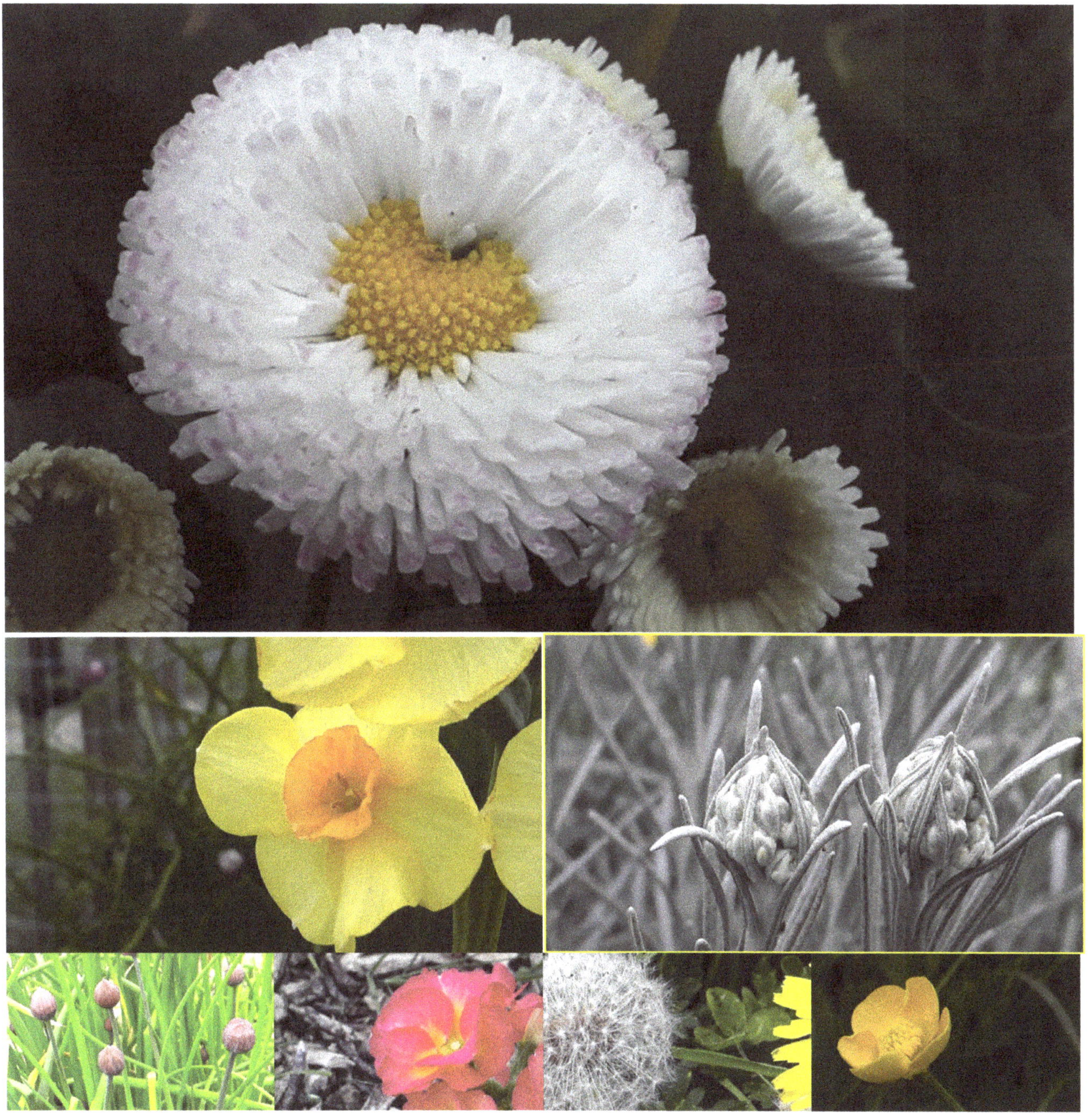

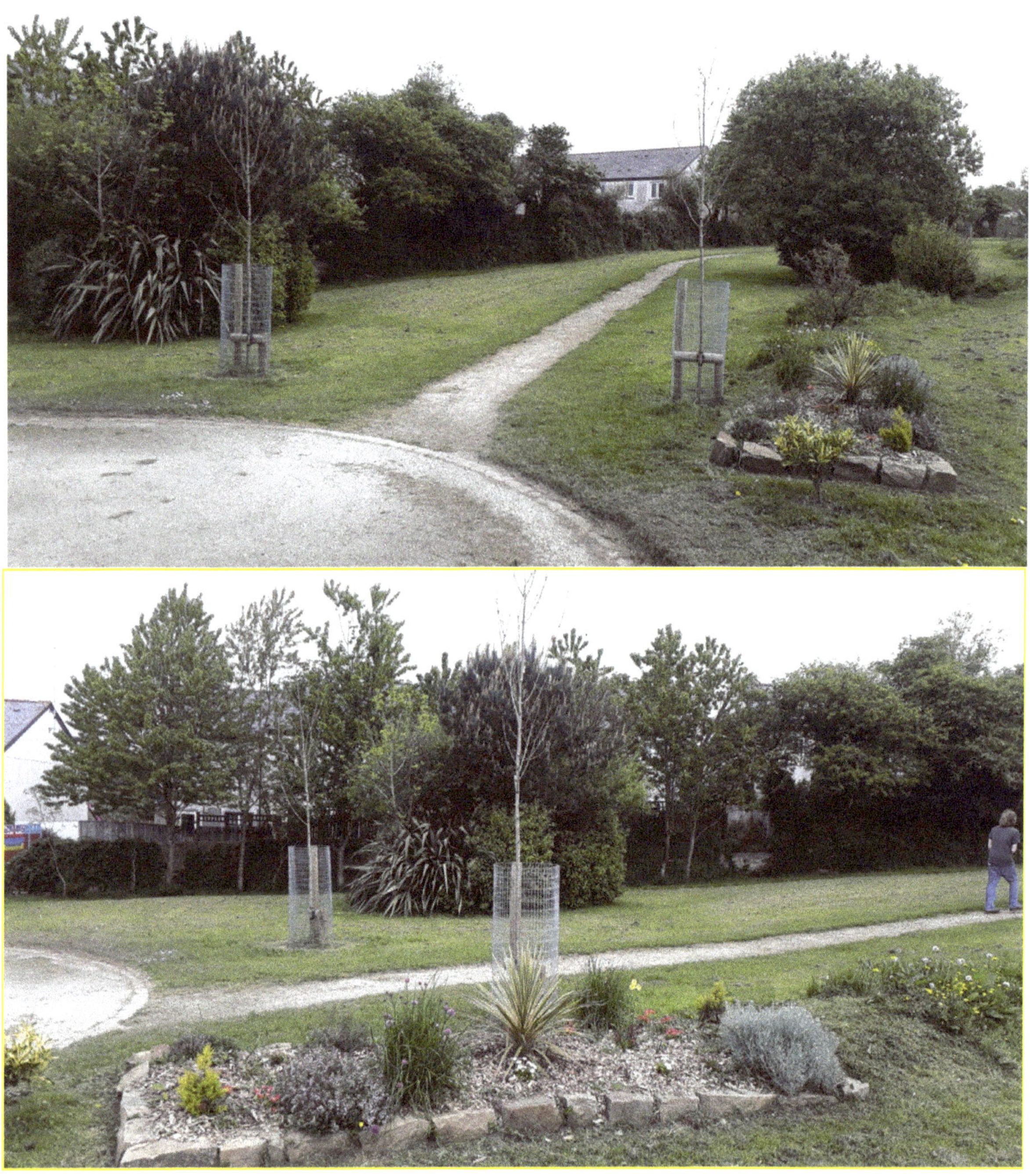

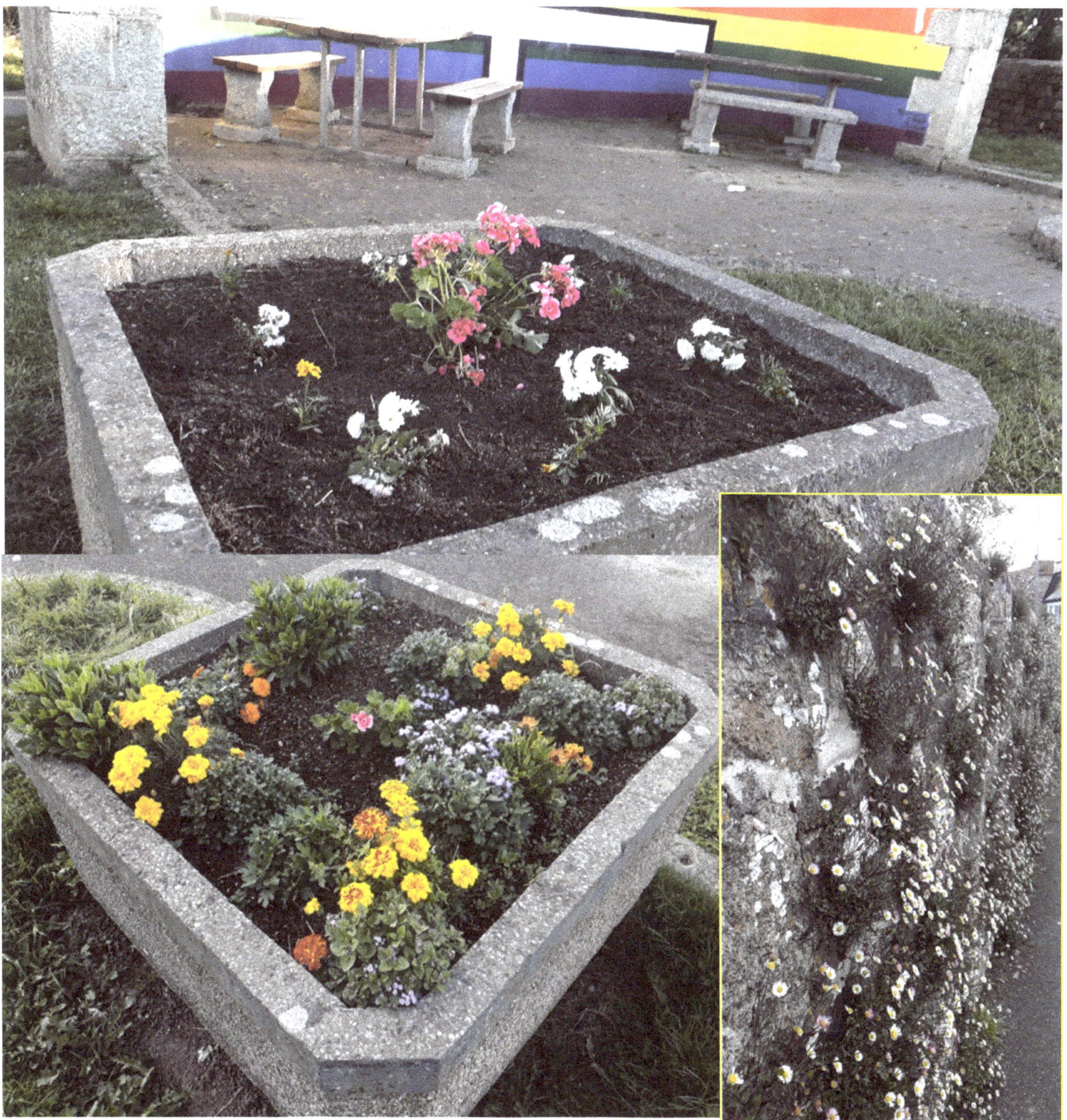

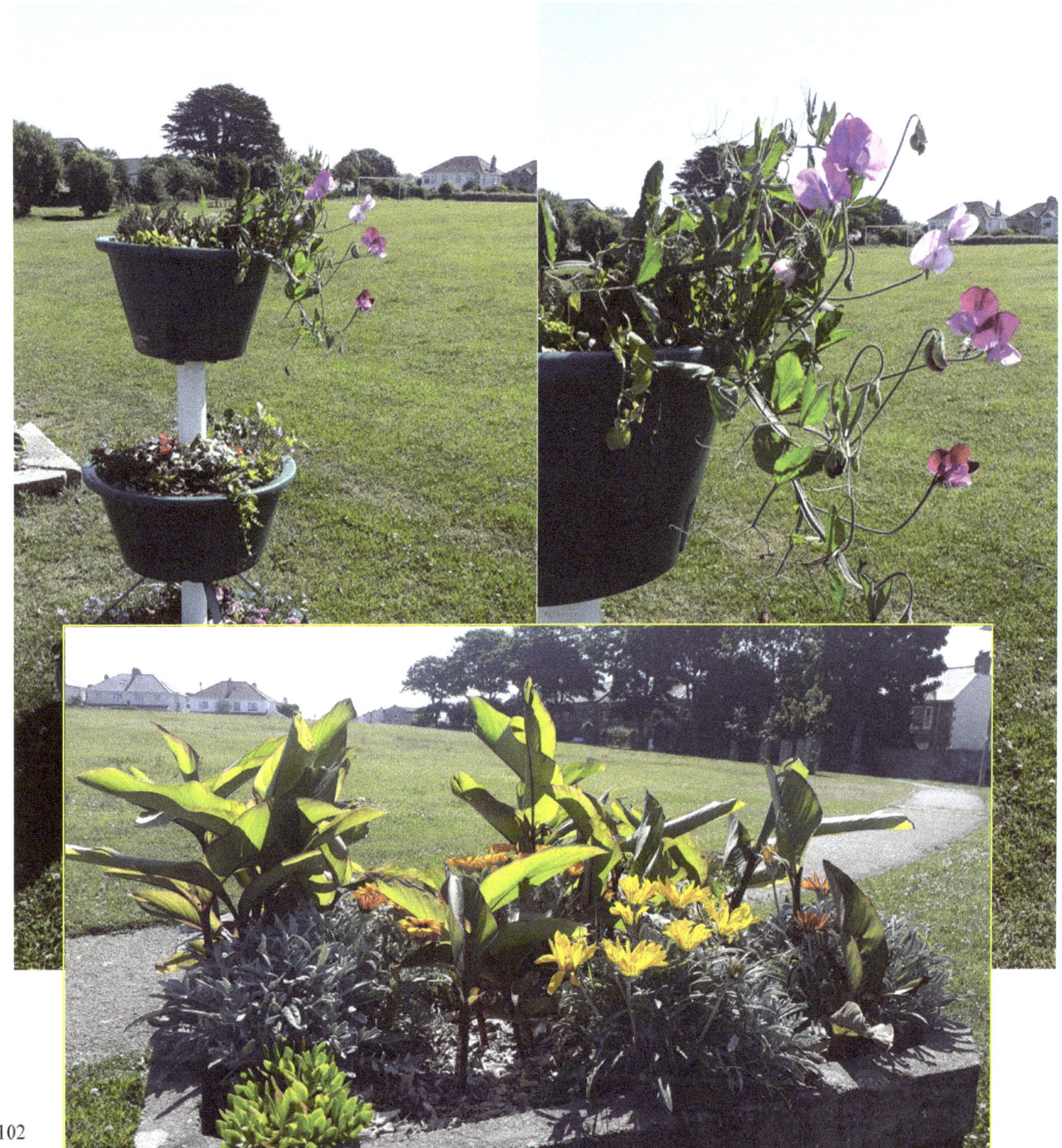

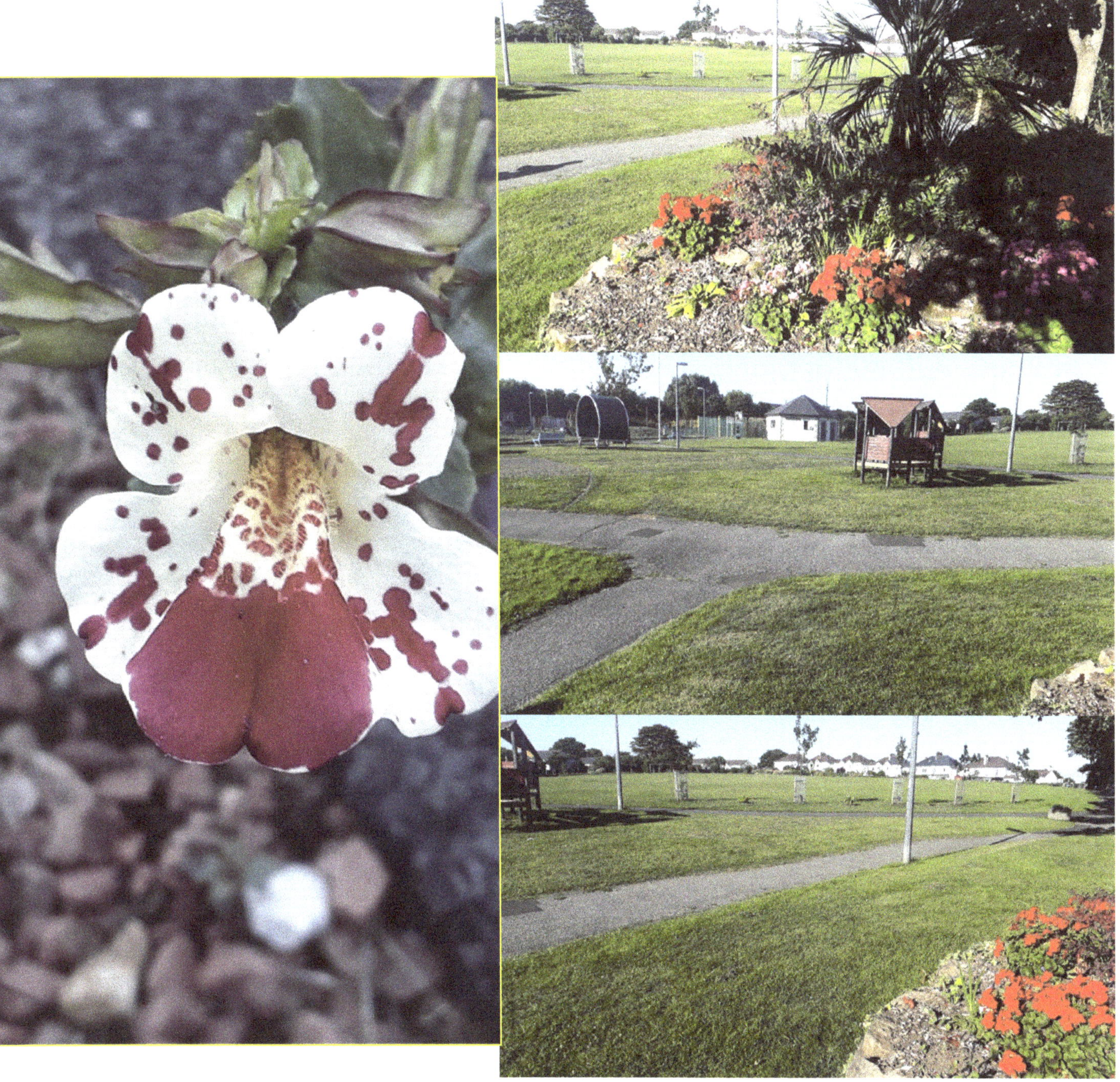

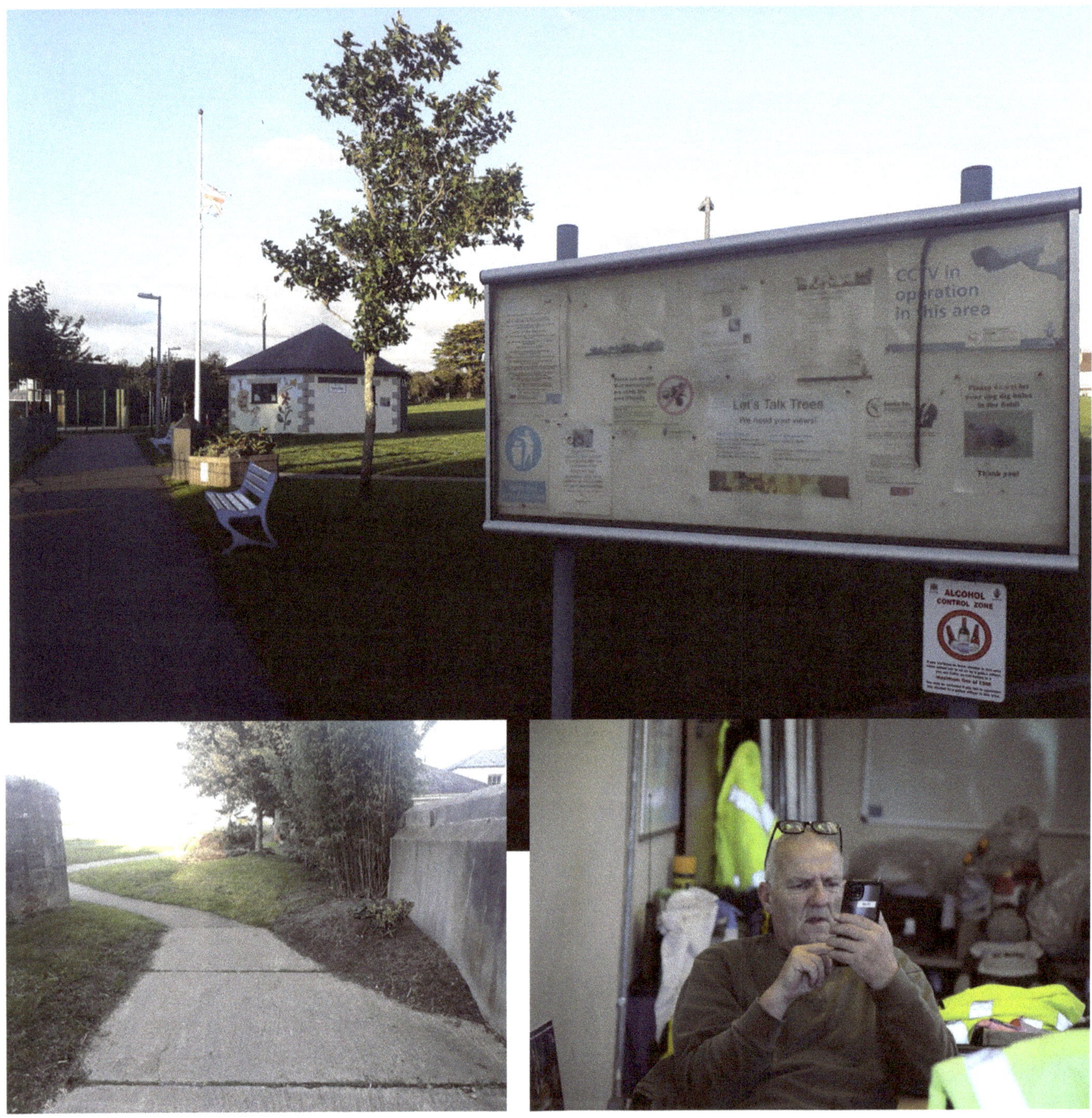
Let's Talk Trees
ALCOHOL
CONTROL ZONE

Business in the Office

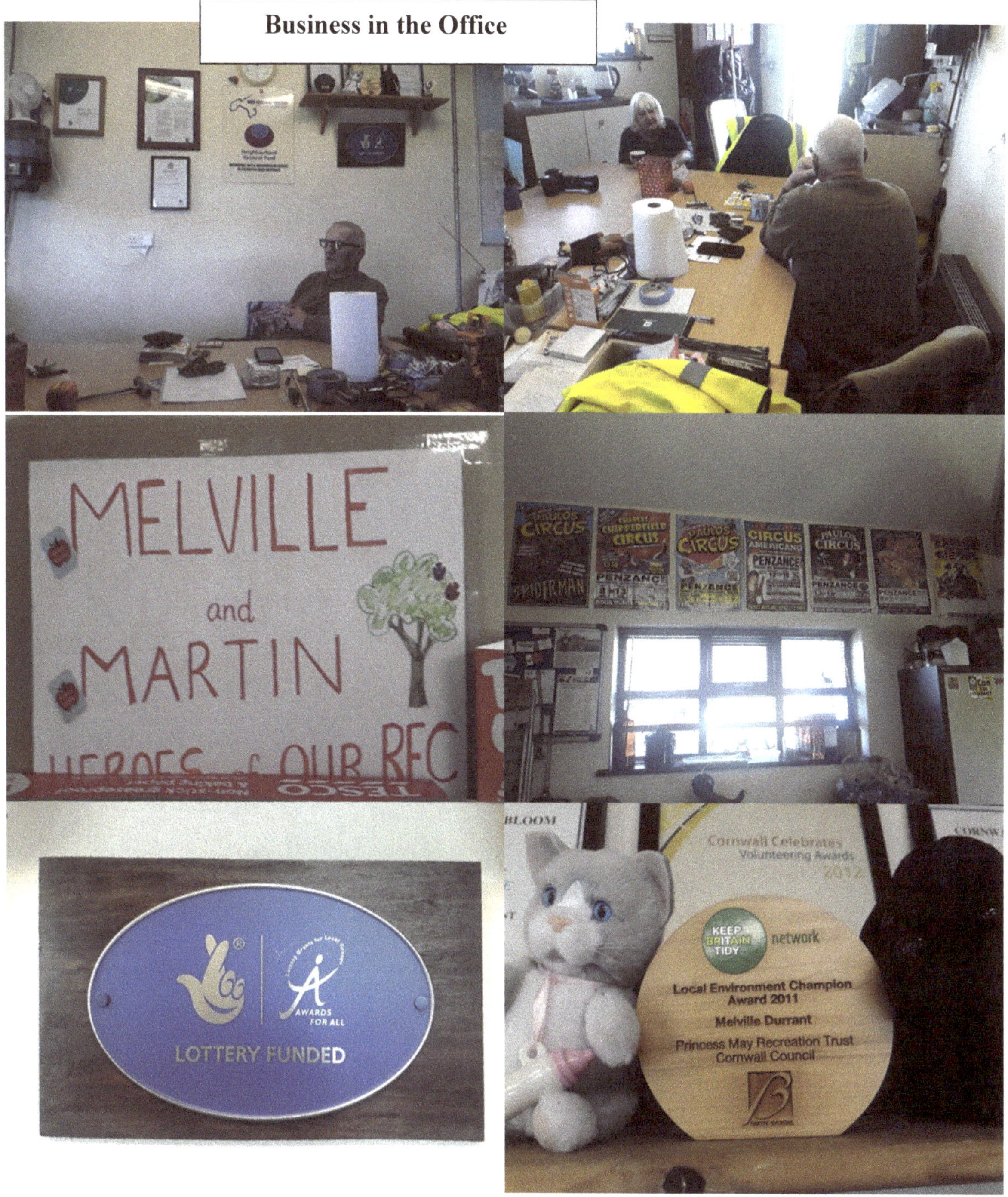

CERTIFICATE OF INCORPORATION
OF A
COMMUNITY INTEREST COMPANY
Companies House
LOCAL ENVIRONMENT CHAMPION
Melville Durrant
KEEP BRITAIN TIDY
network
Local Environment Champion Award 2011
Melville Durrant
Princess May Recreation Trust
Cornwall Council
IT'S YOUR
NEIGHBOURHOOD
BRITAIN
IN BLOOM
SOUTH WEST
RHS
Penzance - Princes May Recreation Ground
Level 4 - Thriving

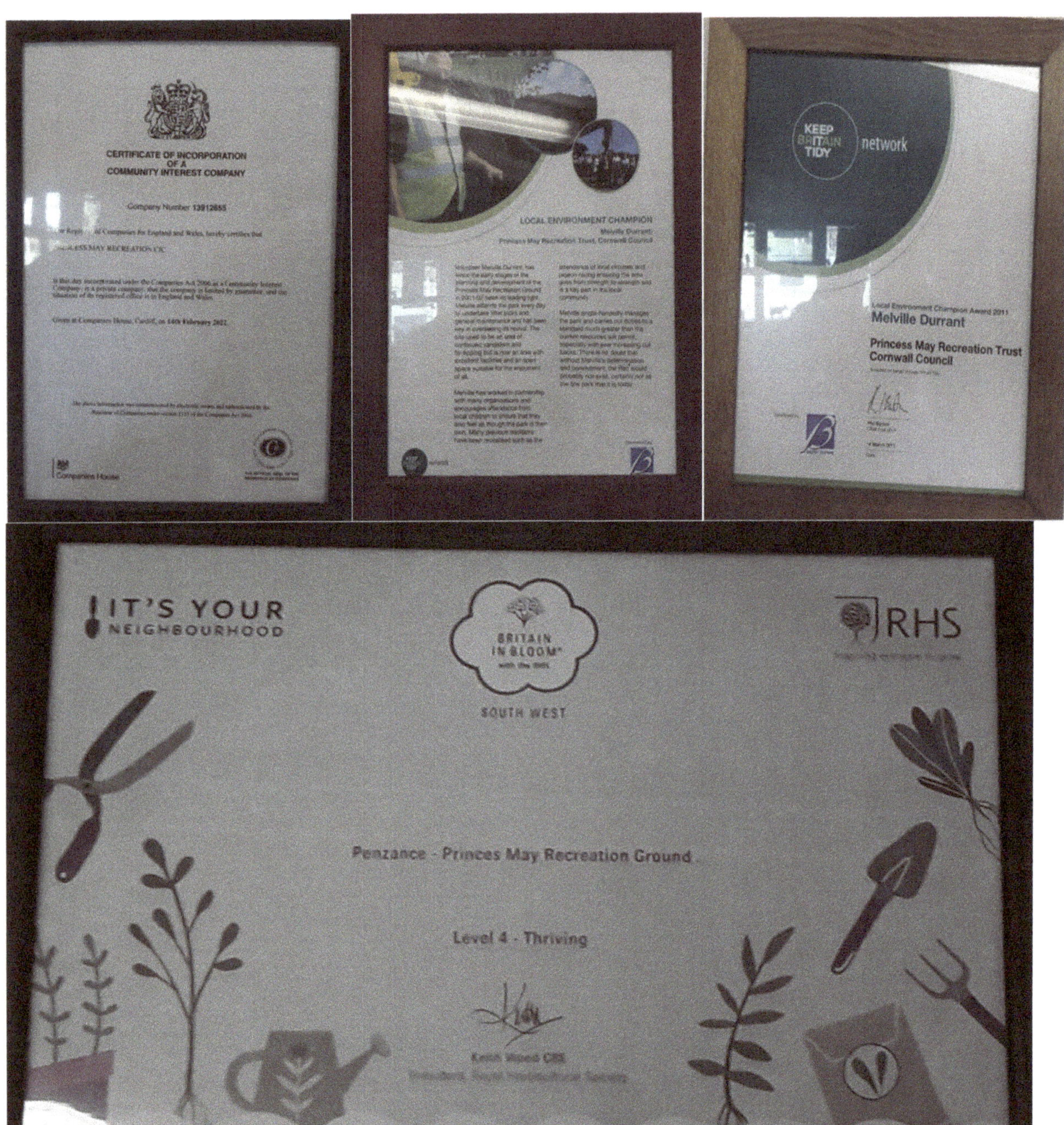

Pride & Joy

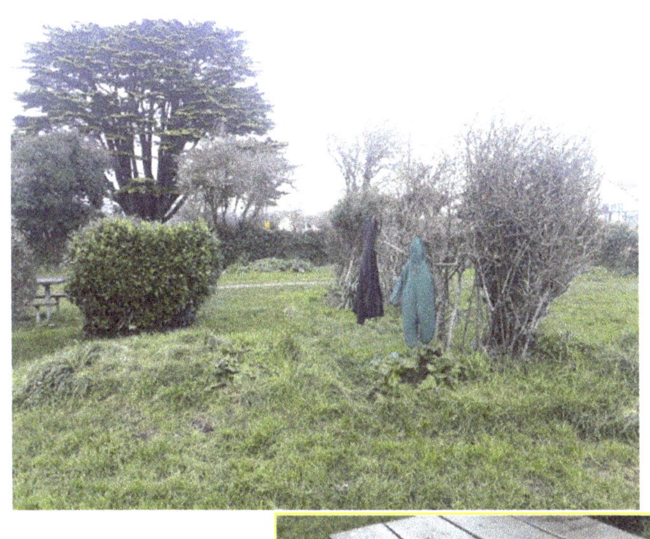

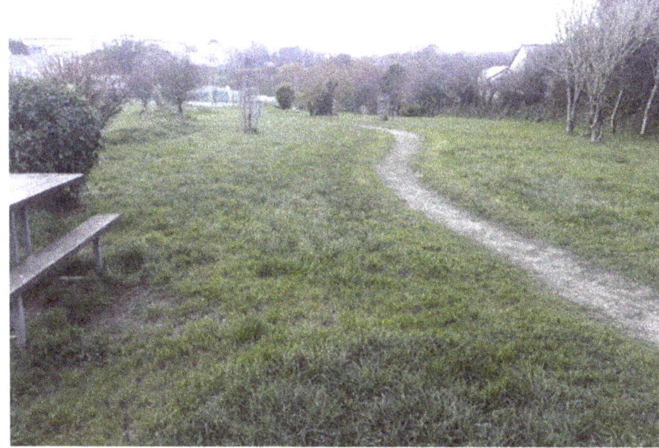

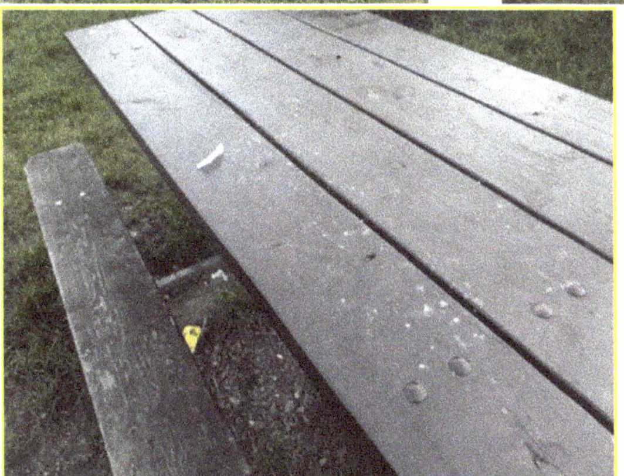

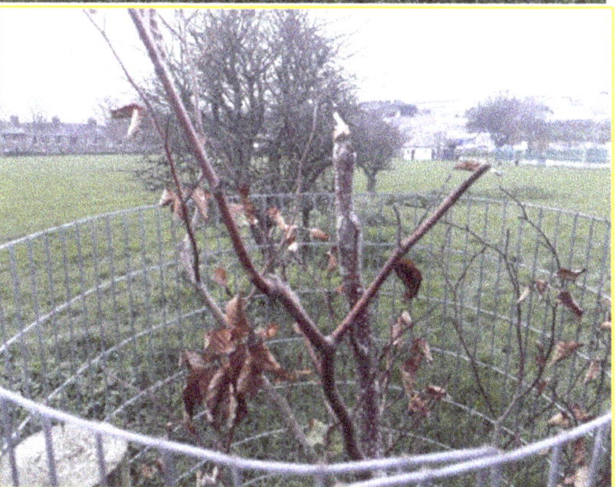

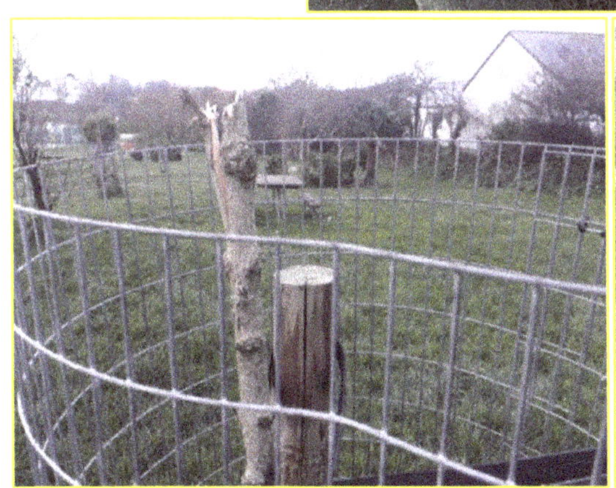

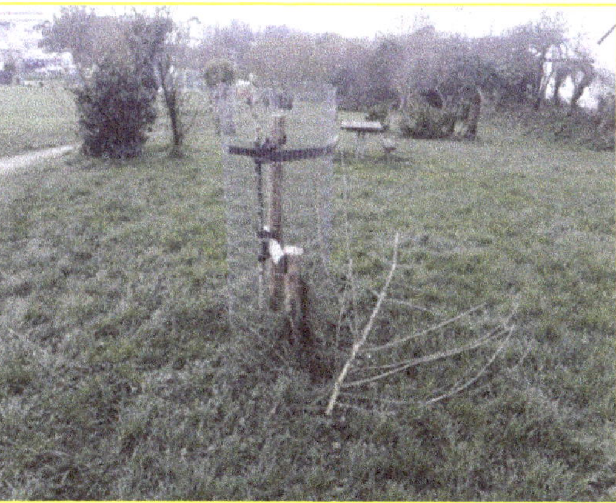

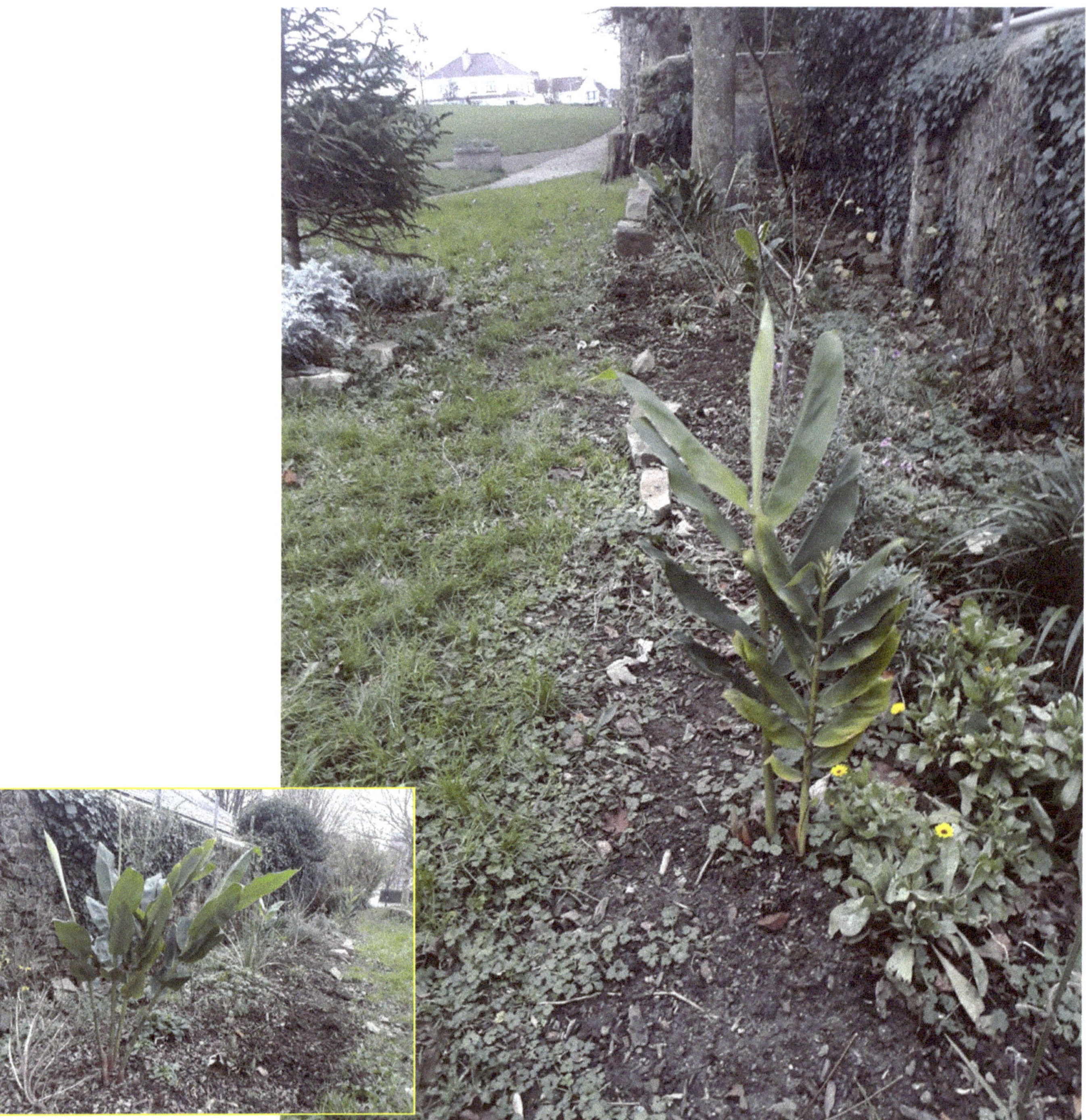

Doggy Treats

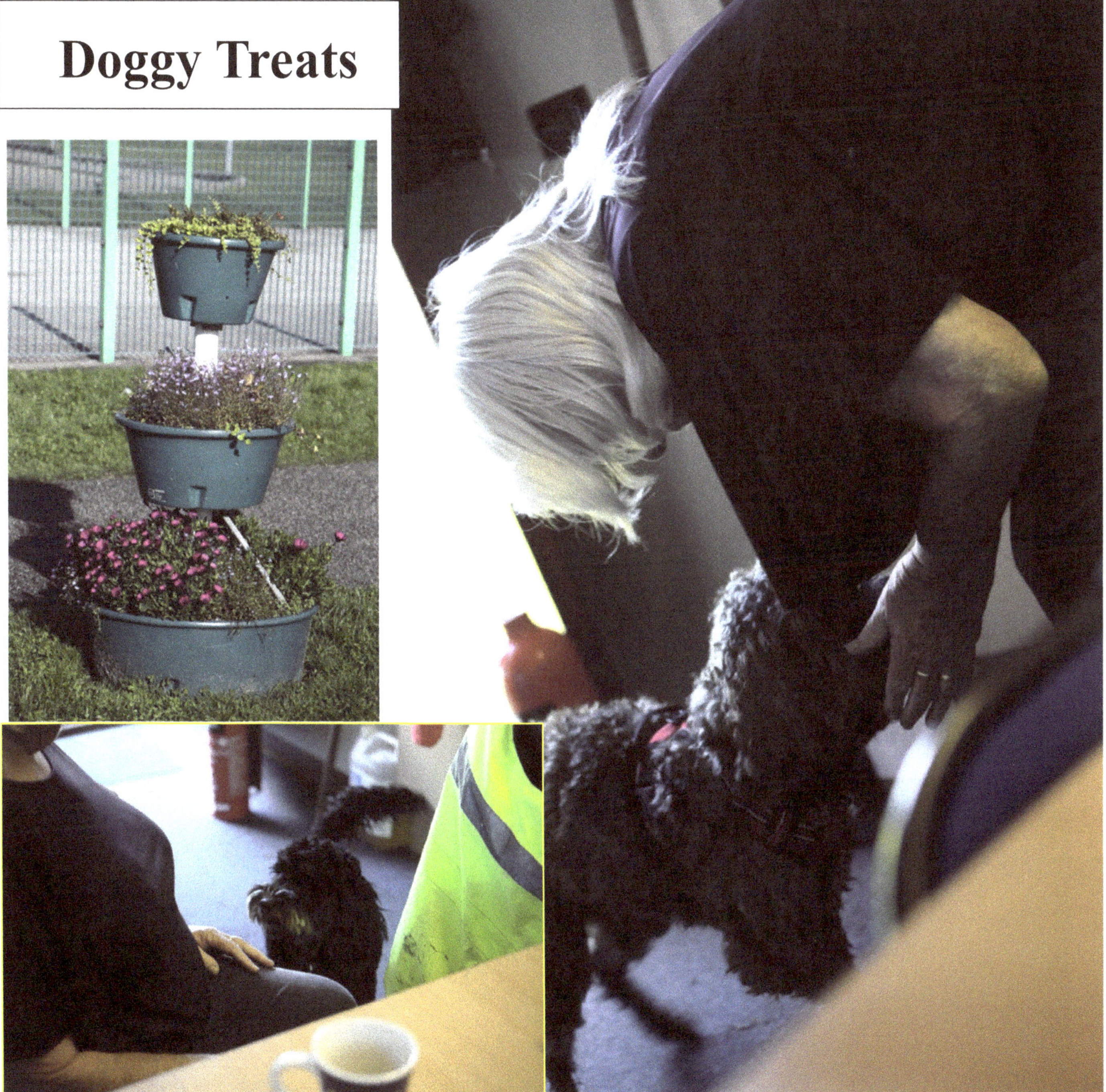

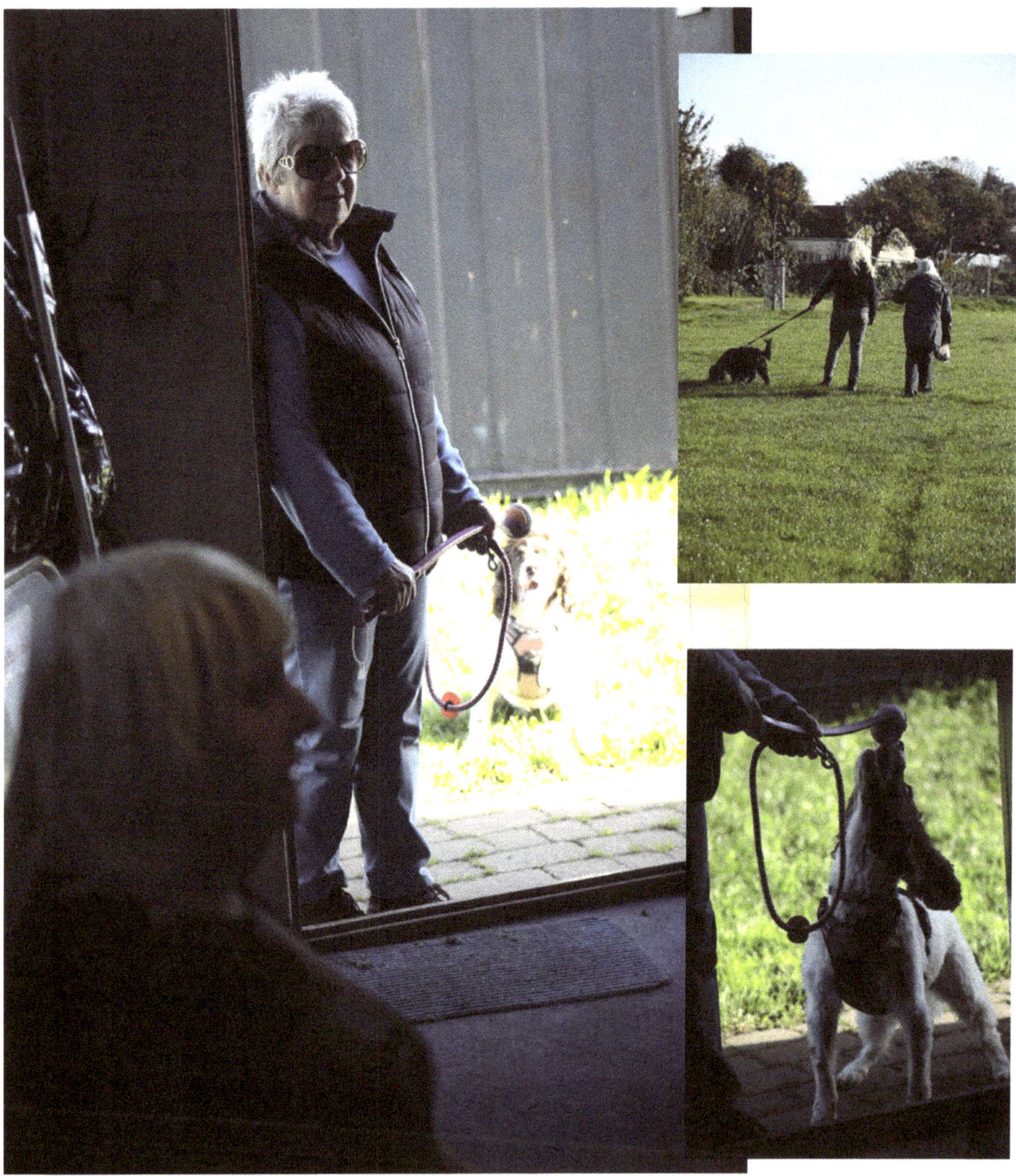

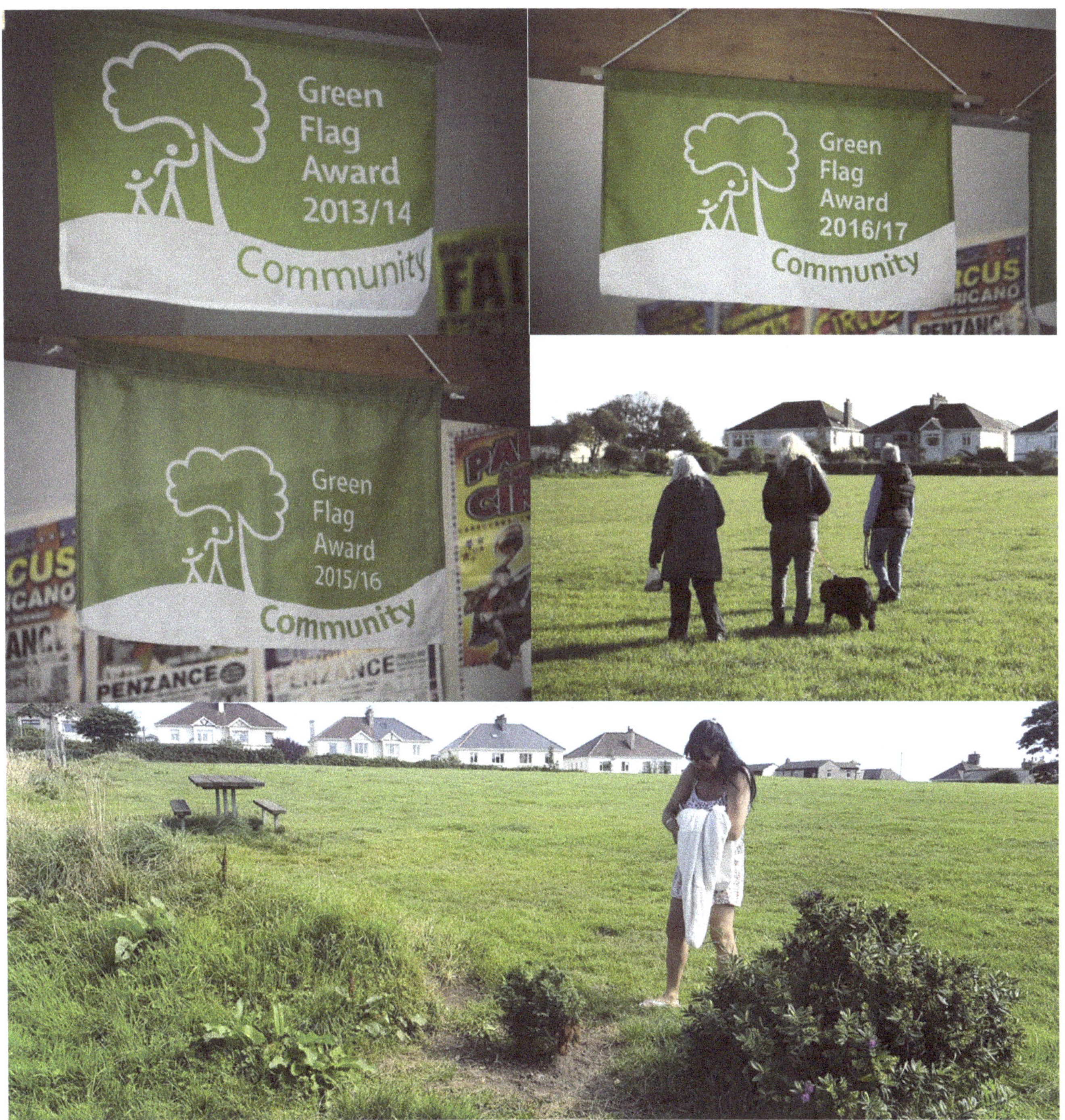
Green
Flag
Award
2013/14
Community
Green
Flag
Award
2016/17
Community
Green
Flag
Award
2015/16
Community
PENZANCE

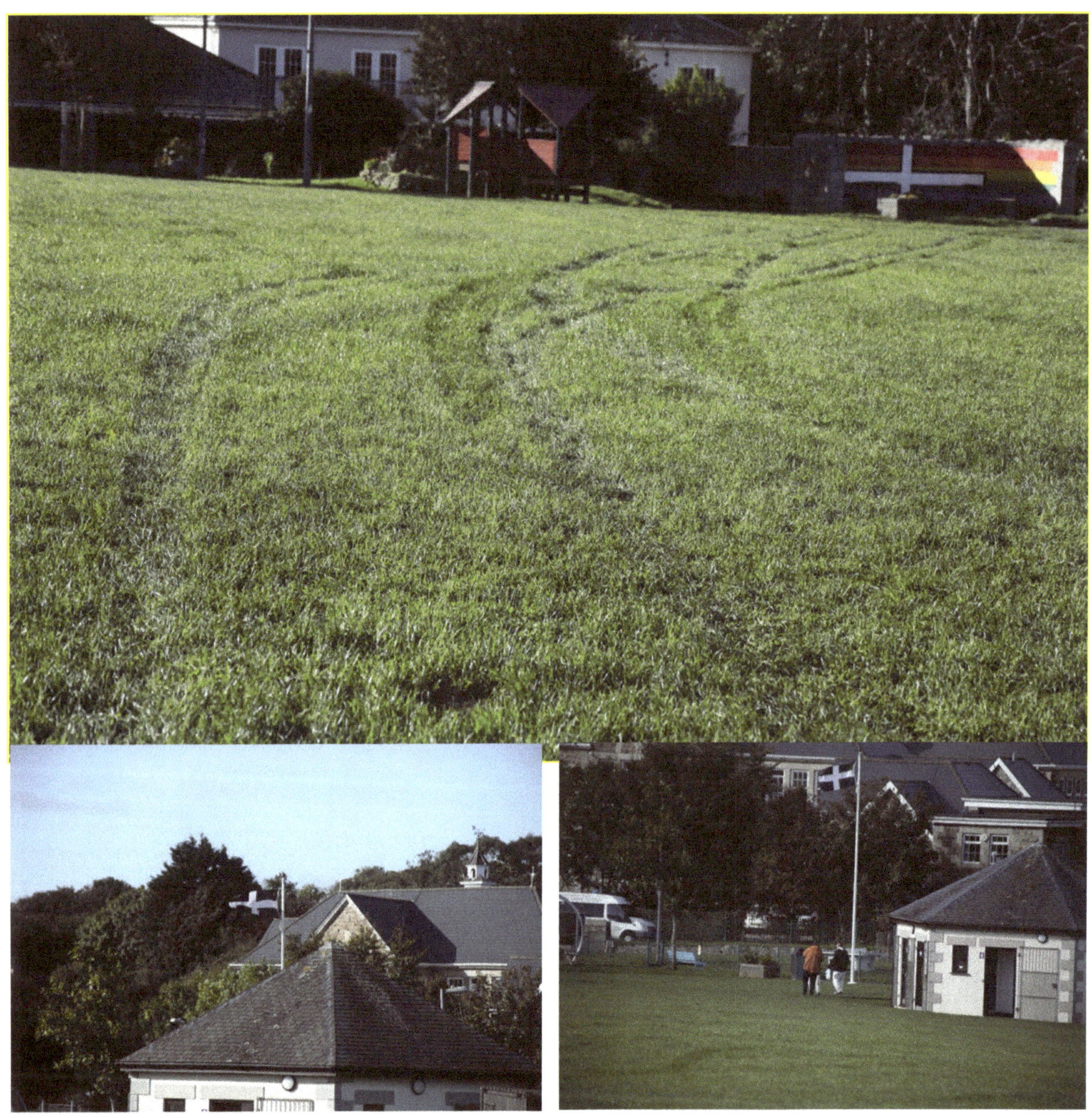

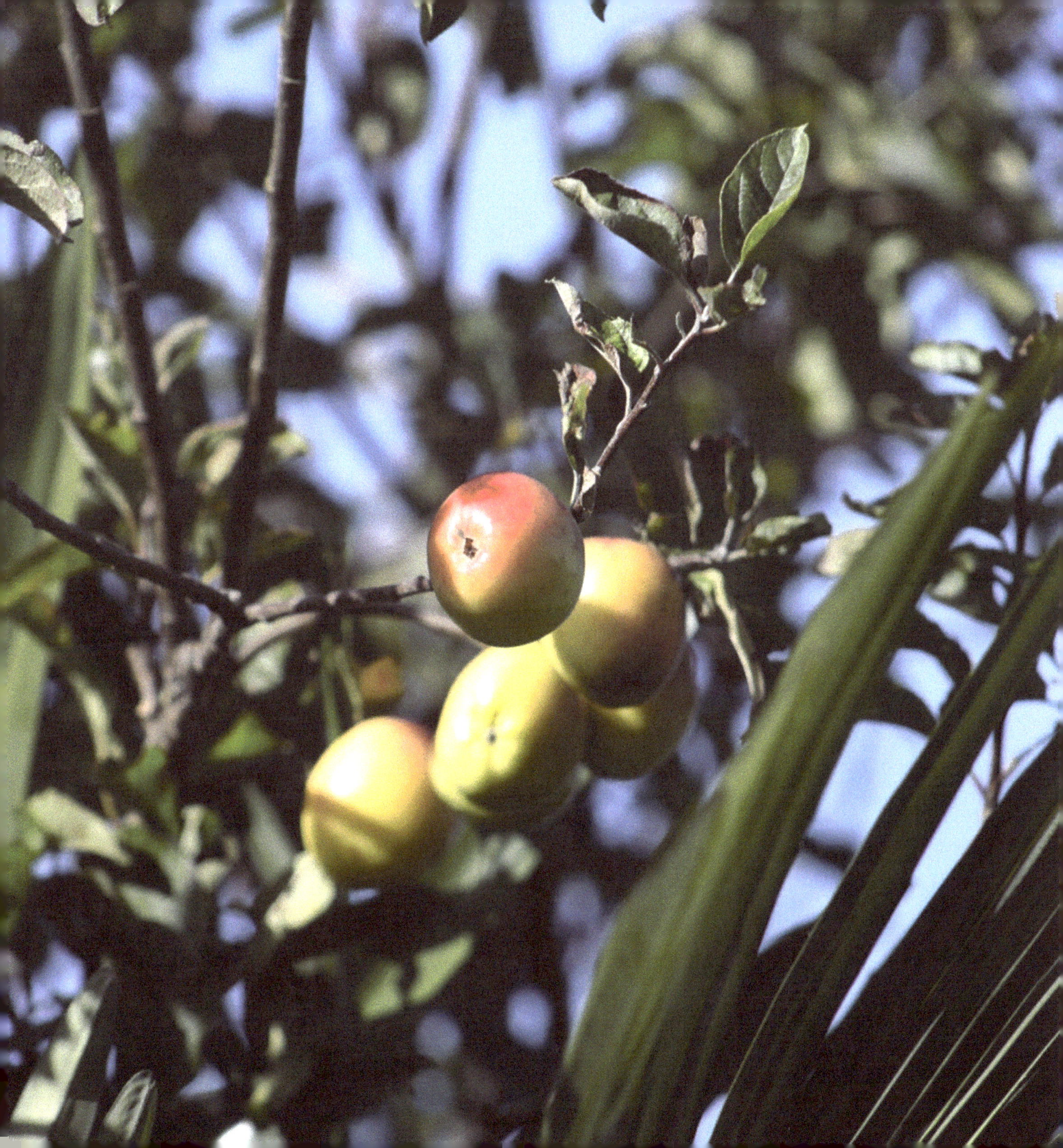

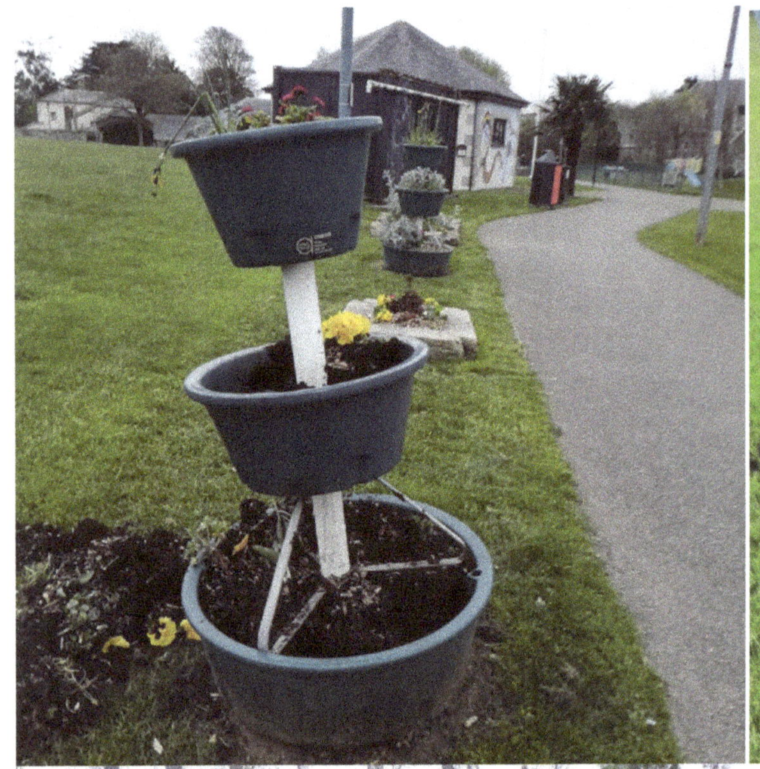
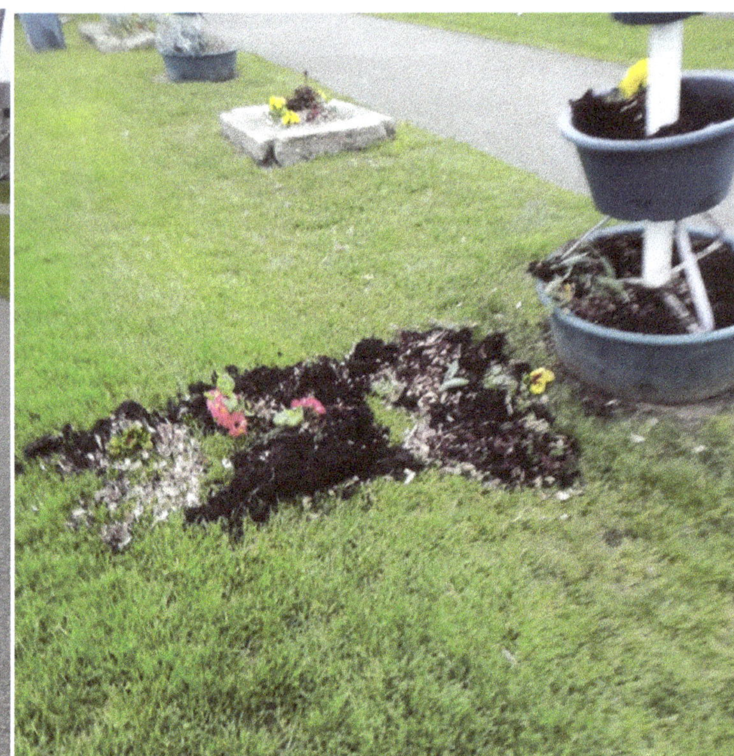
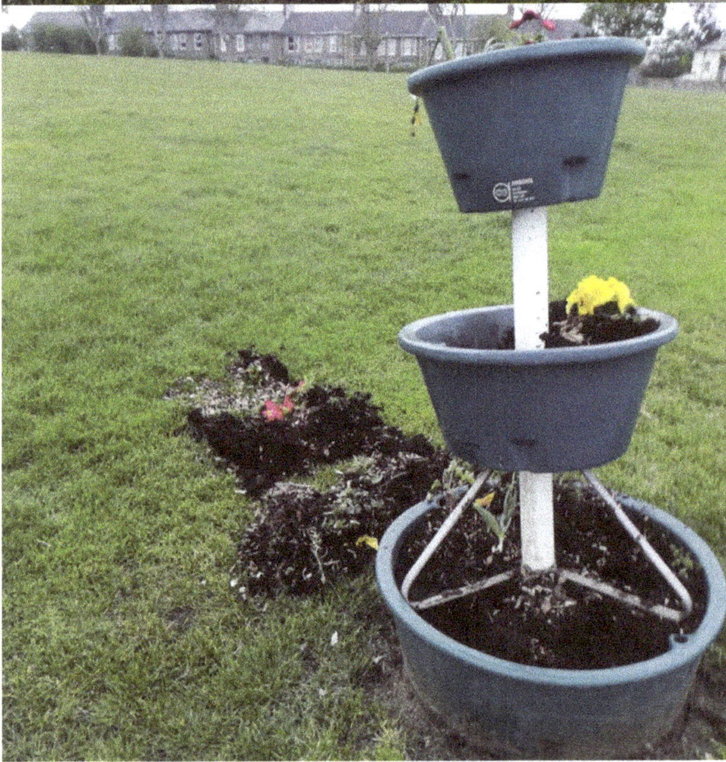
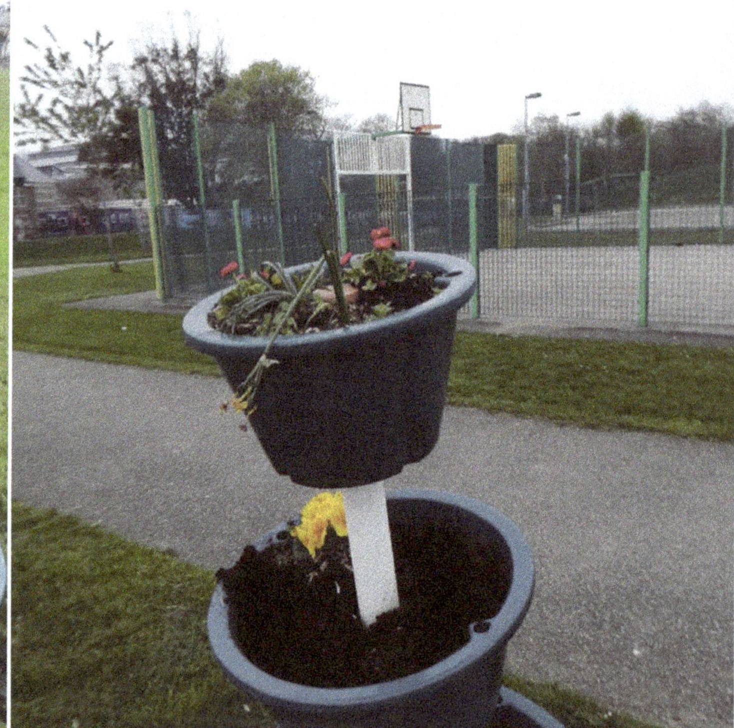

2023

The Princess May Recreation Ground in Penzance, while primarily a local community space, has hosted several memorable events over the years. Some of these events include:

1. **Sports Tournaments and Matches**: The ground has been the site of numerous local sports tournaments, particularly football and cricket matches, drawing spectators and fostering community spirit.
2. **Community Fairs and Festivals**: Various local fairs, fetes, and festivals have been held at the ground, providing entertainment and a gathering place for the community. These events often include games, stalls, performances, and food, creating a festive atmosphere.
3. **Charity Events**: The ground has hosted charity events, such as fun runs, fundraisers, and other activities aimed at supporting local causes and organizations.
4. **Celebratory Gatherings**: National celebrations, such as the Queen's Jubilees or other royal events, have seen the community come together at the ground to commemorate these occasions with picnics, concerts, and public gatherings.
5. **Historical Commemorations**: Occasionally, the ground has been used for events that commemorate historical dates or figures, tying in with its historical naming after Princess May.

These events have contributed to the ground's reputation as a central and versatile venue for the people of Penzance, making it a cherished part of the local community.

The Princess May Recreation Ground in Penzance is a significant part of the local community, reflecting both historical and contemporary value. Here are a few additional points that might be of interest:

1. **Community Engagement**: The recreation ground has long been a hub for local engagement, hosting a variety of events that bring the community together, from sports activities to cultural festivals.
2. **Historical Significance**: Named in 1893 to honour Princess May (later Queen Mary), the ground reflects a common practice of commemorating royal events and figures, showcasing the historical ties between local and national narratives.
3. **Modern Use**: Today, the recreation ground continues to serve as an essential public space, providing a venue for sports, leisure activities, and community gatherings. Its continued use underscores its importance to the people of Penzance.

4. **Environmental Contribution**: As a green space, it plays a role in promoting environmental well-being, offering a natural area for relaxation, exercise, and socializing.
5. **Local Heritage**: The recreation ground is part of Penzance's heritage, contributing to the town's identity and serving as a reminder of its historical connections to the broader national context.

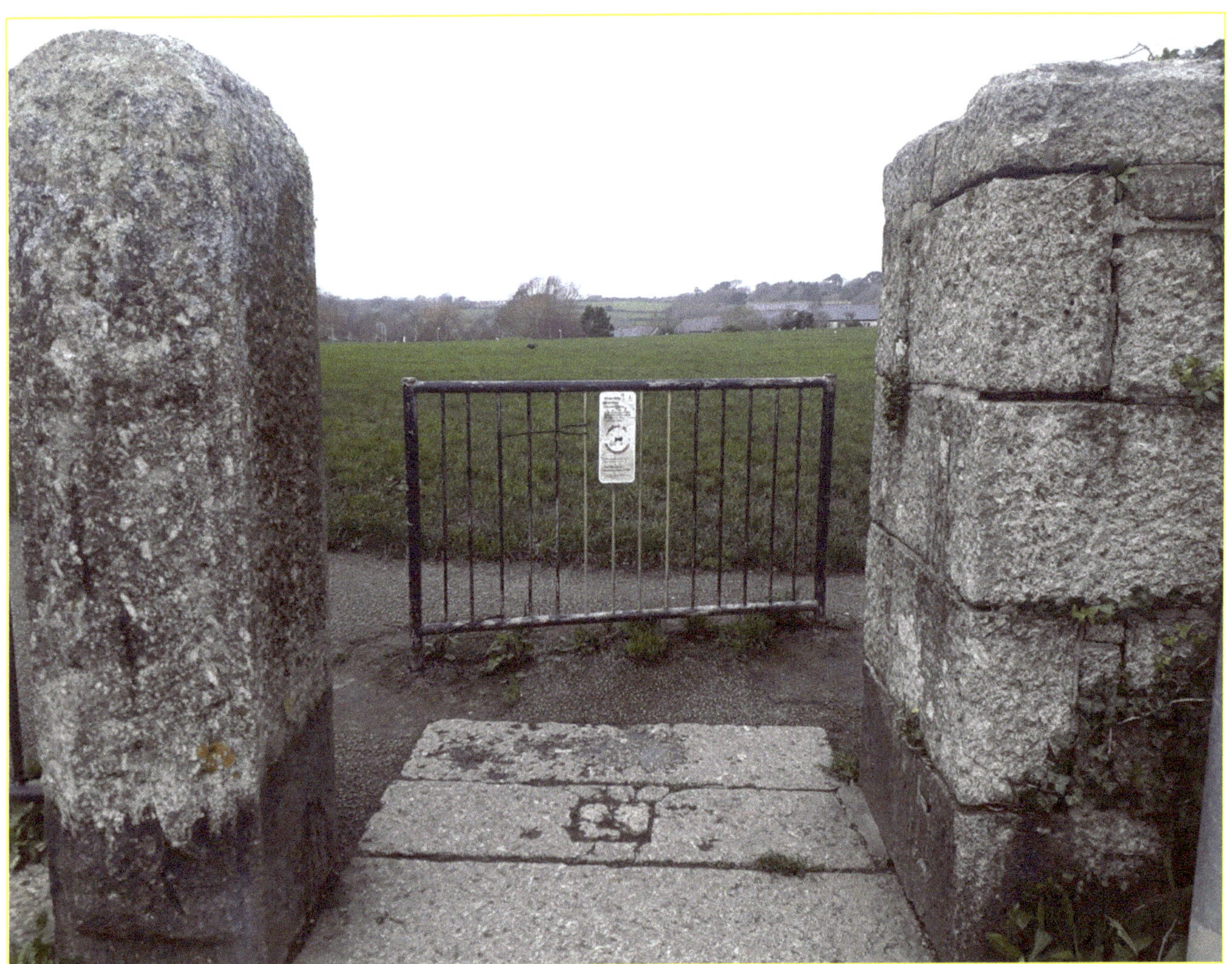

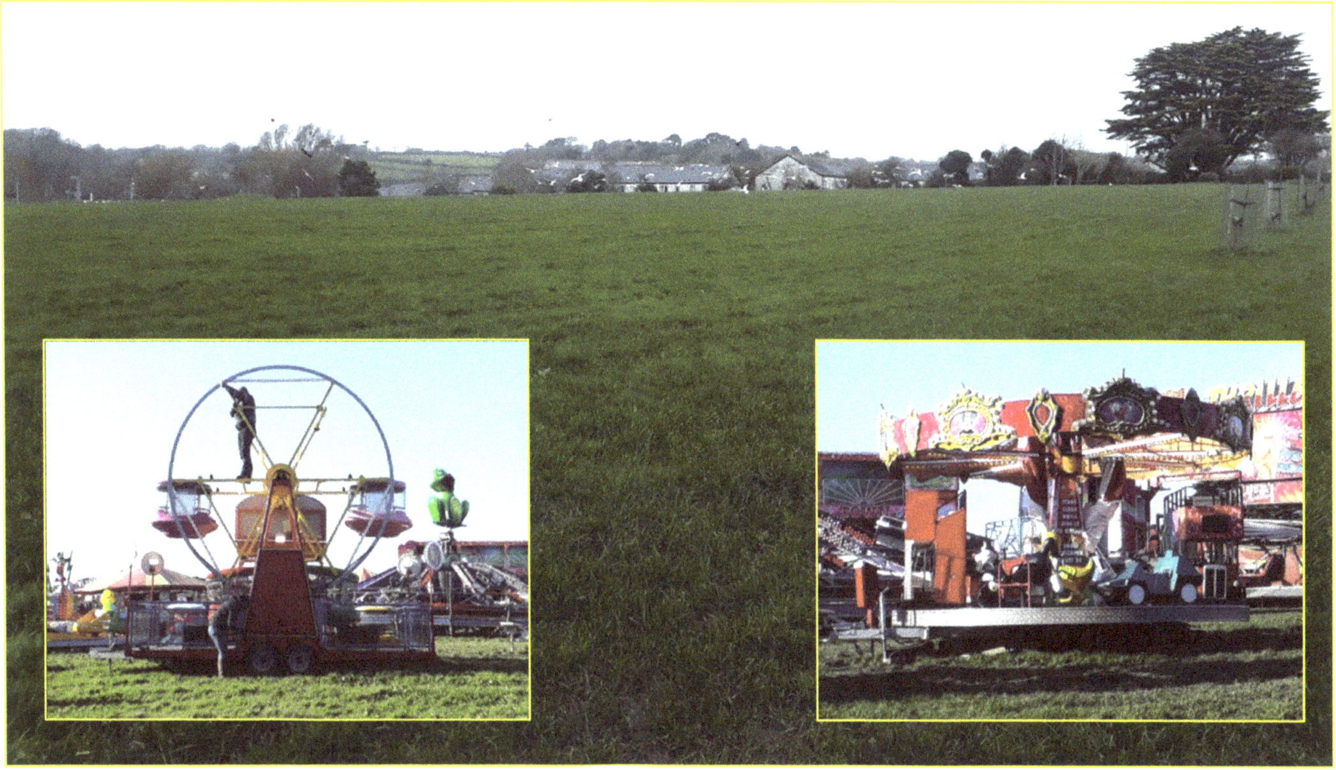

Current Officers of PRINCESS MAY RECREATION
CIC Company number 13912655

- Jean Andrews
- Martin Durrant
- Melville John Durrant (late)
- Andrew Moss Robinson
- Hazel Robinson
- Brian Tempest

https://find-and-update.company-information.service.gov.uk/company/13912655/officers

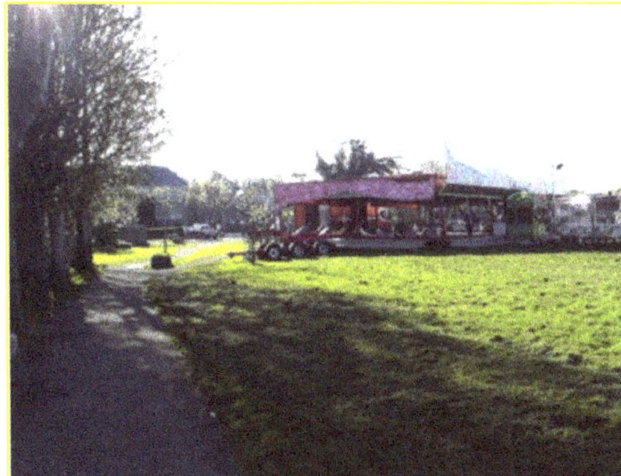

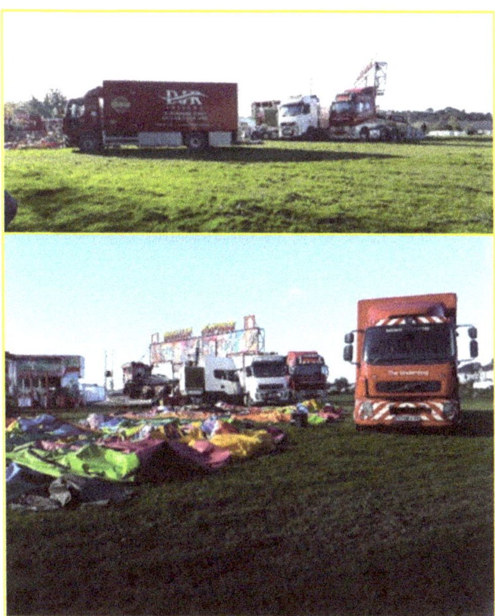

2024

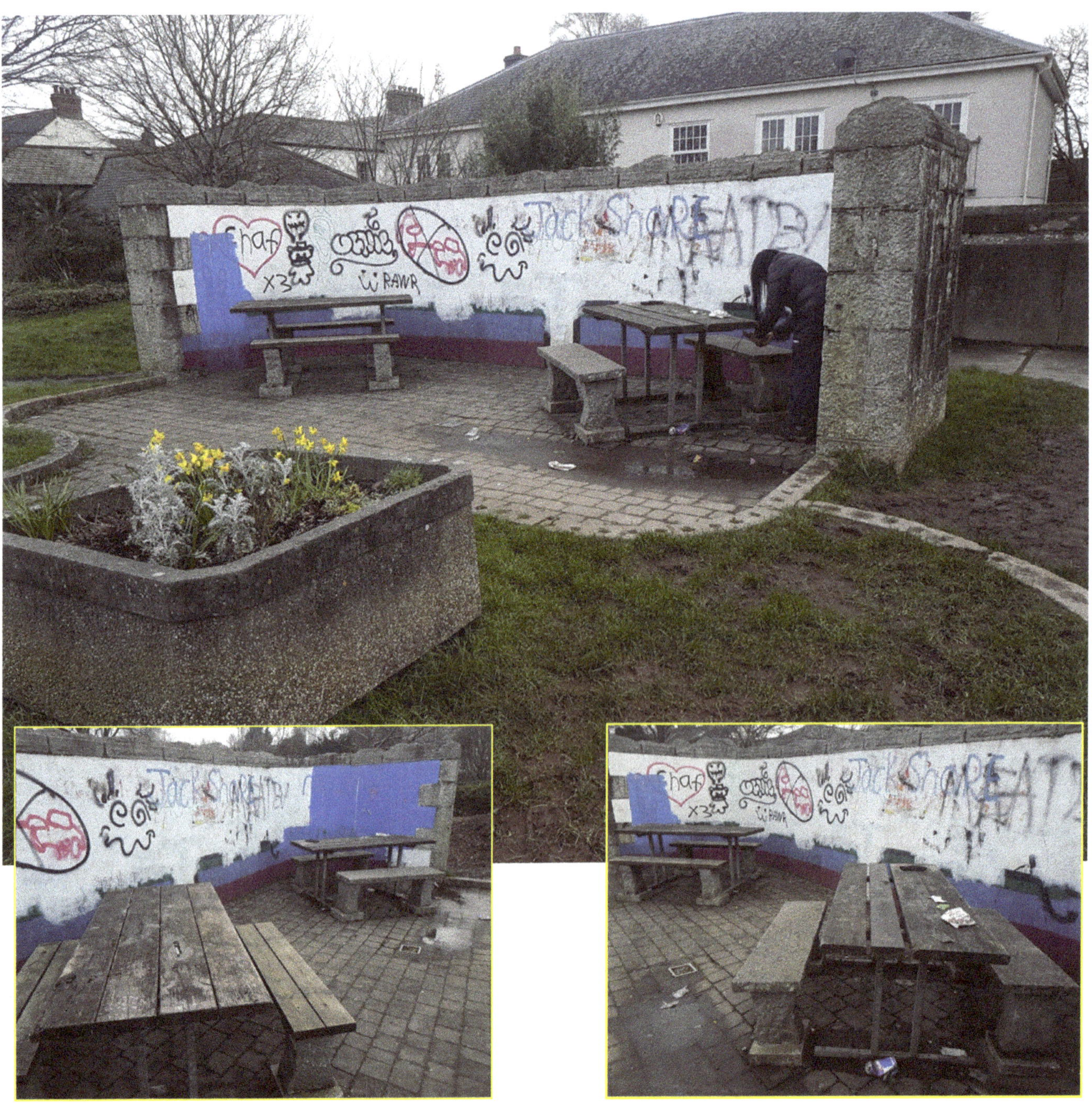

Roll on the sun!

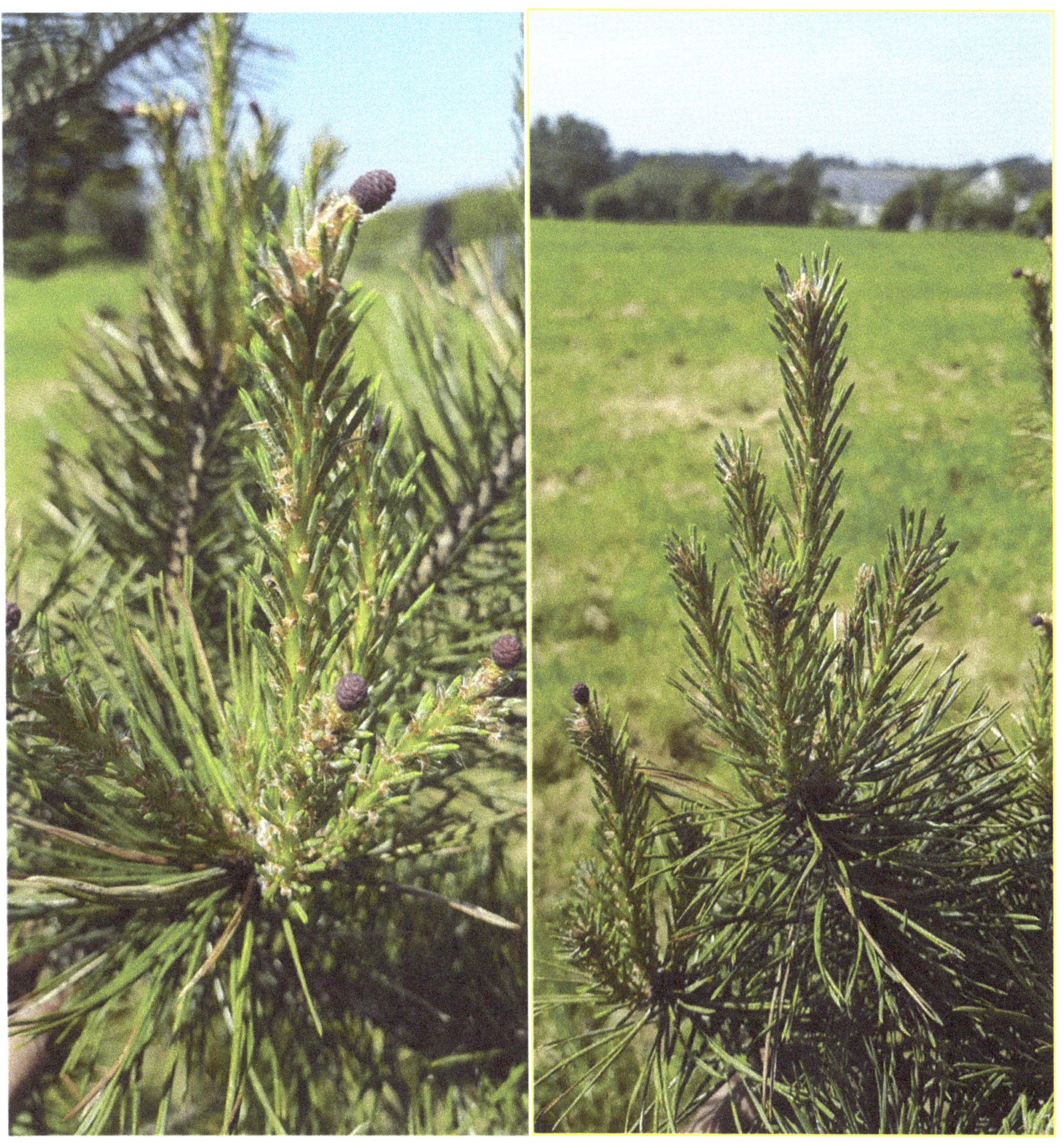

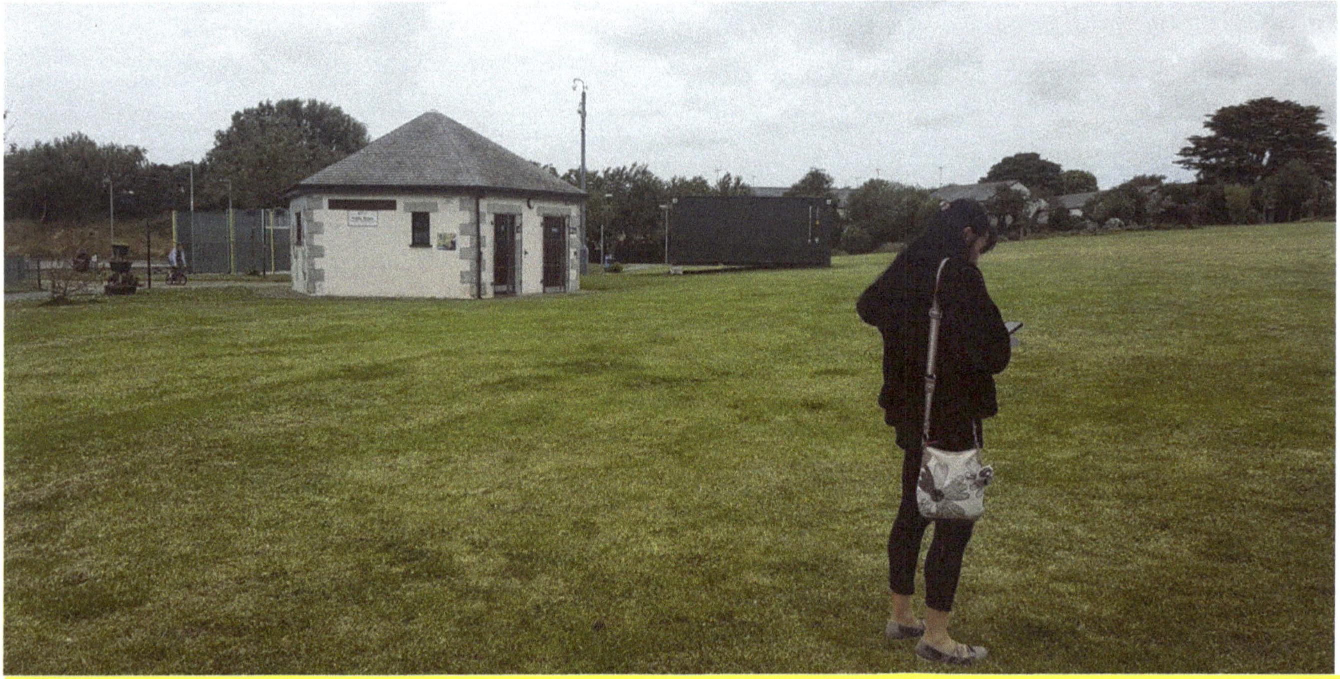

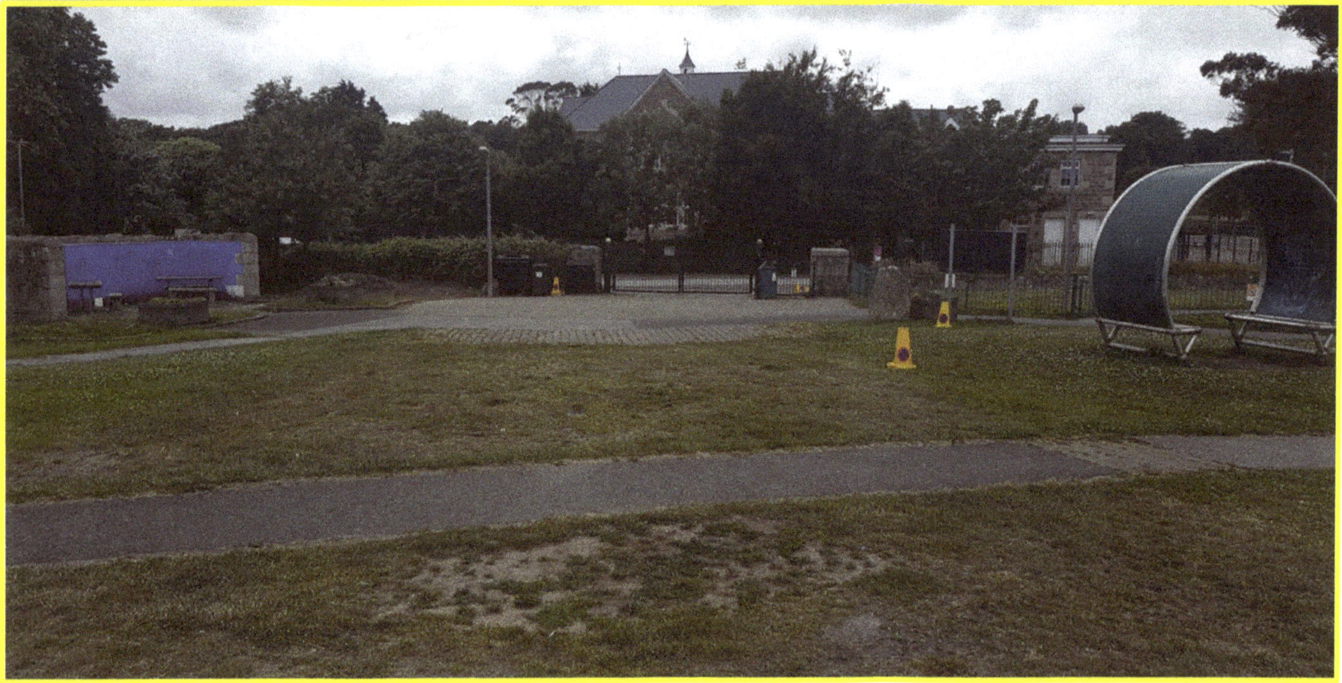

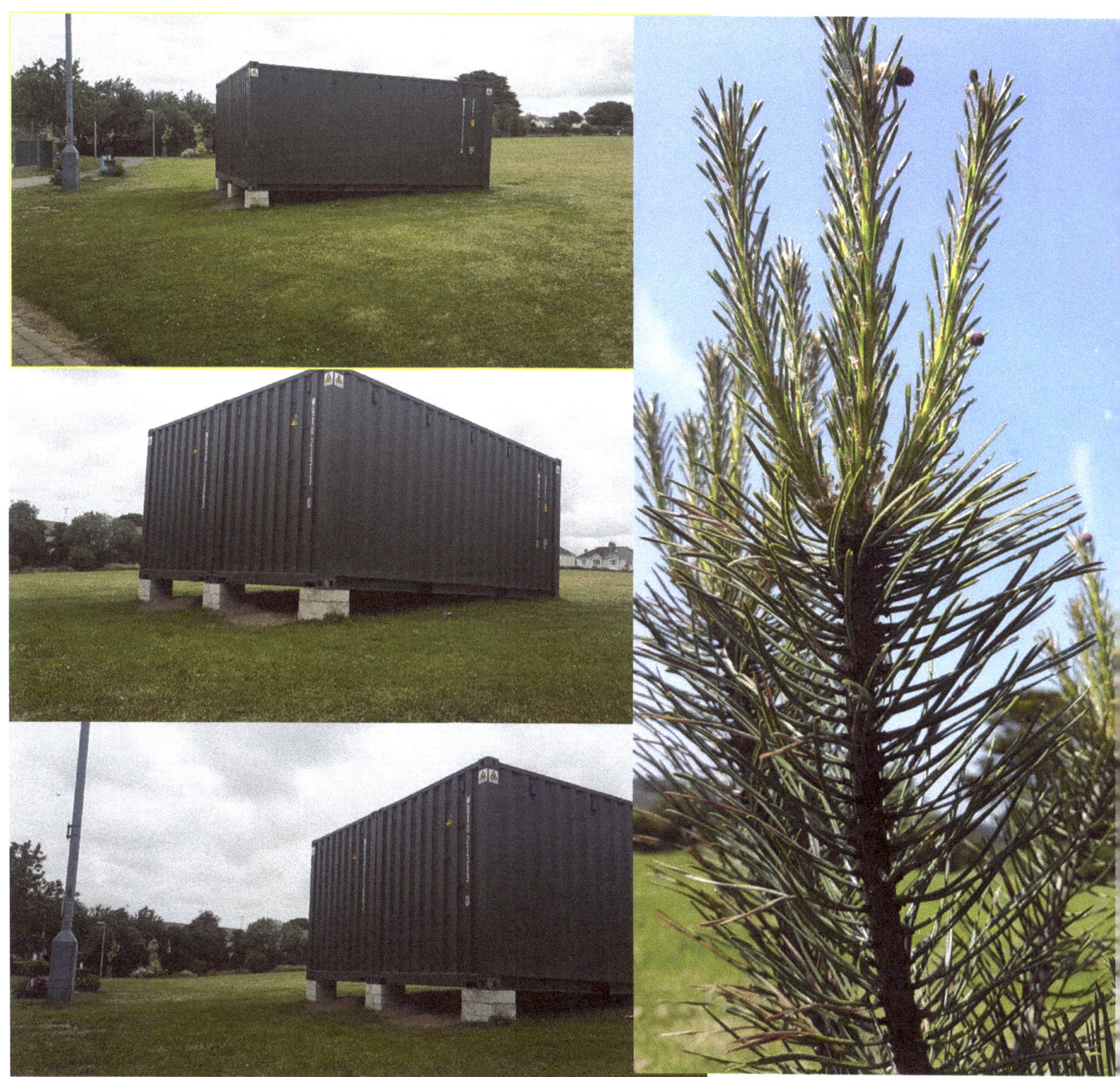

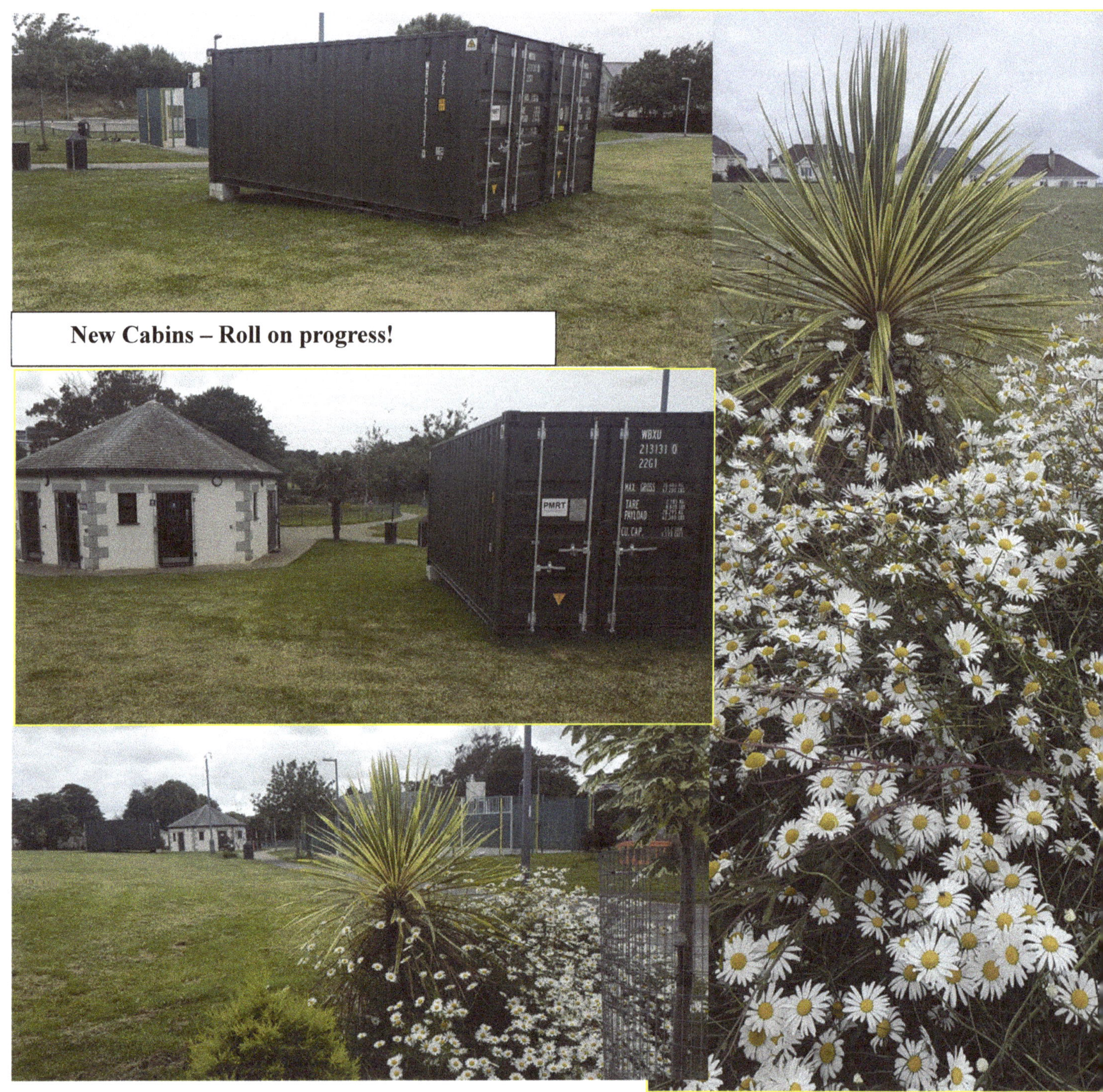

New Cabins – Roll on progress!

RIP Melville Durrant

Since I started this project to help Melville to give some positive light on the recreation ground, Melville Durrant had a heart attack while driving and died at the scene. I only communicated with him on the Thursday, sending interview questions to add to this book, letting him know that, by him answering the questions best as possible, then he will be helping me to help him. I also sent the link to this cover on his phone, but he couldn't open it, he messaged me saying that he couldn't open it, and I told him not to worry I was going to be back from London, when, by then I should have the physical copy of the book, so I will show him it. I am sad that he could not see the work I have done to help. I was in shock when I got a text on Friday morning, 2.8.24 from my wife Julie, that he was no more, he had an accident.

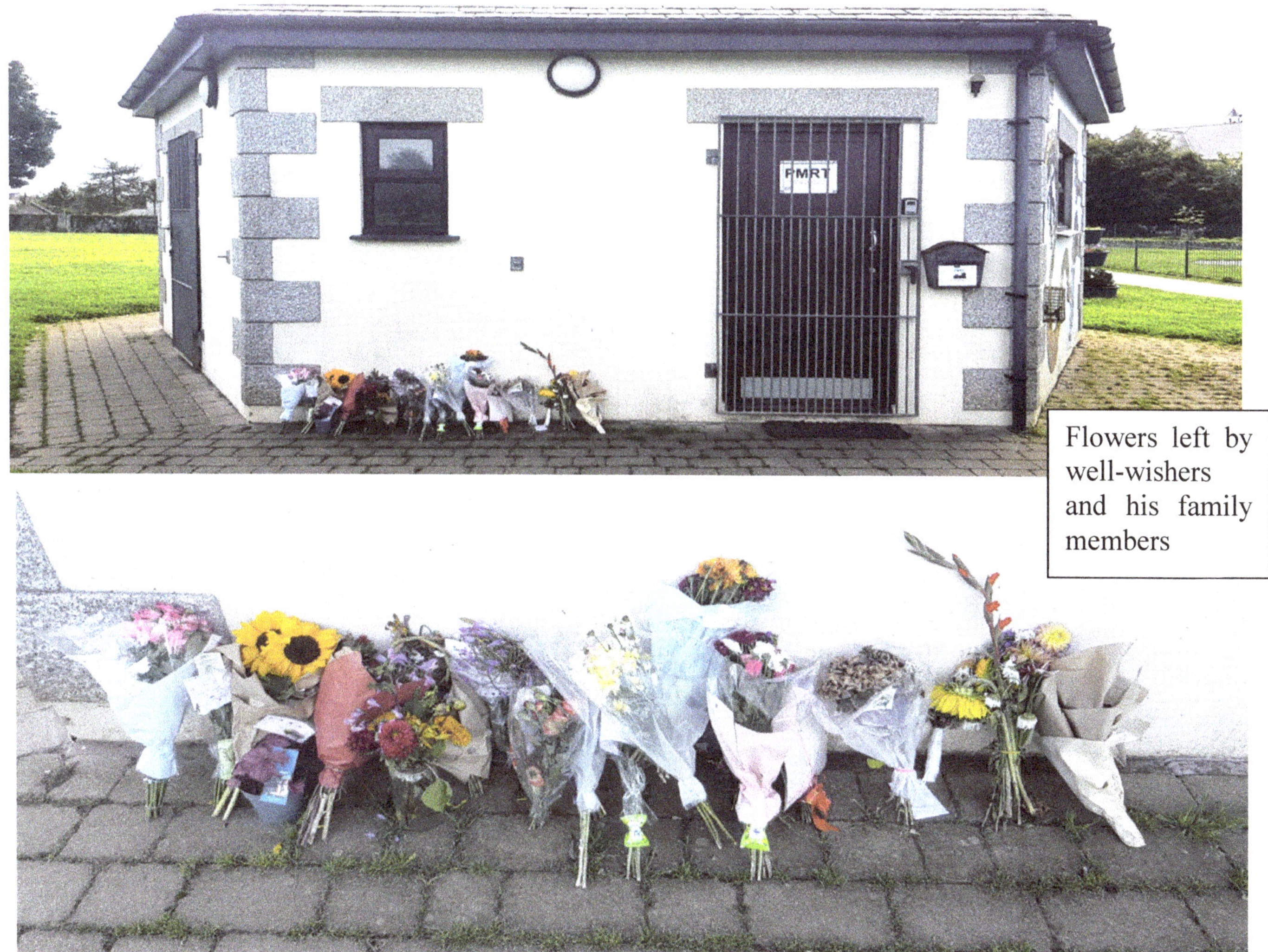

Flowers left by well-wishers and his family members

Other Publications

If you liked this information book about Penwith, Penzance, Cornwall, you will like other titles that have been published about Penwith that gets over looked.

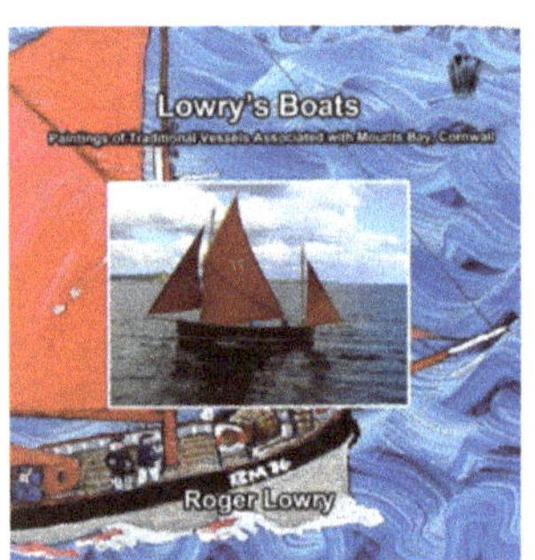 Lowry's Boats	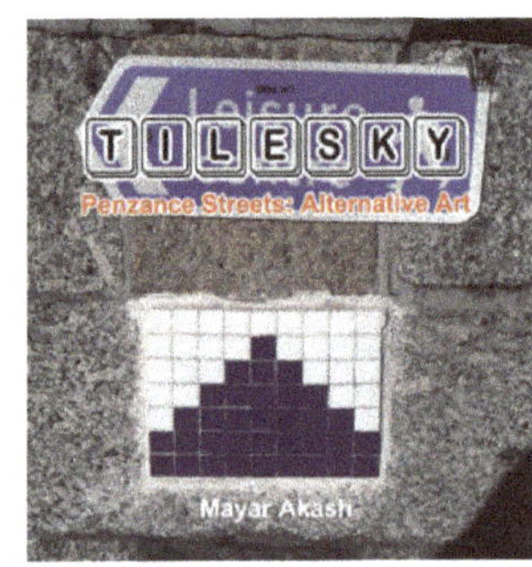 Who is Tileski?	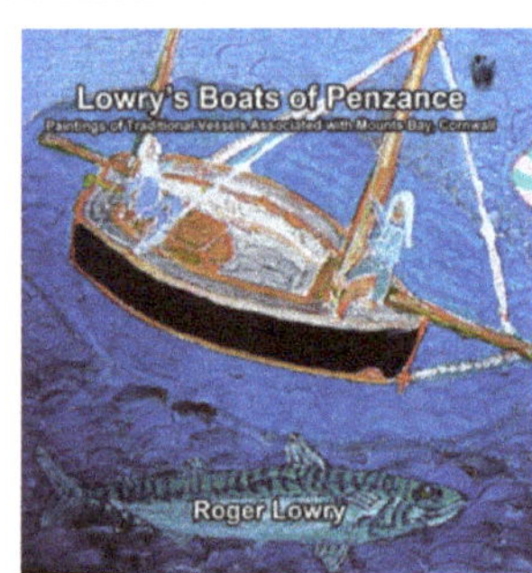 Lowry's Boats of Penzance
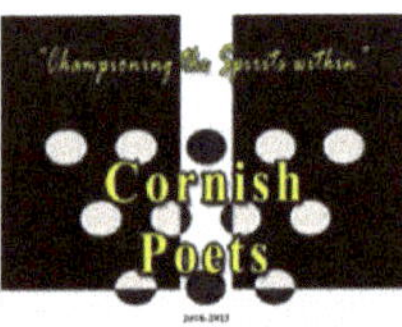 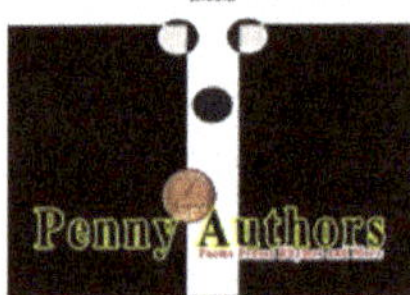 Cornish Poets	Check out the website for more information on the latest publications and future titles.	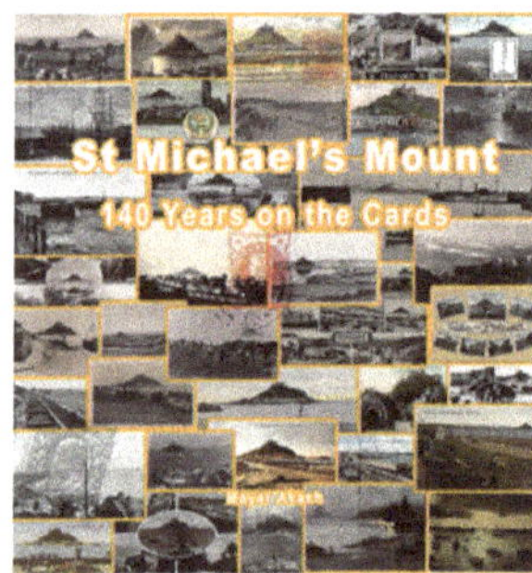 140 Years of St Michael's Mount On the cards
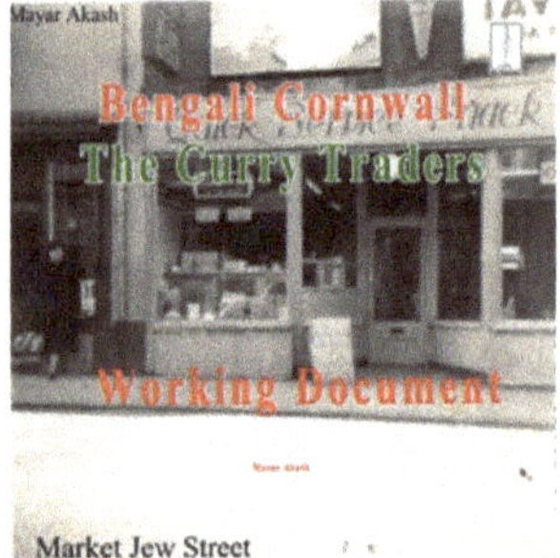 Bengali Cornwall, The Curry Traders	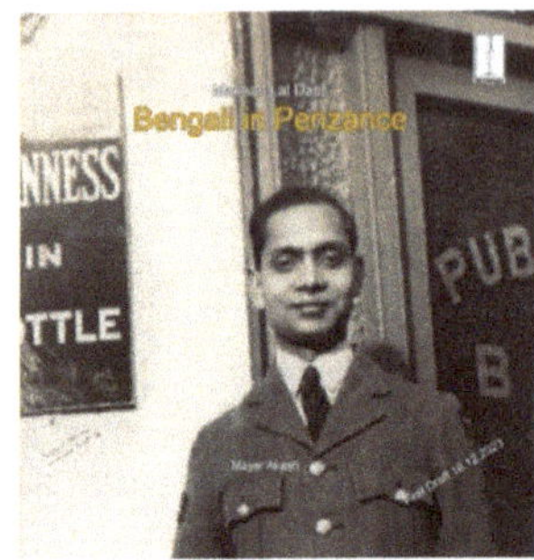 Bengali Penzance	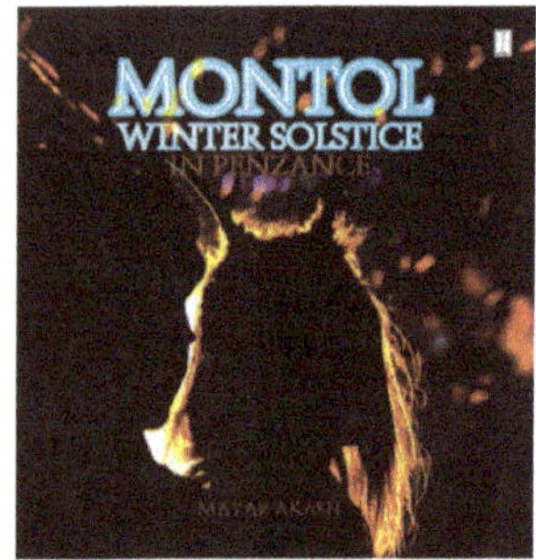 Montol, Winter Solstice

www.mapublisher.org.uk

www.ingramcontent.com/pod-product-compliance
Lightning Source LLC
LaVergne TN
LVHW060640110826
845147LV00018B/1015

* 9 7 8 1 9 1 5 9 5 8 1 7 4 *